A TEXT BOOK OF
ENGINEERING CHEMISTRY

For
Semester - I & II

FIRST YEAR DEGREE COURSE IN ENGINEERING

ACCORDING TO NEW REVISED SYLLABUS OF
SHIVAJI UNIVERSITY, KOLHAPUR
(EFFECTIVE FROM ACADEMIC YEAR - JULYU 2013-14)

COMMON FOR ALL DEGREE ENGINEERING BRANCHES

Dr. M. H. Pendse
M.Sc. Ph.D
Head, Chemistry Deptt.,
Walchand College of Engineering,
Sangli. (Dist. Sangli)

Dr. C. M. Bhavsar
M.Sc. Ph. D.
Applied Science Deptt.
Formerly. G. H. Raisoni
College of engineering
Wagholi, Pune.

Dr. S. S. Joshi
M.Sc. Ph.D
Vice Principal, Tatysaheb Kore
Institute of Engineering & Technology,
Warananagar, (Dist. Kolhapur)

Dr. S. D. Kulkarni
M.Sc., Ph.D., SET
Assistant Professor,
Department of Chemistry,
Sir Parashurambhau College, Pune

NIRALI PRAKASHAN

ENGINEERING CHIMISTRY (FE. SU)　　　　　　　　　　　　　　ISBN : 978-93-83525-68-3

First Edition : September 2013

© : **Authors**

The text of this publication, or any part thereof, should not be reproduced or transmitted in any form or stored in any computer storage system or device for distribution including photocopy, recording, taping or information retrieval system or reproduced on any disc, tape, perforated media or other information storage device etc., without the written permission of Authors with whom the rights are reserved. Breach of this condition is liable for legal action.

Every effort has been made to avoid errors or omissions in this publication. In spite of this, errors may have crept in. Any mistake, error or discrepancy so noted and shall be brought to our notice shall be taken care of in the next edition. It is notified that neither the publisher nor the authors or seller shall be responsible for any damage or loss of action to any one, of any kind, in any manner, therefrom.

Published By :	Printed By :
NIRALI PRAKASHAN	**REPRO INDIA LTD.**
Abhyudaya Pragati, 1312, Shivaji Nagar,	50/2 T.T.C. MIDC,
Off J.M. Road, PUNE – 411005	Industrial Area, Mahape, Navi Mumbai
Tel - (020) 25512336/37/39, Fax - (020) 25511379	Tel - (022) 2778 2011
Email : niralipune@pragationline.com	

DISTRIBUTION CENTRES
PUNE

Nirali Prakashan
119, Budhwar Peth, Jogeshwari Mandir Lane
Pune 411002, Maharashtra
Tel : (020) 2445 2044, 66022708, Fax : (020) 2445 1538
Email : bookorder@pragationline.com

Nirali Prakashan
S. No. 28/25, Dhyari,
Near Pari Company, Pune 411041
Tel : (022) 24690204 Fax : (020) 24690316
Email : dhyari@pragationline.com
bookorder@pragationline.com

MUMBAI
Nirali Prakashan
385, S.V.P. Road, Rasdhara Co-op. Hsg. Society Ltd.,
Girgaum, Mumbai 400004, Maharashtra
Tel : (022) 2385 6339 / 2386 9976, Fax : (022) 2386 9976
Email : niralimumbai@pragationline.com

DISTRIBUTION BRANCHES

NAGPUR
Pratibha Book Distributors
Above Maratha Mandir, Shop No. 3, First Floor,
Rani Jhanshi Square, Sitabuldi, Nagpur 440012,
Maharashtra, Tel : (0712) 254 7129

BENGALURU
Pragati Book House
House No. 1, Sanjeevappa Lane, Avenue Road Cross,
Opp. Rice Church, Bengaluru – 560002.
Tel : (080) 64513344, 64513355,
Mob : 9880582331, 9845021552
Email:bharatsavla@yahoo.com

JALGAON
Nirali Prakashan
34, V. V. Golani Market, Navi Peth, Jalgaon 425001,
Maharashtra, Tel : (0257) 222 0395
Mob : 94234 91860

KOLHAPUR
Nirali Prakashan
New Mahadvar Road,
Kedar Plaza, 1st Floor Opp. IDBI Bank
Kolhapur 416 012, Maharashtra. Mob : 9855046155

CHENNAI
Pragati Books
9/1, Montieth Road, Behind Taas Mahal, Egmore,
Chennai 600008 Tamil Nadu, Tel : (044) 6518 3535,
Mob : 94440 01782 / 98450 21552 / 98805 82331, Email : bharatsavla@yahoo.com

RETAIL OUTLETS
PUNE

Pragati Book Centre
157, Budhwar Peth, Opp. Ratan Talkies,
Pune 411002, Maharashtra
Tel : (020) 2445 8887 / 6602 2707, Fax : (020) 2445 8887

Pragati Book Centre
Amber Chamber, 28/A, Budhwar Peth,
Appa Balwant Chowk, Pune : 411002, Maharashtra,
Tel : (020) 20240335 / 66281669
Email : pbcpune@pragationline.com

Pragati Book Centre
676/B, Budhwar Peth, Opp. Jogeshwari Mandir,
Pune 411002, Maharashtra
Tel : (020) 6601 7784 / 6602 0855

PBC Book Sellers & Stationers
152, Budhwar Peth, Pune 411002, Maharashtra
Tel : (020) 2445 2254 / 6609 2463

MUMBAI
Pragati Book Corner
Indira Niwas, 111 - A, Bhavani Shankar Road, Dadar (W), Mumbai 400028, Maharashtra
Tel : (022) 2422 3526 / 6662 5254, Email : pbcmumbai@pragationline.com

Preface...

It gives immense pleasure to present the book **'Engineering Chemistry'** to the students of first year degree course in engineering. The subject matter in the book is in accordance with the new revised syllabus prescribed by Shivaji University, Kolhapur implemented from August 2013.

The book has been written strictly as per the university syllabus and will be useful for faculty as well as student community.

The subject matter is presented in a lucid, fluent and comprehensive manner. All efforts have been taken to present the text matter in Simple Language. Illustrative Figures, Exercise and Solved Problems have been added.

We take this opportunity to express our sincere thanks to **Shri. Dineshbhai Furia, Shri. Jignesh Furia** for publishing this book in time.

We specially appreciate special efforts taken by **Shri. M. P. Munde,** and Staff of **Nirali Prakashan, Pune.**

We are also thankful to **Mr. Virdhaval Shinde** (Branch Manager, kolhapur office) and **Mr. Ashok Nanaware** (Marketing Executive, Sangli District) for their valuable help and efforts for promotion of this book.

Any misprints or errors that have inadvertently crept in during the publication is solely our responsibility and we apologise for the same. We assure that constructive suggestions will be given attention for next reprint.

19th **September 2013**

Authors

Syllabus ...

Section - I

Unit 1 : Water (7)

Introduction, impurities in natural water, water quality parameters, total solids, acidity, alkalinity, chlorides, and dissolved oxygen (definition, causes, significance), hardness of water (causes, types, units of hardness), ill effects of hard water in steam generation in boilers, numerical on hardness, treatment of hard water (ion exchange and reverse osmosis).

Unit 2 : Instrumental Methods of Chemical Analysis (7)

Introduction, advantages and disadvantages of instrumental methods.

(a) **pH-metry :** Introduction, pH measurement using glass electrode, applications of pH-metry.

(b) **Spectrometry :** Introduction, Laws of spectrometry (Lambert's and Beer-Lambert's law), Single beam spectrophotometer (schematic, working and applications).

(c) **Chromatography :** Introduction, types, gas-liquid chromatography (GLC), basic principle, instrumentation and applications.

Unit 3 : Advanced Materials (7)

(a) **Polymers :** Introduction, plastics, thermosoftening and thermosetting plastics, industrially important plastics like phenol formaldehyde, urea formaldehyde and epoxy resins, conducting polymers (doping, conjugation, conductivity), examples and applications, biodegradable plastics.

(b) **Nanomaterials :** Introduction, synthesis and applications.

(c) **Composite materials :** Introduction, constituents, types of composites, advantages, composition, properties and uses of fibre reinforced plastics (FRP) and glass reinforced plastic (GRP).

Section - II

Unit 4 : Fuels (7)

Introduction, classification, calorific value, definition, units (calorie, kcal, joules, kilojoules), characteristics of good fuels, comparison between solid, liquid and gaseous fuels, types of calorific value (higher and lower), Bomb calorimeter and Boy's calorimeter. Numericals on Bomb and Boy's calorimeter. Fuel cells : Introduction, classification, advantages, limitations and applications.

Unit 5 : Corrosion (7)

Introduction, causes, classification, atmospheric corrosion (oxidation corrosion), electrochemical corrosion (hydrogen evolution and oxygen absorption mechanism), factors affecting rate of corrosion. Prevention of corrosion by proper design and material selection, hot dipping (galvanizing and tinning), cathodic protection, metal spraying and electroplating.

Unit 6 : Metallic Materials and Green Chemistry (7)

(a) **Metallic materials :** Introduction, alloy definition and classification, purposes of making alloys. Ferrous alloys : Plain carbon steels (mild, medium and high), stainless steels. Non-ferrous alloys : Copper alloy (Brass), Nickel alloy (Nichrome), Aluminium alloy (Duralumin and Alnico). Tin alloy (Solder metal).

(b) **Green chemistry :** Definition, goals of green chemistry, significance, basic components of green chemistry research, industrial applications.

Contents ...

Unit 1 :	Water	1.1 – 1.28
Unit 2 :	Analytical Chemistry	2.1 – 2.46
Unit 3 :	Advanced Materials	3.1 – 3.38
Unit 4 :	Fuels	4.1 – 4.24
Unit 5 :	Corrosion and its Prevention	5.1 – 5.28
Unit 6 :	Metallic Materials and Green Chemsity	6.1 – 6.22

Unit 1

Water

- Introduction
- Impurities in Natural Water
- Water Quality Parameters
  - pH
  - Acidity of Water
  - Alkalinity of Water
  - Total Dissolved Salts (TDS)
  - Dissolved Oxygen
  - Chlorides
- Hardness of Water
  - Causes of Hardness
  - Units of Hardness
  - Types of Hardness and its calculations
- Ill Effects of Hard Water in Steam Generation in boilers.
- Treatment of hard Water
  - Ion Exchange Process
  - Reverse Osomosis
- Numerical Problems on Hardness
- Exercise

1.1 Introduction :

Water is essential for the survival of life on the earth. Life has originated and evolved in water. Water acts as a solvent and medium for all living body reactions. Water is essential for human development. All ancient civilization developed on the banks of rivers. The industrial development started with water vapours by James Watt. Water is essential part of all industries.

Although water is abundant on earth's surface only a very small quantity of 5% can be actually used. The water present in seas and oceans cannot be used without treatment. The water present in river, lakes, ponds and underground water can only be used.

Water is a covalent compound containing two O-H bonds and angle between them is 104.5°. The water is polar in nature. The dielectric constant of water is 78.6, hence ionic compounds are easily soluble in it. Intermolecular hydrogen bonding is present in water. It is in the form of stable liquid between 0 - 100°C. Above 100°C it is in the form of steam used for many industrial applications. Below 0°C it is used as solid coolant.

Sources of Water :

Water mainly requires for domestic, agriculture and industrial purposes. The natural water available may be classified into four types.

1. Surface Water :

Water available on the surface of earth is called surface water. It is further divided into two parts.

  (i) **Still water :** The water present in lakes, ponds, reservoirs (dams etc.) is called still water.

  (ii) **Flowing water :** The water present in rivers and streams is called flowing water.

2. Under Ground Water :

The part of rain water penetrates the earth soil and goes deep in the earth and collects at one place or flows. The water is available from underground shallow and deep springs and wells. The water is also available from lower measures of coal mines.

3. Rain Water :

The rain water is another source of water obtained naturally in definite period. It is the purest form of natural water. It is collected in lakes, reservoirs, ponds, and sea. Some part of it penetrates the earth soil. The rain water can be collected and used as source of water.

It is difficult to collect rain water and is expensive process. Rain water supply cannot be regular. The use of rain water for industries is not practicable. The industrial gases like CO_2, SO_2, CO, nitrogen oxide etc. pollute the rain water.

4. Sea Water :

Sea water is the most impure source of water available. The impurities are carried by rivers and collected into sea. The sea water contains about 3.5% dissolved solid. The sodium chloride present in sea water is approximately 2.5%. Sea water also contains potassium chloride, magnesium chloride, magnesium sulphate, calcium sulphate, magnesium bromide etc. Therefore, sea water cannot be used for industrial purposes. It can be used for cooling purposes only.

1.2 Impurities in Natural Water :

The rain available naturally is purest form of water. The rain water reach to earth through atmosphere and flows on surface of earth or penetrates through crust. The rain water is contaminated during this travel and becomes impure. The different impurities present in water are classified into following types :

(A) Suspended Matter :

The water appear turbid due to presence of suspended particles

(i) Inorganic impurities : These impurities include clay, sand, fine particles suspended in water.

(ii) Organic impurities : These impurities include vegetable and animal matter, oil droplets, colouring matter, amino acids etc.

(B) Dissolved Matter :

(i) Dissolved gases : The rain drops absorb atmospheric gases like CO_2, N_2, O_2, NH_3, H_2S, SO_2, oxide of N_2 etc. These gases dissolve in water and becomes acidic. The lake water contains more CO_2 because of degradation of organic matter at the bottom. The colour and odor of water in due to dissolved matter in it. Underground water is generally colourless and odorless but some underground water has rotten egg smell due to dissolved H_2S gas. The water from well located near oil fields are contaminated with dissolved methane.

(ii) Dissolved inorganic salts : When rain water flows on ground different inorganic salts from rocks and earth must dissolve in water. The dissolved salts producing different cations and anions in water and contaminate the water.

The cations like Ca^{2+}, Mg^{2+}, Na^+, K^+, Fe^{2+}, Fe^{3+}, Al^{3+}, Zn^{2+}, Cu^{2+} etc. and anions like SO_4^{2-}, HCO_3^-, Cl^-, CO_3^{2-}, NO_3^-, F^-, NO_2^- etc. may be present in water.

(C) Dissolved Organic Salts :

Many organic salts dissolve in water. It includes pesticides, detergents, synthetic organic compounds, plant nutrients etc.

1.3 Water Quality Parameters :

Different quality parameters of water are as follows :

1.3.1 pH :

pH is defined as negative logarithm of concentration of hydrogen ions.

$$pH = -\log[H^+]$$

It is the measure of concentration of hydrogen ions in water. Acidic solutions have pH < 7, alkaline solutions have pH > 7 and neutral solution has pH = 7. Therefore pH is also the measure of acidity and alkalinity of water. pH of water is determined by instrument pH meter using calomel and glass electrodes.

Minerals and salts dissolve in natural sources of water and may become acidic or alkaline. The measurement of pH of water indicates acidic or alkaline nature of water. The water used for domestic and industrial purposes should have pH nearly 7. The pH of water lower than 7 causes corrosion and pH greeter than 7 produces incrustation, sedimentation deposit and difficulty in chlorination. In lime-soda process, removal of Ca^{2+} is favoured at high pH value. The solution of pH should be constant while governing the nature of coagulant and charge determination of colloidal impurities in water. Pathogenic bacteria do not survive in highly acidic or highly alkaline solutions.

1.3.2 Acidity of Water :

Pure water is neutral and its pH should be 7. But generally water present in rivers near industries is acidic. The acidic nature of water may be due to hydrolysis of acidic salts present in dissolved state or due to presence of acid and acidic substances. The commonly occurring acidic substances in water are different acids, sulphates, nitrates and chlorides of Mg, Cu, Fe, Mn, K^+ and Na^+. Water has acidity due to (i) industrial effluents, (ii) pickling liquors, (iii) acid mine drainage and (iv) humic acid.

Definition of Acidity : The concentration of different acidic substances in water is referred to as acidity. Acidity measures the effects of different compounds and conditions in water. It is defined as the strength of water to neutralize hydroxyl ions (OH^-) It is expressed in terms of ppm of calcium carbonate equivalent.

Mineral and Total Acidity : Acidity of water can be estimated by volumetric method. It consists of titration of fixed volume of water sample with standard sodium hydroxide (NaOH) solution, using either methyl orange or phenolphthalein indicator.

The amount of sodium hydroxide (NaOH) required for the sample of pH below 4.5 (pH < 4.5) to reach pH 4.5 which is the end point of methyl orange corresponds to **mineral acidity**.

The amount of sodium hydroxide (NaOH) required for the sample to reach the pH 8.3 which is the end point of phenolphthalein corresponds to **total acidity**.

Experimental Procedure :

1. Fill the burette with 0.02 M NaOH solution.
2. Take 50 cm^3 water sample which is dechlorinated in a titration flask.
3. Add two drops of methyl orange indicator.
4. Run the NaOH solution from burette in titration flask till the yellow colour changes to orange.
5. Record the burette reading as 'X' cm^3.

Calculation of Mineral Acidity :

Mineral acidity is calculated as :

$$\text{Normality of water} = \frac{\text{Normality of NaOH} \times \text{Volume of NaOH}}{\text{Volume of water}}$$

$$N_1 = \frac{0.02 \times X}{50}$$

$$\text{Mineral acidity} = N_1 \times 50 \; CaCO_3 \text{ eq. g/L} = N_1 \times 50 \times 1000 \; CaCO \text{ eq. mg/L}$$

$$= \frac{0.02 \times X \times 50000}{50} \; CaCO_3 \text{ eq. mg/L}$$

$$= 0.02 \times X \times 1000 \; CaCO_3 \text{ eq. mg/L}$$

$$\text{Mineral acidity} = 20 \times X \text{ ppm } CaCO_3 \text{ eq.}$$

Total Acidity : Total acidity corresponds to mineral acidity and CO_2 acidity.

The amount of sodium hydroxide (NaOH) required for the sample to reach the pH = 8.3 which is the end point of phenolphthalein indicator corresponds to total acidity.

Experimental Procedure (At Room Temperature) :

1. Fill the burette with 0.02 M NaOH solution.
2. Take 100 cm^3 or the water sample in tall cylinder which decrease the surface of the sample minimizes the loss of carbonic acid during titration.
3. Add 2-3 drops of phenolphthalein indicator. The solution is colourless.
4. Run the 0.02 N NaOH solution from the burette till the colour changes to pink.
5. Record the burette reading as Y cm^3.

Calculation of Total Acidity :

$$\text{Normality of water} = \frac{\text{Normality of NaOH} \times \text{Volume of NaOH}}{\text{Volume of water}}$$

$$N_1 = \frac{N_2 \times V_2}{V_1}$$

$$N_1 = \frac{0.02 \times Y}{100}$$

$$\text{Total acidity} = N_1 \times 50 \; CaCO_3 \text{ eq. g/L} = N_1 \times 50 \times 1000 \; CaCO_3 \text{ mg eq/L}$$

$$= \frac{0.02 \times Y \times 50 \times 1000}{100} \; CaCO_3 \text{ mg eq/L}$$

$$= 0.02 \times 500 \times Y \; CaCO_3 \text{ mg eq/L} = 10 \times Y \; CaCO_3 \text{ mg eq/L}$$

$$\text{Total acidity} = 10 \times Y \text{ ppm } CaCO_3 \text{ eq.}$$

Total acidity at boiling temperature (100°C) is determined by boiling the sample of water (50 cm^3) with 2 drops of phenolphthalein for two minutes and then titrating with standard (0.02 N) NaOH solution. The calculations are identical as given above.

1.3.3 Alkalinity of Water :

Generally, water present in lakes, rivers and underground is slightly basic or alkaline (pH > 7). The basic nature of water is due to hydrolysis of salts that are present in dissolved states or due to presence of alkaline substances. The commonly occurring alkaline substances are hydroxides such as $Ca(OH)_2$, $Mg(OH)_2$ and NH_4OH, bicarbonates such as $Ca(HCO_3)_2$,

$Mg(HCO_3)_2$, $NaHCO_3$ and carbonates such as $CaCO_3$, $MgCO_3$, Na_2CO_3. Hydroxides and carbonates are stronger bases than bicarbonates.

Definition of Alkalinity : The concentration of different alkaline substances in water is referred to as alkalinity. It is defined as the strength of water to neutralise hydrogen ion (H^+) It is expressed in terms of ppm of calcium carbonate equivalent.

Phenolphthalein Alkalinity and Methyl Orange Alkalinity : Alkalinity of water can be estimated by volumetric method. It consists of titration of fixed volume of water sample with standard hydrochloric acid (HCl) solutions using either methyl orange or phenolphthalein indicator.

Initially, fixed volume of water is titrated with strong acid. All hydroxide ions (OH^-) are neutralised and half the carbonate ions (CO_3^{2-}) present in water are neutralized to bicarbonate (HCO_3^-).

The reactions are as follows :

$$OH^- + H^+ \rightarrow H_2O$$

$$CO_3^{2-} + H^+ \rightarrow HCO_3^-$$

As both OH^- and CO_3^{2-} are strong bases and end point is in basic region and hence phenolphthalein can be used as an indicator. The alkalinity due to OH^- and CO_3^{2-} whose neutralization can be indicated by 'phenolphthalein alkalinity'.

After phenolphthalein end point only bicarbonate ions are present which are weak bases. If the same sample is further titrated using methyl orange as an indicator with standard acid, the alkalinity obtained is called methyl orange alkalinity'.

$$HCO_3 + H^+ \longrightarrow H_2CO_3 \longrightarrow H_2O + CO_2$$

Phenolphthalein alkalinity and methyl orange alkalinity = total alkalinity

Experimental Procedure to determine alkalinity :

(I) Phenolphthalein Alkalinity (PA) :

1. Fill the burette with 0.02 M HCl solution.
2. Pipette out 100 cm^3 of water sample of water in 250 cm^3 titration flask (pH > 8).
3. Add two drops of phenolphthalein as an indicator. The colour of solution becomes pink.
4. Run 0.02 M HCl solution from burette till the solution is colourless. Record the burette reading as X cm^3.

Calculations : Normality of water = $\dfrac{\text{Normality of HCl} \times \text{Volume of HCl}}{\text{Volume of water}}$

$$N_1 = \dfrac{N_2 \times V_2}{V_1} = \dfrac{0.02 \times X}{50}$$

Phenolphthalein alkalinity = $N_1 \times 50$ $CaCO_3$ eq/L

$\left(\text{Hydroxide} + \dfrac{1}{2}\text{Carbonate}\right)$ = $N_1 \times 50 \times 1000$ $CaCO_3$ eq. mg/L

$$= \dfrac{0.02\ X}{50} \times 50 \times 1000\ CaCO_3 \text{ eq. mg/L}$$

Phenolphthalein alkalinity = 20.0 $CaCO_3$ eq. mg/L

Phenolphthalein alkanity (PA) = 20 ppm $CaCO_3$ eq.

(II) Methyl Orange Alkalinity (MA) :

1. Use the same burette for filtration.
2. Take the same solution used in titration I. Add two drops of methyl orange indicator. Yellow colour develops in solution.
3. Run the HCl solution from X till the colour changes to orange. Record the burette reading as Y cm^3.

Calculations :

$$V_1 = X$$
$$V_2 = Y - X$$

Normality of water = $\dfrac{\text{Normality of HCl} \times \text{Volume g}}{\text{Volume of water}}$

$$N_1 = \dfrac{0.02 \times Y}{50}$$

Methyl orange alkalinity = $N_1 \times 50$ eq $CaCl_3$ g/L

$\left(\begin{array}{l}\dfrac{1}{2}\text{bicarbonate from carbonate}\\+\text{ bicarbonate}\end{array}\right)$ = $N_1 \times 50 \times 1000$ eq. $CaCO_3$ mg/L

$$= \dfrac{0.02 \times Y \times 50 \times 1000}{50} \text{ eq. } CaCO_3 \text{ mg/L}$$

$$= 0.02 \times Y \times 1000 \text{ eq } CaCO_3 \text{ mg/L}$$

$$= 20 \times Y \text{ eq mg/L}$$

Methyl orange alkalinity (MA) = $20 \times Y$ ppm eq. $CaCO_3$

The amount of individual ions present in the water sample can be calculated using the table given below.

Table 1.1 : Concentration of hydroxyl, carbonate and bicarbonate ion concentration from PA and MA

Volume of Acid / cm^3	Alkalinity ppm	C_{OH^-} / ppm	$C_{CO_3^{2-}}$ / ppm	$C_{HCO_3^-}$ / ppm
$V_1 = 0$	PA = 0	0	0	PM
$V_1 = V_2$	PA = MA	MA	0	0
$V_1 = \frac{1}{2} V_2$	PA = $\frac{1}{2}$ MA	0	2PA	0
$V_1 > \frac{1}{2} V_2$	PA > $\frac{1}{2}$ MA	2PA – MA	2MA – PA	0
$V_1 < \frac{1}{2} V_2$	PA < $\frac{1}{2}$ MA	0	2PA	MA – 2PA

1.3.4 Total Dissolved Salts (TDS) :

Pure water is colorless, odourless and tasteless. It is a universal solvent. Therefore water has tendency to pick up and dissolve solid impurities.

The dissolved solids can be salts, metals, minerals, cations, anions etc.

Definition :

The term total dissolved salts refer to bicarbonates, chlorides and sulphates of magnesium, calcium, sodium, and potassium and nitrates (inorganic salts) and small amount of dissolved organic matter in water. In other words TDS is sum of cations and anions in water.

TDS in water is due to many factor such as,

- Natural sources of water
- Industrial waste water
- Chemical used in water treatment
- Nature of pipelines
- Agricultural run off

Method of Determination of TDS :

(I) Gravimetric Method :

- Weigh the ceramic dish = w_1 g.
- Take measured volume of water sample (250 cm^3) in a beaker.
- Filter it through a standard glass fiber filter and collect the filtrate in a previously weighed dish.

- Place the dish in a oven set at a temperature of 103°C. Keep the dish in oven till all the water in evaporated.
- Increase the temperature to 150°C to remove trapped water. The solid present in water remains in the dish.
- Cool the ceramic dish and weigh it = w_2 g.
- Weight of dissolved solid present is w g = ($w_2 - w_1$) g.
- The dissolved solids in the sample is $\frac{w}{250}$ g cm^{-3}
- The TDS of water sample is $(4 \times w) \times 10^3$ mg per litre or $(4 \times w) \times 10^3$ ppm.

(II) Conductivity Method :

This is very fast method of determination of TDS of water. In this method specific conductance of water is measured.

- The sample of water is taken in a 100 cm^3 beaker.
- A conductivity probe is dipped in the water.
- It is connected to conductivity bridge.
- The digital display directly gives the TDS.

(Scale of specific conductance is modified to read TDS directly).

Health and other effects :

The limit of TDS is 500 ppm as a part of secondary drinking standard.

- TDS is not heath hazard. It is secondary drinking water standard.
- Water with higher TDS interfere in washing clothes.
- Water with higher TDS corrode pipelines.
- Water with higher TDS has salty (brackish) taste and forms scales in containers. It decreases the efficiency of hot water heater.

TDS test is an indicator for general quality of water. TDS test does not show specific quality of water. It does not give exact idea of taste, corrosiveness and hardness.

1.3.5 Dissolved Oxygen (DO) :

The oxygen present in atmosphere is not readily soluble in water. The oxygen dissolves in water to some extent.

When air dissolves in water, oxygen exists in water. Because of O_2 present in water, aquatic life survives.

The solubility of oxygen is directly proportional to partial pressure. The dissolved oxygen saturation value is designated as DO. The DO at 20°C is calculated by knowing partial pressure which is equal to 0.2094 atmosphere pressure at 20°C and Henry's law constant equal to 43.8 mg L^{-1} atm.

$$DO = 43.8 \times 0.2094 = 9.17 \text{ mg L}^{-1}$$

The DO depends on temperature and decreases with rise in temperature as shown in Table 1.2.

Table 1.2 : DO values at different temperature

Temperature /°C	0	10	20	30	40
DO saturation value / mg L^{-1}	14.62	11.33	9.17	7.63	6.41

The DO saturation value also decreases with rise in salt concentration as shown in Table 1.3.

Table 1.3 : Effect of Chloride concentration on DO values

Chloride concentration / mg L^{-1}	0	1000	5000	10000
DO values / mg L^{-1}	9.17	9.08	8.73	8.3

DO values decreases with altitude as shown in table. Higher altitude with lowered atmospheric pressure have a profound effect on DO values. DO at particular can be obtained knowing the height of the place.

Table 1.4 : Effect of altitude on DO values at 20 °C

Height / meter	0	500	1000	2000	3000
DO / mg L^{-1}	9.17	8.63	8.10	7.14	6.29

The decrease in DO value decreases with organic matter content indicates the pollution load on receiving water bodies. This is of great significance for water treatment.

The dissolved oxygen is corrosive to many metals such as steel, iron, galvanized iron, brass etc. The container prepared from these metals are generally used for storing water. The corrosion increases at low pH and high temperature. The water used in low pressure boilers should have oxygen content less than 0.05 ppm and for high pressure boiler less than 0.01 ppm.

The corrosion due to dissolved oxygen is controlled by deaeration of boiler feed water or sodium sulphide treatment.

$$Na_2SO_3 + \frac{1}{2}O_2 \rightarrow Na_2SO_4$$

Procedure for Estimation of Dissolved O$_2$ (Winkler's Method) :

The analysis is performed immediately after removing the stopper in the field or sight. The reagents are added by burette dipping its end in water. Nitrates, sulphides, sulphites, Fe (II) compounds, organic matter etc. are oxidized by $KMnO_4$ in presence of H_2SO_4. Mn (OH$_2$) readily adsorbs dissolved oxygen.

1. Take 250 cm^3 the water sample. Add 0.7 cm^3 of concentrated H_2SO_4 and 1 cm^3 $KMnO_4$.

2. Stopper the bottle and shake well

3. If violet colour disappears add more 1 cm³ KMnO$_4$ and shake. Repeat the procedure till colour of KMnO$_4$ persists for 20 minutes.

4. Add 1cm³ MnSO$_4$ and 5cm³ KI solution and shake it, when Mn(OH)$_2$ precipitates and settle down.

5. Add 1cm³ concentrated sulphuric acid and shake well

6. Dissolved oxygen liberates free iodine from KI. These (1) to (6) steps are performed in field.

7. Fill the burette with 0.025 N Na$_2$S$_2$O$_3$ solution.

8. Take 200 cm³ of sample of water with liberated iodine in a conical flask.

10. Titrate it with Na$_2$S$_2$O$_3$ till the blue colour changes to colorless.

11. Record the burtte reading = Y cm³

Calculation of DO :

$$\text{ppm of dissolved } O_2 = \text{Volume of Na}_2S_2O_3 \times \text{Normality of Na}_2S_2O_3 \times 0.08 \times \frac{10^6}{\text{Volume of sample}}$$

$$= \frac{Y \times 0.025 \times 0.008 \times 10^6}{250} = Y$$

1.3.6 Chlorides :

Chlorides are present in water in the forms of sodium chloride (NaCl), calcium chloride (CaCl$_2$) and magnesium chloride (MgCl$_2$). When chloride present in drinking water below 250 ppm level is harmless. The industrial waste water, domestic sewage water contain more chloride than raw water. When chloride contain is higher than 250 ppm level, impart particular taste to water hence higher content of chloride in drinking water is unacceptable and indicate pollution. The presence of higher chloride in boiler feed water is also undesirable. The magnesium chloride (MgCl$_2$) present in boiler feed water, undergoes hydrolysis at high temperature and pressure of boilers producing hydrochloric acid which corrode the metal parts of boiler. Higher content of chloride in water is also harmful to agricultural crops.

Determination of Chloride (Mohr's Method) :

The sample of water is titrated with standard silver nitrate solution using K$_2$CrO$_4$ as indicator.

$$Ag^+ + Cl^- \rightarrow AgCl \downarrow$$

$$2Ag^+ + CrO_4^{2-} \rightarrow Ag_2CrO_4 \downarrow \text{ (red)}$$

Procedure :

(i) Pipette out 100 cm^3 of sample in a conical flask.

(ii) Adjust pH of the solution with the help of H_2SO_4 or NaOH solution.

(iii) Add 1 cm^3 of K_2CrO_4 (5%) solution in the sample Stir well.

(iv) Run the standard (N_1) silver nitrate solution from the burette till the permanent red colour appears in solution. This is the end point of titration.

(v) Record the burette reading 'X'.

Calculations (chloride content) :

$$1000 \text{ cm}^3 \text{ 1 N AgNO}_3 = 35.5 \text{ g of chloride}$$

$$\times \text{cm}^3 \text{ N}_1 \text{ AgNO}_3 = \frac{35.5 \times N_1}{1000} \times X \text{ g of chloride in 100 cm}^3 \text{ sample}$$

$$\text{g per litre} = \frac{35.5 \times N_1}{1000} \times X \times 10 \text{ g} = 0.355 \times N_1 \times X \text{ g}$$

1.4 Hardness :

We use water for domestic purposes like cooking, cleaning, washing cloths, drinking gardening etc. We use different sources of water like well, water from municipal supply, bore well etc. It is our observation that water from certain wells do not produce lather with soap while some produce lather with soap. We can distinguish hard water and soft water on this property of producing lather with soap.

Soft water : When soap is dissolved in water then lather or foam is formed which is called **soft water**. Rain water and distilled water are soft water as they form lather with soap. Such water does not contain impurities.

Hard water : When soap is dissolved in water does not form lather instead scum or curd like insoluble substance is formed which is called **hard water**. Hard water contains soluble impurities.

1.4.1 Causes of Hardness of Water :

Main causes of hardness are absorption of CO_2 from air and dissolution of soluble salts in water.

• When rain water comes on surface of earth from atmosphere, carbondioxide present in air dissolve in rain water and became acidic. When such water flows over surface containing $CaCO_3$ and $MgCO_3$ react to form soluble Ca $(HCO_3)_2$ or Mg $(HCO_3)_2$ and dissolve slowly in water. Thus rain water is changed to hard water.

$$H_2O + CO_2 \rightarrow H_2CO_3$$
$$H_2CO_3 + MgCO_3 \rightarrow Mg(HCO_3)_2$$
$$H_2CO_3 + CaCO_3 \rightarrow Ca(HCO_3)_2$$

- The earth surface contains salts of sulphates and chlorides of Ca and Mg and some salts of Fe and Mn which are soluble in water. When rain water flows on the surface, these salts dissolve in water and water becomes hard.

Thus hard water contains bicarbonates (HCO_3^-), carbonates (CO_3^{2-}) sulphate (SO_4^{2-}), nitrates (NO_3^-) and chlorides (Cl^-) of monovalent cations like K^+, Na^+ and bivalent cation such as Ca^{2+}, Mg^{2+}, Fe^{2+} and Mn^{2+}.

Hard water when reacts with soap which is sodium seterate produce scum as shown in the reaction as,

$$2C_{17}H_{33}COONa + Ca(HCO_3)_2 \rightarrow (C_{17}H_{33}COO)_2Ca + 2NaHCO_3$$
(soap)　　　　(hard water)　　　　(scum or curd)

Hard water is not suitable for drinking and industrial purposes.

1.4.2 Types of Hardness

There are two types of hard water.

1. Temporary Hard Water :

It is also called as carbonate hardness. If the hardness of water is due to presence of bicarbonates (HCO_3^-) and carbonates (CO_3^{2-}) salts such as $Mg(HCO_3)_2$, $Ca(HCO_3)_2$, $MgCO_3$, $CaCO_3$ etc. is called temporary hardness. $CaCO_3$ and $MgCO_3$ are slightly soluble.

This type of hardness can be removed simply by boiling the water. During boiling the bicarbonates and carbonates are converted into the form that is insoluble in water such as hydroxides. The insoluble precipitate can be removes by filtration process. Since, the hardness can be removed by simple method it is called temporary hardness.

Reactions :

$$Mg(HCO_3)_2 \xrightarrow[100°C]{heat} Mg(OH)_2 \downarrow + 2CO_2$$

$$Ca(HCO_3)_2 \xrightarrow[100°C]{heat} Ca(OH)_2 \downarrow + 2CO_2$$

$$MgCO_3 + H_2O \xrightarrow[100°C]{heat} Mg(OH)_2 \downarrow + CO_2$$

2. Permanent Hard Water :

If the hardness of water is caused by the presence of dissolved salt of metals other than bicarbonates and carbonates, the salts which are present in water are generally nitrates, sulphates and chlorides. The salts which cause permanent hardness are $Ca(NO_3)_2$, $Mg(NO_3)_2$, $CaSO_4$, $MgSO_4$, $CaCl_2$, $MgCl_2$, $FeCl_2$, $CuCl_2$ etc.

The hardness of water cannot be removed just by boiling. It requires special chemical treatment.

Total Hardness : Total hardness of water is sum of temporary hardness and permanent hardness.

Total Hardness = Temporary Hardness + Permanent Hardness

Units of Total Hardness : Hardness is usually expressed in terms of dissolved magnesium and calcium salts calculated as calcium carbonate equivalents. Hardness is most frequently expressed as part per million i.e. ppm.

One ppm is a unit weight of solute per million units of solution. The density of solution is assumed to be equal to 1.0 g cm^{-3} since it is very dilute.

$$1 \text{ ppm} = 1 \text{ mgL}^{-1} = \frac{1 \times 10^{-3} \text{ g}}{1 \times 10^3 \text{ cm}^3} = \frac{1}{10^6} \text{ g cm}^{-3}$$

$$1 \text{ ppm} = 10^{-6} \text{ g cm}^{-3}$$

$$1 \text{ ppm} = \frac{10^{-6} \text{ g of solute}}{1 \text{ cm}^3 \text{ of solvent}}$$

Table 1.5 : Degree of hardness of water

Quality of water	ppm of $CaCO_3$
Soft	upto 100
Moderately hard	100 – 150
Hard	150 – 300
Very hard	> 300

1.4.3 Experimental Procedure to Determine Total Hardness of Water (EDTA Method) :

The most common analytical method of estimation of total hardness of water is complexometric titration (volumetry). In this titration, disodium salt of ethylene diamine tetra–acetic acid (EDTA) is used as complexing agent represented as Na_2H_2Y and H_2Y is complex forming ion. The structure of sodium salt of EDTA is as given below.

$$\begin{array}{c}
\text{HO–C(=O)–H}_2\text{C} \diagdown \qquad \diagup \text{CH}_2\text{–C(=O)–OH} \\
\text{N–CH}_2\text{–CH}_2\text{–N} \\
\text{NaO–C(=O)–H}_2\text{C} \diagup \qquad \diagdown \text{CH}_2\text{–C(=O)–ONa}
\end{array}$$

EDTA forms a complex with monovalent and divalent cations. The structure of EDTA complex with divalent metal ion is as follows:

[Structure of EDTA-metal complex with charge 2−, showing central metal M coordinated to N, N, and four carboxylate O atoms via CH₂ groups]

The complex formation takes place at pH = 10. Therefore basic buffer solution of NH_4Cl and NH_4OH may be used to maintain the constant pH during titration. Eriochrome black T (H_2D^-) is used as an indicator in the titration. The indicator is blue due to HD^- in pH range 7-11. HD^{-2} forms unstable complex with metal ions which are red in colour.

$$MD^- \text{ (red)} + H_2Y^{2-} \longrightarrow MY^{2-} \text{ (blue)} + H^+ + HD^{2-}$$

Experimental Procedure :

The experiment to find out total hardness is performed in two parts:

Part I : Standardization of EDTA solution using Standard ZnSO₄ solution:

1. Prepare the standard 0.05 M zinc sulphate by dissolving 1.347 g of $ZnSO_4.6H_2O$ (molecular weight of $ZnSO_4$ = 269.54 g) in distilled water and diluting to 100 cm³.

2. Fill the burette with given EDTA solution.

3. Pipette out 25 cm³ of 0.05 M $ZnSO_4$ solution in a titration flask.

4. Add to it 10 cm³ of buffer solution of pH = 10.

5. Add 5 drops of Eriochrome black T indicator, wine red colour develops in the solution.

6. Run the EDTA solution from burette till wine red colour changes to clear blue. Record the burette reading as X cm3. Find the molarity of EDTA solution using the relation,

$$M_2 = \frac{M_1 V_1}{V_1} = \frac{0.05 \times 25}{X}$$

Part II : Determination of total Hardness of Water :
1. Fill the burette with EDTA of know molarity.
2. Pipette out $25 cm^3$ of given water sample. Add to it $10 cm^3$ of buffer solution and 5 drops of Eriochrome black T indicator.
3. Run the EDTA solution till the solution is clear blue. Record the burette reading as $Y\ cm^3$.

$$\text{Morality of water} = \frac{\text{Morality of EDTA} \times \text{Volume of EDTA}}{\text{Volume of water}}$$

$$M_3 = \frac{M_2 \times Y}{25}$$

Total hardness of water $= M_3 \times 100\ CaCO_3$ eq gL^{-1}

$\qquad\qquad\qquad\qquad\quad = M_3 \times 100 \times 1000\ CaCO_3$ eq mgL^{-1}

Total hardness of water $= M_3 \times 10^5$ ppm $CaCO_3$ eq.

1.5 Ill Effects of Hard Water In Stean Generation in boilers :

When hard water is used in boilers it may produce following troubles :

- Scale and sludge formation
- Corrosion
- Priming and foaming
- Caustic embrittlement

[A] Scale and sludge formation :

Water continuously vaporizes in boiler and concentration of salts in water increases. If the water is hard the concentration of salts is very high. Finally two types of precipitates are produced. One is soft, loose and slimy precipitate ($CaCl_2$, $MgCl_2$, $MgCO_3$ etc.) which is non adherent and can be easily removed even by blowing is called sludge.

Sludge is bad conductor of heat and waste the heat. Excessive formation of sludges disturb the working of boilers. It settles in pipe connection, plug opening, gauge connection and even choke the pipes. They are formed on colder portion of boiler and decreases the efficiency boiler.

The other type of precipitous ($CaSO_4$, $Mg(OH)_2$ $CaCO_3$, Silicates of Mg and Ca etc.) is hard and stick very firmly stick to the heated inner surface of the boiler called scales. These are difficult to remove by blow-down operation. The scale formation decreases the efficiency of boiler and crate some chances of explosion. Scales are bad conductor of heat and heat cannot pass through it easily result in wastage of fuel. Over heating due to scale formation makes the maternal of boiler soft and weaker.

[B] Boiler corrosion :

Corrosion is the chemical process of decay or destruction of a metal due to surrounding medium or environment. It occurs when water contained different impurities like dissolved gases, dissolved salts and acidity or alkalinity of water.

- **Dissolved gases :** When dissolved oxygen is present (8 cm^3 dm^{-3}) in boiler water, corrosion of iron occurs and boiler material is affected.

$$4\,Fe + 4\,H_2O + 2O_2 \rightarrow 4\,Fe(OH)_2$$
iron ferrous hydroxide

$$4\,Fe(OH)_2 + O_2 \longrightarrow 2\,Fe_2O_3\,2H_2O$$
ferric oxide or rust

The dissolved oxygen can be removed by adding exact amount of sodium sulphite (Na_2SO_3) or sodium sulphide (Na_2S) or hydrazine.

When hard water containing bicarbonates of Ca and Mg and dissolved CO_2 may attack the boiler due to the formation of weak carbonic acid as,

$$Ca(HCO_3)_2 \longrightarrow CaCO_3 + H_2O + CO_2 \uparrow$$

$$Mg(HCO_3)_2 \longrightarrow MgCO_3 + H_2O + CO_2 \uparrow$$

$$CO_2 + H_2O \longrightarrow H_2CO_3$$

Calculated quantity of Ammonia can be used to remove CO_2, O_2 and CO_2 by deaeration process.

- **Dissolved salts :** Presence of Magnesium chloride ($MgCl_2$) in a water produces hydrochloric acid due to hydrolysis reaction as,

$$MgCl_2 + 2\,H_2O \longrightarrow Mg(OH)_2 + 2HCl$$

The hydrochloric acid is a strong acid and attack the iron metal of boiler like a chain reaction giving HCl continuously as,

$$Fe + 2HCl \longrightarrow FeCl_2 + H_2 \uparrow$$

$$FeCl_2 + 2\,H_2O \longrightarrow Fe(OH)_2 + 2HCl$$

Therefore presence of traces of magnesium chloride causes corrosion of boiler to large extent and may damage it. The acidity of water is therefore neutralized by adding alkaline salt or ammonia.

- **Acidity or alkalinity of water :** If the pH of water used in the boiler is less than 7 (acidic water), then it causes corrosion to higher extent. If the water is too alkaline (pH > 11) it causes corrosion to very high extent. The alkaline water of pH = 7 to 9.5 may cause corrosion to very small extent.

[C] Priming and foaming :

Priming is the process in which some particles of liquid water (small droplets) are mixed with steam when steam is generated at very rapid rate in boiler and pass from boiler along with steam. The priming is due to suspended solid particles in water or very high velocity of steam or faulty boiler design.

Disadvantages of priming :

- More heat is required to adjust the steam pressure in boiler. Then efficiency of steam production is lowered.

- Dissolved salt as well as water may enter the machine parts and lowers the life of it.
- The level of water in boiler may not be judged.

Priming can be avoided by

- Using pure water in boiler
- Using steam purifier and
- Maintaining constant rate of steam
- Keeping low levels in boilers.

Foaming is the process of formation of bubbles or foam at the surface of water in the boilers which cannot break easily. Foaming is due to higher quantity of dissolved matter in water which reduces the surface tension of water. Foaming can be avoided by

- Adding castor oil
- Adding antifoaming agent
- Carrying blow down operations to predetermined interval

[D] Caustic embrittlement :

It is also called as caustic corrosion. Caustic corrosion is caused when

- boiler operates at high pressure and
- highly alkaline solution is used in the boiler. When the water softened by adding Na_2CO_3 is used in the high pressure boiler, Na_2CO_3 is decomposed to NaOH as,

$$Na_2CO_3 + H_2O \longrightarrow 2NaOH + CO_2 \uparrow$$

NaOH formed makes the water more alkaline. If minute cracks are present on inner lining of boiler, water (alkaline) flows through such cracks by capillary action. The alkaline water evaporates here and solid NaOH (caustic soda) left behind. The layers of caustic soda increases as the process continues. The caustic soda attack the surrounding part of the crack and dissolves iron metal of the boiler. This causes embrittlement of boiler parts particularly at joints, bends, rivets etc. and may cause failure of boiler.

The process of caustic embrittlement avoided by

- The use sodium phosphate instead of Na_2CO_3 for softening water.
- The use of additives in boiler water such as lignin or tanin in which block the linkages of boiler.
- The alkalinity of water is adjusted to pH 7 to 9.

1.6 Treatment of Hard Water :

The hardness of water depends on the amount or concentration of dissolved impurities present in water. The process of softening water is the removal of dissolved salts from it. The soft water is required by almost all industries for boilers. Some industries required deionised water. The industries like distilleries, canning, paper, textiles, brewing etc. require soft water. The battery industries require deionized water. Soft water of different purity can be prepared using different methods. Among these lime-soda process is commonly used which is chemical water softening method. The soft water obtained by cold lime-soda process is ~ 50-

60 ppm hardness. The dissolved salts are completely removed to produce deionised water. The two important method of softening water are,

(i) Ion exchange process (ii) Revers Osmosis.

Principle :

1.6.1 Ion Exchange Process :

Ion exchange resins : Synthetic ion exchange resins find applications in water softening for industrial purpose. The ion exchange resins are macro molecules of high molecular weight have three dimensional networks called matrix to which large polar

Strong anion exchange resine in OH^- form

Strong anion exchange resine in H^+ form

exchange groups are attached. They have cross-linked structure. They are insoluble in water and have porous structure. They swells when solvent is taken up. The commercial resins are granular type. Depending on the electrical charge the ion exchange resin can exchange their cation or anion from the solution hence ion exchangers are grouped as (i) cation ion exchanger and (ii) anion ion exchangers and also (i) strong ion exchanger and (ii) weak ion exchanger.

The strong cation exchangers have groups like SO_3^-, etc. and weak cation exchangers have groups COO^-, $-HPO_2^-$. The strong anion exchangers have groups like P^+, $-CH_3$, $N^+(CH_3)_3$, $N^+(CH_4)_2 CH_2 CH_2 OH$. The weak anion exchangers have groups like $-NH_2$ etc.

Ion Exchange Reaction : The ion exchange resin can be represented as $R^+ A^-$ or $R^- A^+$. In ion exchange reaction there is exchange of the ions of same sign between a solution and a solid (exchanger) in contact with it.

$$R^- A^+ + B^+ \rightleftharpoons R^- B^+ + A^+$$
$$\text{solid} \quad \text{solution}$$

And
$$R^+ A^- + B^- \rightleftharpoons R^+ B^- + A^-$$
$$\text{solid} \quad \text{solution}$$

The solid is called exchanger and mobile ions on exchanger (A^+ or A^-) and ions in solution (B^+ or B^-) are called counter ions.

The essential properties for ion exchange resin :

The following properties are required with ion exchangers for effective water softening.

- Ion exchangers should be easily available and cheap.
- Ion exchangers should not be toxic and should not impart colour to water.
- Ion exchangers should be physically stable and resistive to chemical attack.
- Chemical attack ion exchangers should be insoluble in water and should have high exchange capacity (mill equivalent g^{-1} of exchanger).
- Ion exchanger should be capable of regeneration.

Water treatment by ion exchange process :

(I) Water softening :

In this method cations present in water are removed using cation exchange resin either in Na^+ form or H^+ form. Ca and Mg in the form of bicarbonate, sulphate and chloride can be removed using cation exchangers.

$$R^- Na^+ + Ca^{2+} (HCO_3^-, SO_4^{2-}, Cl^-) \longrightarrow (R^-)_2 Ca^{2+} + Na^+$$

$$R^- Na^+ + Mg^{2+} (HCO_3^-, SO_4^{2-}, Cl^-) \longrightarrow (R^-)_2 Mg^{2+} + Na^+$$

$$R^- H^+ + Ca^{2+} \longrightarrow (R^-)_2 Ca^{2+} + H^+$$

$$R^- H^+ + Mg^{2+} \longrightarrow (R^-)_2 Mg^{2+} + H^+$$

In water softening method a vessel containing ion exchange resin bed is used. At the top of the vessel stop cock to pass hard water and another stop cock to pass acid or alkali for regeneration of ion exchangers are provided. At the bottom stop cock to remove soft water is attached as shown in the Fig. 1.6. In this method the water that is soften using lime-soda method is used to gent complete soft water. When the such water enters the top of vessel pass through resin bed. The ion exchange reaction occurs and Ca^{2+} and Mg^{2+} ions are removed and soft water comes to the bottom of the vessel and removed by lower cock. When the resins are saturated with ions the Na^+ form of ion exchanger is regenerated by passing concentration pure NaOH solution or H^+ form of exchanger is regenerated by passing concentrated solution of pure HCl solution at the top of the vessel. The solution is removed. The resin is repeatedly washed with water and then reused.

(II) Demineralisation process by ion exchange reaction :

It is possible to remove completely dissolved salts from water using cation and anion exchange resins and deionised water of highest purity is obtained.

(i) Construction and working : This method consists of two vessel connected to each other one containing cation exchanger bed and other containing anion exchange bed. The first vessel has two stop cocks one for hard water and other for acid required for regeneration of cation exchanger. When water flows through cation exchange bed, cations are removed as:

$$2R^- H^+ + Ca^{2+} \longrightarrow (R^-)_2 Ca^{2+} + 2H^+$$

$$2R^- H^+ + Mg^{2+} \longrightarrow (R^-)_2 Mg^{2+} + 2H^+$$

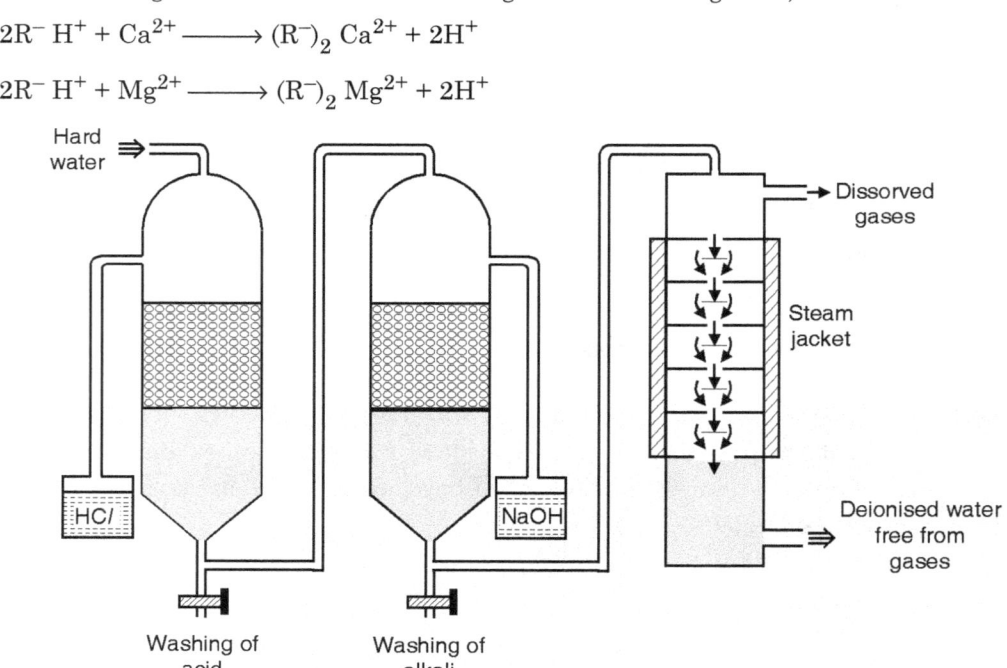

Fig. 1.6 : **Apparatus for demineralization by ion exchange process**

After removal of cations, water comes to the bottom of first vessel from where it comes to the top of second vessel which contains anion exchanged bed. When water flows through anion exchanger bed, the anions are removed as,

$R^+ OH^- + Cl^- \longrightarrow R^+ Cl^- + OH^-$

$2R^+ OH^- + CO_3^{2-} \longrightarrow (R^+)_2 CO_3^{2-} + 2OH^-$

$2R^+ OH^- + SO_4^{2-} \longrightarrow (R^+)_2 SO_4^{2-} + 2OH^-$

The treated water comes to the bottom of second vessel and then comes to the top of third vessel.

This vessel is fitted with degasifier unit to remove CO_2 to obtain deionised water. The deionised water is removed from the bottom of third vessel.

(ii) Regeneration of ion exchangers : After long use, resins lose the capacity of exchanging H^+ and OH^- ions. Then the ion exchangers are regenerated.

(a) The cation exchanger is washed with concentrated HCl when the following reactions take place.

$(R^-)_2 Ca^{+2} + 2H^+ \longrightarrow 2R^- H^+ + Ca^{2+}$

$(R^-)_2 Mg^{2+} + 2H^+ \longrightarrow 2R^- H^+ + Mg^{2+}$

After treatement of HCl, cation exchanger is repeatedly washed with deionized water.

(b) The an ion exchanger is washed with concentration NaOH when following reactions take place

$(R^+) Cl^- (+ OH^- \longrightarrow (R^+) OH^- + Cl^-, (R^+)_2 CO_3^{2-} + 2 OH^- \to 2 (R^+) OH^- + CO_3^{2-}$

After treatment of NaOH, an ion exchanger is repeatedly washed with deionized water.

After regeneration it can be used again.

Advantages of the method :

(i) The highest purily water is obtained having residual hardness about 2ppm only. The water can be used in boilers operating at high pressure.

(ii) The process is useful for both acidic and alkaline water.

(iii) It is a clean process because impurities like sludges does not form.

Disadvantages of the method :

(i) The equipments are costly.

(ii) The resins required for this method have high cost.

(iii) The turbid solution reduce the output of the process. The turbidity should not exceed 10ppm. If turbidity is higher should be removed by coagulation first and then used for ion exchange treatment.

1.6.2 Reverses Osmosis Method

Osmosis:

The unidirectional flow of solvent through the semipermeable membrane is called osmosis.

Semipermeable membrane allows solvent to flow through it but does not allow solute to pass through it (see Fig. 1.2).

When two solutions of different concentrations are separated by semipermable membrane, in two compartments the equilibrium is achieved by movement of solvent from low solute concentraiotn area to the high evolute concentration area. This process is termed as osmosis. The pressure applied to high concentration side to stop the flow of solvent from low concentration is called osmotic pressure.

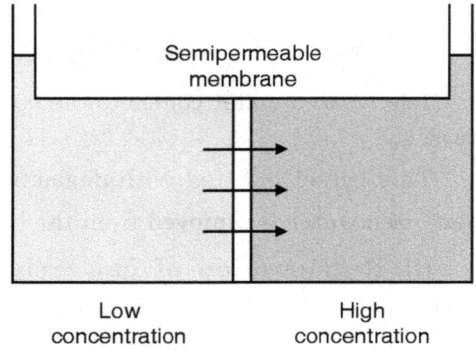

Fig. 1.2 : Osmosis process

When the osmosis process is reversed is called reverse osmosis.

Reverse osmosis :

Reverse osmosis is the process of forcing a solvent from a region of high solute concentration through a semipermeable membrane to a region of low solute concentration by applying external pressure in excess of the osmotic pressure.

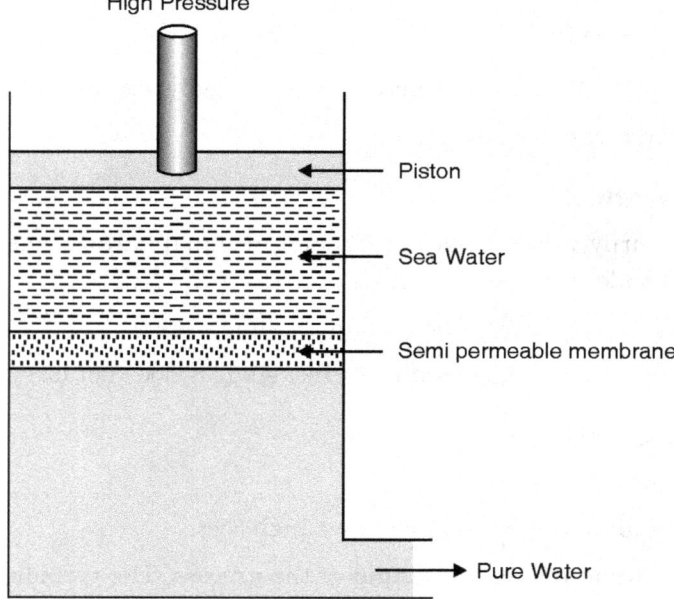

Fig. 1.3 : Reverse Osmosis Method

(i) It consists of tank with two compartments seperated by special semi permable membrane

(ii) The semi permiable membrane in RO is thin film of cellulose acetate or polymethacrylate or polyamide polymer. Where seperation occurs. The membrane size is such that 50nm to 2×10^{-4} nm. It allows solvent to pass but prevent the passage of solute. The membrane should be strong to withstand the applied pressure.

(iii) In one compartment impure water (sea water or brakish water) is taken. In this compartment concentration is high. To this compartment high pressure of the order of 40-70 bar, in case of sea water 30-250 bar and 2-17 bar for brakish water is applied with the help of piston.

(iv) The pure water is forced through semipermeable membrane in other compartment.

(v) The ionic and nonionic salts remain in first compartment.

(vi) The desalined water coming out from RO system is corrosive. It is stabilized by adding lime or caustic to adjust the pH at 6.8 to 8.1 to meet the potable water specification and corrosive control to prevent corrosion of concrete lined surfaces.

(vii) The water coming after pH adjustment is free from pathogenic organisms but not bacteria protozoa and virus. Therefore disinfection is done by treatment of water by means of UV radiation from UV lamp or chlorination process.

Advantages :

(i) This method removes ionic, non ionic, matter as well as colloidat and high molecular weight organic substances. It removes colloidal silica also.

(ii) The maintence cost is the replacement of semipermable membrance which has life of two years.

(iii) The replacement time of membrane is small and uninterrupted water supply can be provided.

(iv) RO systems are used to convert sea water to drinking water.

(v) The method uses no electricity and chemicals therefore envoronmental friendly.

Disadvantages :

(i) Method requires pretreatment of feed water to remove species that adhere or precipitate on membrane and foul its surface.

1.7 Numerical Problems On Hardness

Hardness Calculations :

$$\text{Calcium carbonate equivalents} = \text{weights of the substance} \times \frac{\text{Eq. weight of CaCO}_3}{\text{Eq. weight of substance}}$$

Temperoary Hardness :

1. $Mg(HCO_3)_2$ = Weight of $Mg(HCO_3)_2 \times \dfrac{50}{73}$

2. $Ca(HCO_3)_2$ = Weight of $Ca(HCO_3)_2 \times \dfrac{50}{81}$

3. $MgCO_3$ = Weight of $MgCO_3 \times \dfrac{50}{44}$

4. $CaCO_3$ = Weight of $Mg\ CaCO_3 \times \dfrac{50}{50}$

Permanent Hardness :

1. $CaSO_4$ = Weight of $CaSO_4 \times \dfrac{00}{68}$

2. $MgCl_2$ = Weight of $MgCl_2 \times \dfrac{50}{47.5}$

3. $CaCl_2$ = Weight of $CaCl_2 \times \dfrac{50}{55.5}$

4. $FeCl_2$ = Weight of $FeCl_2 \times \dfrac{50}{63.43}$

5. $CuCl_2$ = Weight of $CuCl_2 \times \dfrac{50}{67.75}$

6. $Mg(NO_3)_2$ = Weight of $Mg(NO_3)_2 \times \dfrac{50}{74}$

7. $MgSO_4$ = Weight of $MgSO_4 \times \dfrac{50}{60}$

The salts does not contribute to hardness.

(a) NaCl

(b) KCl

Numerical Problems

Example 1 :

A water sample was found to contain following salts
($Ca(HCO_3)_2$ = 16.0 mg/litre, $MgCl_2$ = 19.5 mg / lit. $Mg(HCO_3)_2$ = 18.6 mg/lit.
$CaCl_2$ = 14.1 mg/lit. Calculate temperoary, permanent and total hardness.

Sol. :

1. Hardness of $Ca(HCO_3)_2$ = $16.0 \times \dfrac{50}{81}$ = 9.876

2. Hardness of $MgCl_2$ = $19.5 \times \dfrac{50}{73}$ = 12.740

Temperoary Hardness = 9.876 + 12.740 = 22.616 mg/lit = 22.616 ppm

3. Hardness of $MgCl_2$ = $19.5 \times \dfrac{50}{47.5}$ = 20.526

4. Hardness of $CaCl_2$ = $14.1 \times \dfrac{50}{55.5}$ = 12.703

Permanent hardness = 20.526 + 12.703 = 33.229 mg/lit. = 33.229 ppm.

Result : Total hardness = Temperoary Hardness + Permanent hardness
= 22.616 + 33.229 = 55.845 ppm.

Example 2 :

Calculate temperoary, permanent and total hardness of water sample in ppm from the following data :

(a) $Mg(HCO_3)_2$ = 8.4 mg/lit   (b) $Ca(HCO_3)$ = 38.0 mg/lit

(c) $MgCl_2$ = 20 mg/lit   (d) $MgSO_4$ = 8 mg/lit

(e) $CaCl_2$ = 8 mg/lit   (f) KCl = 50 mg/lit

Sol. : (a) Hardness of $Mg(HCO_3)_2$ = $8.4 \times \dfrac{50}{73}$ mg/lit = 5.753 ppm

(b) Hardness of $Ca(HCO_3)_2$ = $38 \times \dfrac{50}{81}$ mg/lit = 23.457 ppm

Temperoary hardness = (a + b) = 5.753 + 23.457 = 29.21 ppm.

(c) Hardness of $MgCl_2$ = $20 \times \dfrac{50}{47.5}$ mg/lit = 21.053

(d) Hardness of $MgSO_4$ = $28 \times \dfrac{50}{60}$ mg/lit = 23.333 ppm.

(e) Hardness of $CaCl_2$ = $48 \times \dfrac{50}{55.5}$ mg/lit = 43.243 ppm.

Permanent hardness = (c + d + e)
= 21.053 + 23.333 + 43.243 = 87.629 ppm.

KCl does not contribute to hardness

Result : Total hardness = Temperoary Hardness + Permanent hardness
= 29.21 + 87.629 = 116.839 ppm.

Exercise

Long Answer Questions

1. Discuss the different sources of water.
2. Explain the common impurities present in natural water.
3. Define acidity. What is mineral acidity and total acidity? Give the experimental procedure to determine total acidity.
4. Define alkalinity. Distinguish between phenolphthalein and methyl orange alkalinity. Discuss the experimental determination of phenolphthalein and methyl orange acidity.

5. Explain the term dissolved oxygen. Give the method to estimate dissolved oxygen.
6. What is soft and hard water ?
7. Explain the different types of hardness of water. What is the unit of hardness ? Discuss the EDTA method to determine total hardness of water.
8. Discuss in short ill effects of hard water.
9. Discuss ill effects of hard water in different industries.
10. What is the difference between sledges and scales ? Mention the disadvantages caused by them.
11. Discuss water softening treatment by ion exchange process.

Short Answer Questions

1. What in pH ? How it explains water quality ?
2. Explain the term acidity of water.
3. Explain the term alkalinity of water.
4. Write a note on Winkler's method.
5. In which forms chlorides are present in water ? What are the effects of presence of chloride? Explain the experimental method to determine chloride in water.
6. What is soft and hard water ?
7. Discuss the experimental procedure to determine total hardness of water.
8. What are the ill effects of hardness for domestic purposes ?
9. Discuss ill effects of hard water in steam generation.
10. What are the different troubles caused by use of hard water in boilers ?
11. Explain the causes of corrosion of boiler.
12. What are priming and foaming ? What are the disadvantages of priming ? How are priming and foaming avoided.
13. Write a note on caustic embrittlement.
14. Explain the process of disinfection by chlorine.
15. Discuss the process of reverse osmosis for desalination of water.
16. What are cation and anion exchange resins ? What are essential properties of ion exchange resins ? What is ion exchange reaction?

Problems

1. Find the total hardness of water when 25 cm^3 of the water sample requires 1.9 cm^3 of 0.05 M EDTA solution.
   Ans.: 380 ppm
2. Calculate temporary, permanent and total hardness if 50 cm^3 water sample consumed 15 cm^3 of 0.01 m EDTA solution before boiling and 5 cm^3 after boiling.
   Ans.: Total hardness - 300ppm, permanent hardness - 100ppm, Temporary hardness - 200ppm

University Questions

1. Explain with suitable diagram, industrial softering of hard water by continuous lime soda, process / hot lime soda process.
2. Ill effects of using hard water in industries.
3. What are bad effects of scales and sluge formation in steam generating boilers.
4. What are the ill effects of hard water in domestic uses ?
5. Describe the following parameters of water.
   (i) Acidity (ii) Dissolved oxygen.
6. Write short notes on :
   (a) Disinfection by chlorine.
   (b) Zeolite process.
   (c) Alkalinity of water
   (d) Hot soda lime process
   (e) Sedimentation and Coagulation

Problems

1. Calculate temperoary, permanent and total hardness of water sample in ppm having following data after analysis in mg/lit.
   (i) $Mg(HCO_3)_2$ = 7.3 mg/lit   (ii) $Ca(HCO_3)_2$ = 40.5 mg/lit
   (iii) $MgCl_2$ = 19 mg/lit.   (iv) $CaCl_2$ = 55.75 mg/lit.

2. A sample of water analysis has been found to containfollowings in ppm. Calculate the temperoary, permanent and total hardnes of water in ppm.

   $Mg(HCO_3)_2$ - 10.75 ppm (mol. wt. 146)
   $Ca(HCO_3)_2$ - 9.5 ppm (mol. wt. 162)
   $CaSO_4$ - 5.3 ppm (mol. wt. 136)
   $MgCl_2$ - 4.2 ppm (mol. wt. 95)

❐❐❐

Unit 2

Analytical Chemistry

- Introduction
- Advantages and disadvantages of Instrumental methods.
- pHmetry :
  - Introduction
  - pHmeasurement using glass electrode
  - Applications of pHmetry
- Spectrometry
  - Introduction
  - Laws of spectrometry (Lamber and Beer Lambert law)
  - Single beam spectrophotometer (schematic working and application)
- Chromatography
  - Introduction
  - Types
  - Gas–liquid chromatography (GLC) basic principle, instrumentation and applications.
- Exercise

2.1 Introduction – Analytical Chemistry :

Analytical chemistry is the important branch ot chemistry developed and gained importance in last fifty years. Analytical chemistry is a branch of chemistry concerned with characterization of chemical composition of matter. It deals with the separation and analysis of chemical substances. Analysis is concerned with chemical composition and determination of chemical structure as well as measurement of physical properties. It deals with both qualitative and quantitative aspect. The qualitative analysis gives us information about the nature of the sample by knowing about the presence and absence of certain components. The quantitative analysis deals about the content present in the sample.

Many simple detection procedures are used in qualitative analysis. The inorganic qualitative analysis using hydrogen sulphide is the systematic procedure of identifying a cation or anion of inorganic substance either single or mixture of two or more substances. In organic qualitative analysis, the organic compounds are detected either single or in mixture. These procedures are useful for learning the analytical procedures for students.

The spot tests are simple and rapid method of detecting many molecules and ions. In forensic laboratories the thin layer and paper chromatography are used in detecting different blood groups and different ink. Some spectroscopic methods like emission spectroscopy finds its use in fast detection of some inorganic compounds. Such many methods are used in qualitative analysis.

There are large number of methods developed which are non-instrumental or chemical and instrumental in quantitative analysis. It was mainly used for inorganic substance. But it is useful for the analysis of organic substances also. Now-a-days it is no more for chemistry only. It finds applications almost in every field of science and technology. It is applicable for the analysis of food, air, fertilizers, soil, plant, pharmaceuticals, blood, urine, body fluids like hormones, vitamins, hair, alloys, ores, water etc.

Methods Used in Quantitative Analysis :

The measurement of physical and physico-chemical properties of the substance before, during and after the chemical reaction provide lot of information about the analytical method to be selected. A general Classification of quantitative methods in terms of physical and chemical properties are given in the table 2.1.

Table 2.1: Classification of Quantitative Methods of Analysis

Sr. No.	Analytical Method	Characteristic Property of Method
1.	Gravimetric	Weight of pure substance or of stoichiometric compound containing in it.
2.	Volumetric	Volume of standard reagent solution reacting with the substance.
3.	Spectrometric	Intensity of electromagnetic radiation absorbed or emitted by the substance.
4.	Electrochemical	Electrical properties of the solution of the substance.
5.	Radiochemical	Intensity of nuclear radiation emitted by the substance.
6.	Mass spectrometric	Abundance of molecular fragments derived by the substance.
7.	Chromatographic	Physicochemical properties of individual substances after separation.

The methods of analysis in quantitative analysis are also Classified as non–instrumental or chemical methods and instrumental methods. Volumetric and gravimetric methods are chemical methods which are important and widely used. Chemical methods are quickly adopted to analyse new type of substances. These methods are used even today because of simplicity ease and reproducibility.

Instrumental Methods

Instrumental methods are based on the measurement of some physical property, of the substance by instrument to determine its chemical composition. These methods are accurate, fast and lead to automation. In instrumental analysis descrete samples are used or monitored continuously. This is useful when quality of the product, safety of a chemical substance and effect on environment is involved. A number of purely instrumental methods have been investigated. The instruments require calibration for each type of sample. Some instrumental methods show the accuracy and precision equivalent to chemical methods. Instrumental methods and chemical methoc supplement each other. Both techniques have been extensively used in good analytical, laboratories. Table 2.2 gives the list of teh instrumental methods and physical property used.

Instrumental methods mainly include optical and electrochemical methods. Optical methods are based on the interaction of desired constituent with electromagnetic radiation. This involves UV, IR and visible spectrophotometry, emission spectroscopy. Scattering of radiation is related with nephalometry and turbidimetry and Raman spectroscopy. Electrochemical methods are based on the relationship between electrical properties like voltage, current or resistance and chemical reactions. Conductometry, potentiometrv, polarography, voltametry, amperometry and colorimetry are included in this Class. These methods of analysis of high degree of accuracy and capable of measuring concentration as low as 10^{-10} molar.

In addition, properties such as dielectric constant, fluorescence, radioactivity, magnetic susceptibility are also used in analytical methods.

Table 2.2 : Instrumental method and physical property

	Physical Property	Instrumental Method
1.	Absorption of radiation	(i) Ultra violet, visible infrared spectro photometry
		(ii) Atomicabsention spectroscopy
		(iii) Nuclear magnetic responance sepctroscopy
2.	Emission of radiation	(i) Emission spectroscopy
		(ii) Flame photometry
		(iii) Fluorometry
		(iv) Radiochemicel methods

	Physical Property	Instrumental Method
3.	Scattering of radiation	(i) Turbidimetry (ii) Nephelometry (iii) Raman Spectroscopy
4.	Electrical Potential	Potentiometry
5.	Electrical Conductance	Conductometry
6.	Electrical Current	(i) Polarography (ii) Amparometry (iii) Coulometry
7.	Quantity of electricity	(i) Coulometry (ii) Electrogravimetry
8.	Refraction of radiation	(i) Refractometry (ii) Interferometry
9.	Rotation of radiation	Polarimetry
10.	Diffraction of radiation	Xray diffraction method
11.	Thermal Properties	(i) Thermogravimetry (TGA) (ii) Differential Thermatnetry (DTA) (iii) Differential scanning calorimetry (DSC)
12.	Mass to charge ratio	Mass spectrometry

Instruments used in chemical analysis are unique in their function. Instruments do not give direct quantitative data but provides information which can be easily converted into suitable form which corelates with structure and content.

There are following steps to obtain the data using instrumental analysis :

(a) Generation of a signal : Singal generator usually gives the signal which is indicative of the component and its concentration. In pHmeter H^+ ion concentration in the solution acts as a signal generator. In spectrophotometer, colour of the solution and radiation from source constitutes the signal generator.

(b) Transformation of signal into measurable form or unit : The signal generated is converted into a more conveniently measurable signal using transducers. In spectrophotometers radiant energy is converted into electrical energy with help of components like thermocouple, phototube or photo meltiplier tube. In pHmeter glass–calomel system converts the signal to electrical potential.

(c) Amplification of transduced signal : Signal processors generally modifies the transduced signal to make it more convenient for analysis. Generally it involves amplification of the signal. The amplification is done electronically to increase the sensitivity.

(d) Read out device : The transduced and amplified signal is presented as a displacement along the scale or on the chart of the recorder. It involves the deflection of the needle of galvanometer, deflection of light from mirror of the galvanometer etc. It generally converts processed into signal that is observable by the observer.

The modern instruments employ micro–processors, computers, amplifiers, integrated circuits to get rapid and reproducible signal every time.

It is necessary that every instrument should give rapid response which should be quantitative and proportional to the information it recieves. A great deal of electronic circuits are involved in the instrument for generation of signal, its amplification and converting into displayed signal. There is tremendous improvement in the field of electronics and therefore sophistication and modernization of instrument has been occured.

There are some advantages and some disadvantages of instrumental method as discussed below.

Uses of Analytical Chemistry

Chemical analysis is essential aspect of modern technology. The function of analytical chemistry is fundamental and applied. Analytical chemistry is found to be useful in almost all branches of chemistry such as organic, inorganic and biochemistry etc. It is not only useful in chemistry but is interdisciplinary branch of science. It has enormous importance in every branch of science and technology. It touches upon agriculture, medical and clinical, environmental, forensic, metallurgy, pharmaceutical, engineering, astrophysics, electronic, petrochemical, biology, microbiology etc. Analytical chemistry elevates the growth of different branches of science. The important uses of analytical chemistry are as follows :

1. Quality Control : This is related to our day to day life. Analysis of food, water and air are of vital importance. The food we eat, water we drink and air we breath must be of good quality. The standards for these are set and frequent analysis must be performed to confirm that standards are maintained. Quality control is the essential part of all industries. Analysis of raw materials and final products are necessary to check the specifical of raw material and purity of the final product. Quality control of pharmaceuticals and chemicals is very important.

2. Diagnosis : Most of the diseases are diagnosed by chemical analysis. Analysis of glucose in blood and urine is routine for diabetic patients. Enzymes, vitamins, can be estimated by radio immunoassay technique. The condition of thyroid can be diagnosed by the analysis of activity of radioisotope. The damage of liver is indicated by 12% alkaline phosphate in blood serum.

3. Identification of Chemical Composition and Physical Properties : Chemical analysis is useful in finding the chemical composition and physical properties of chemical substances. Identification of impurities of metals is important for their specific uses. The performances of different fuels and catalyst can be tested with chemical analysis.

4. Estimation of Amount of Constituents of Substances : Estimation of different radioisotopes like thorium, uranium and plutonium in different ores by chemical analysis is most important to obtain fuel for reactors to generate electricity. Determination of fat in ice cream, vitamins and proteins in food stuff are other examples.

5. Research : Use of chemical analysis is essential in research work going on in different fields of science and technology. Instrumental methods promote the quality and quantity of research work and development by avoiding the tedious and manual methods.

The applications of analytical chemistry in some important fields are as summarised below :

1. Petrochemical : Petrochemist uses gas–liquid chromatography to detect and isolate hundreds of components of petroleum.

2. Agriculture : Analysis of different fertilizers for N, P, K and micronutrients helps farmers to choose particular fertilizer to improve the growth of crop.

3. Environmental science : Mass spectrometry is used in the detection of traces of impurities in air and drinking water.

4. Pharmaceutical : Spectrophotometry and chromatography techniques are used in pharmaceutical and microbiological laboratories to constituents of medicines and other product and check the quality of final product.

5. Archeology : Archeologists use radio chemical methods to determine age of specimens. Carbon – 14 dating is used to determine age of archeological carbon sample. Naturally occurring radio nuclides like ^{238}U, ^{232}Th etc. are useful to determine age of rock samples.

6. Forensic : It is related with crimes. Presence of trace elements from gun powder on a defendent's hands and place of crime proves the firing of a gun. Poison by arsenic can be detected and estimated by neutron activation analysis.

7. Medicine : There is unlimited scope in this field for diagnosis using different analytical technique including radio analytical technique. Estimation of glucose, vitamin, enzyme hormones, steroids, drugs, in blood serum and K^+, Na^+ and Ca^{2+} ions in body fluids can be performed by different techniques. Determination of volume of blood, obstruction in blood flow, location of brain tumour etc. are possible by radio analytical techniques.

2.2 Advantages and Disadvantages of Instrumental Methods :

2.2.1 Advantages of Instrumental Methods :
(i) For instrumental analysis a small amount of the sample is needed for analysis.

(ii) Sample analysis by instrumental method is fast as compared to other methods.

(iii) The complex mixture can be analysed even without seperation of the mixture.

(iv) The results obtained are reliable and accurate by instrumental method.

(v) When non instrumental method is not available for analysis, instrumental method can be used.

(vi) Instrumental analysis is important in many fields like chemistry, medicine, phamaceutical, forensic science, biology, engineering etc.

2.2.2 Disadvantages of instrumental methods :
(i) The sensitivity and accuracy of the results depends on the type of the instrument used for analysis.

(ii) There is frequent need of checking the results with other method.

(iii) The instrumental methods of analysis are generally costly because of cost of instrument, cost of maintenance and trained personnel required for instrument handling.

(iv) For handling sophisticated instrument specialized training for handling instrument is required.

(v) The instrumental method may not be specific in some cases.

2.3 pHmetry :

2.3.1 Introduction :

pHmetry is the technique in which pH of the sample solution is measured with the help of the instrument called pHmeter.

Hydrogen ion concentration :

The number of gram ions of hydrogen present in one litre of the solution is called hydrogen ion concentration of the solution.

In pure water, hydrogen ion concentration is 1×10^{-7} g ion per litre. The hydroxy ion concentration in water is also 1×10^{-7} g ion per litre because the ionic product of water K_w is 1×10^{-14}.

$$K_w = [H^+][OH^-]$$

$$K_w = 1 \times 10^{-14}$$

$$[H^+] = [OH^-] = 1 \times 10^{-7}$$

Thus, when H^+ ion concentration is 1×10^{-7} g ion per litre the solution is neutral. If $[H^+] < 1 \times 10^{-7}$ the solution is acidic and $[H^+] > 1 \times 10^{-7}$ the solution is alkaline. It is clear from above discussion that every aqueous solution (acidic, alkaline or neutral) contains both H^+ and OH^- ions. But the product of both ions is always equal to $K_w = 1 \times 10^{-14}$. In other words the concentratin of H^+ and OH^- ions in aqueous solution varies over wide range of 1 M to 1×10^{-14} M.

Definition of pH :

Sorensen defined pH as negative logarithm of H^+ ions concentration expressed in molarity.

$$pH = -\log [H^+] \qquad \ldots(1)$$

Similarly pOH can be expressed as,

$$pOH = -\log [OH^-]$$

For any aqueous solution,

$$K_w = [H^+][OH^-]$$

$$= 1 \times 10^{-14} \text{ at } 15°C$$

Using defination of pH and pOH,

$$pK_w = pH + pOH = 14$$

Where $pK_w = -\log K_w$

Thus, neutral solution has pH = 7

for acidic solution pH < 7

and for alkaline solution pH > 7

The pH values of some of the aqueous solutions of 0.1N acids and 0.1N bases are given in the Table 2.3

Table 2.3

No.	Acids	pH	Bases	pH
1.	HCl (Hydrochlonic acid)	1.0	$NaHCO_3$ (Sodium bicarbonate)	8.4
2.	H_2SO_4 (Sulphuric acid)	1.2	NH_3 (Amonomia)	11.3
3.	CH_3COOH (acetic acid)	2.9	Na_2CO_3 (Sodium Carbonate)	11.6
4.	H_3BO_3 (boric acid)	5.2	NaOH (Sodium Hydroxide)	13.0

Methods of Determination of pH :

There are two important methods of determination of pH.

(i) pH indicator method : In this method indicators are used. Indicators show change of colour depending on degree of acidity of the solution. Indicator changes colour over limited range of pH characteristic of the indicator. The indicator show one colour in extreme acidic solution having undissociated form HI_n^- and other colour in extreme alkaline solution having I_n^- form. The pH is given by the equation,

$$pH = pKa + \log \frac{[I_n^-]}{[HI_n]}$$

Ka is dissociation constant of the indicator. The range is approximately 2 pH units given by pKa ± 1.

e.g. Methyl orange – pH range 3.1 to 4.4, Phenolphthalein 8 to 10. The universal indicator which is the mixture of different indicator can be used for the determination of pH in complete pH scale 1 to 14. Few drops of indicator are added into test solution and colour develped is matched with standard colour chart.

(ii) Potentiometric method : This method is one of most extensive application of emt measurement which gives accurate pH.

In this method a cell is set up which consists of two electrodes and solution whose pH is to be determined. One of the electrode is reversible to H^+ ions and other electrode is reference electrode. Usually saturated calomele electrode (SCE) is used as reference electrode. This electrode can be dipped directly into the solution or agar–agar KCl salt bridge is employed to connect the two electrodes. The emf of the cell is measured using potentiometer. Knowing emf of the electrode reversible to H^+ ions, pH of the solution can be determined.

$$E_{cell} = E_1 + E_{SCE}$$
$$E_1 = E_{cell} - E_{SCE}$$

Different types of electrodes reversible to H^+ ions can be used.

(i) Hydrogen electrode

(ii) Quinhydrone electrode and

(iii) Glass Electrode.

We will consider the measurement of pH using glass electrode.

Operational defination of pH : The experimental methods to determine the pH of aqueous solutions do not measure $[H^+]$ directly. The defination, $pH = -\log [H^+]$ is insufficient and we need operational defination of pH.

The following electrochemical cell can be set as,

| Electrode reversible to H^+ | Buffer solution
(i) Known pH (pH_s)
(ii) Unknown pH (pH) | Agar–Agar KCl Salt bridge | SCE |

First emt E_s is measured using know pH solution.

Then emt E_x is measured using unknown pH solution.

$$E_s = E° - \frac{2.303RT}{F} \log [H^+]$$

$$= E° + \frac{2.303RT}{F} pH_s$$

$$E_x = E° - \frac{2.303RT}{F} \log [H^+]$$

$$= E° + \frac{2.303RT}{F} pH$$

Then
$$E_x - E_s = \frac{2.303RT}{F} (pH - pH_s)$$

$$pH = pH_s + \frac{E_x - E_s}{2.303RT/F} \quad \ldots\ldots(2)$$

This equation is operational defination of pH. pH_s vales of buffer solution are obtained from tables.

2.3.2 pH Measurement Using Glass Electrode :

(i) Glass electrode for pH measurement : The glass electrode is widely used for the measurement of pH of the solutions. It works on the principle that the potential is developed on a glass membrane when placed in the solution containing H^+ ions.

Construction of glass electrode :

(i) It consists of a glass tube to which a special glass bulb made from special glass membrane is attached. The composition of lime soda glass is 72% SiO_2 + 22% Na_2O + 6% CaO used for bulb.

(ii) The thickness of glass membrane is 50 μm.

(iii) The bulb is filled with oil 0.1 M HCl solution or suitable buffer solution of constant pH.

(iv) The silver – silver chloride wire is sealed in a thin glass tube and is fitted in the outer glass tube which dips in 0.1 M HCl solution.

(v) The wire is connected to Ag–AgCl wire for electrical contact.

(vi) This arragement is an internal reference electrode $Ag|AgCl_{(s)}|Cl^-$ for making electrical contact with glass membrane.

(vii) The electrode is completely sealed to keep concentration of 0.1 M HCl solution constant.

(viii) The glass electrode is represented as,

H^+ (solution) | glass 0.1M, HCl, $AgCl_{(s)}$ | $AgCl_{(s)}$ Ag

(ix) The potential developed on the electrode depends on the conectration H^+ ions in solution in which glass electrode is dipped.

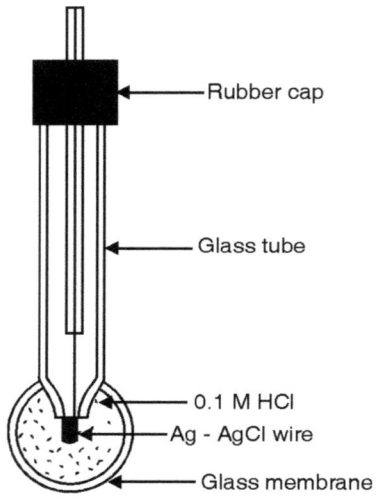
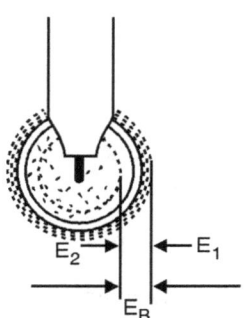

(a) Construction of glass electrode   **(b) Boundary Potential**

Fig. 2.1

Mechanism of glass electrode :

(i) The glass bulb is soaked in water for 12 hours before use.

(ii) The glass bulb forms the hydrated (gel) layer on glass surface.

(iii) The hydrated gel layer acts as semipermiable membrane.

(iv) The exchange of Na^+ ions in glass and H^+ ions in solution takes place.

(v) This ion exchange process can be represented as,

$Na^+ (Gl)^-_s + H^+_{aq} \rightleftharpoons H^+ (Gl)^-_s + Na^+_{aq}$

Exchange of H^+ ions occurs only in the external part of gel layer.

(vi) The phase boundary potential or the potential difference E_B at the interface is the result of difference in potential E_1 developed across gel layer and inner solution in the bulb and E_2 developed across outer solution and gel layer. This boundary potential depends on concentration HCl Solution (C_1) inside the bulb (constant) and concentration of acid solution (C_2) in which glass bulb is immersed.

$$E_B = E_1 - E_2 = \frac{2.303RT}{nF} \log\left(\frac{C_2}{C_1}\right)$$

$$C_1 = \text{Constant} = 0.1 \text{ M}$$

$$E_B = \frac{2.303RT}{nF} \log C_2 - \text{constant A}$$

If $C_1 = C_2$, $E_B = 0$, but it is observed that even when $C_1 = C_2$, a small potential is developed called asymmetric potential (E_{asm})

(vii) The potential of glass electrode (E_a) is given by,

$$E_G = E_B + E_{Ag/AgCl} + E_{asm}$$

$$= \frac{2.303RT}{nF} \log C_2 + (-A + E_{Ag/AgCl} + E_{asm})$$

$$E_G = \frac{2.303RT}{nF} \text{pH} + E_G^°$$

$$E_G = E_G^° + \frac{2.303 \times 8.314 \times 298}{1 \times 96500} \text{pH}$$

$$E_G = E_G^° + 0.059 \text{ pH at } 25°C \qquad \ldots\ldots(3)$$

Where $E_G^° = \text{constant} = (E_{asm} + E_{Ag/AgCl} - A)$

$E_G^°$ is characteristic of each glass electrode

Equation (3) gives the emf of glass electrode.

The potential E_G depends on,

(a) Non uniform composition of glass membrane

(b) Mechanical and chemical attack on external surface.

(c) Strain within membrane.

(d) Degree of hydration of membrane.

(viii) The function of glass electrode stops when glass is dried.

Maintenance of glass electrode :

(i) The glass bulb should not allow to dry.

(ii) The glass bulb should be immersed in distilled water for 12 hours before use. It should be stored in distilled water.

(iii) It should be washed throughly with distilled water after each measurement and several portion of test solution before next measurement.

Advantages of Glass Electrode :

(i) It is convenient and simple to use.

(ii) It is not easily piosoned.

(iii) The equilibrium is rapidly established and results are accurate.

(iv) It can be used when volume of the solution is small.

(v) It can be used in pressure of strong oxidising and reducing agents.

(vi) It can be used in coloured, turbid and colloidal solutions.

(vii) It can be used upto pH 9 and with special glass electrode upto 13 to 14 pH.

Disadvantages of glass electrode :

(i) The glass bulb of the electrode is very fragile and has to be used carefully.

(ii) The glass membrane offer very high electical resistance (~ 100 million Ohm) hence ordinary potentiometer cannot be used for the emf measurement. Therefore special instrument electronic potentiometer called pH meter is required. This is electronic volt meter which require practically no current for their operation.

(iii) Frequent standardization of electrode is necessary because asymmetric potential changes with time.

(iv) The glass electrode cannot be used in dehydrating solution such as pure ethyl alcohol, acetic acid and gelatin.

pH measurement using glass electrode :

(i) The glass electrode is placed in distilled water for 12 hours and stored in distilled water.

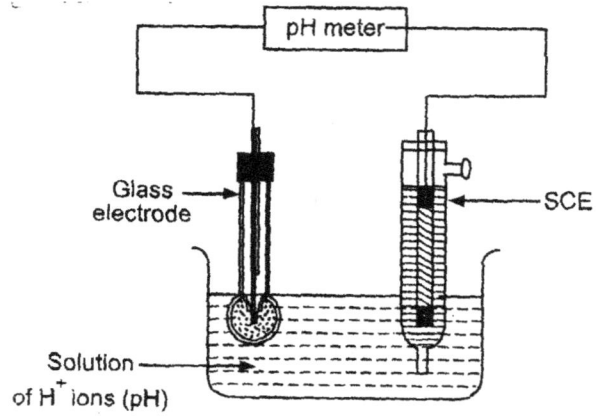

Fig. 2.2 : Cell arrangement for pH measurement

(ii) The solution (unknown pH) is placed in a small beaker.

(iii) The glass electrode and dipping type saturated calomel electrode (SCE) are dipped into the solution.

(iv) The electrodes are connected to pH meter as shown in the Fig. 2.2. Thus a cell is set up for pH measurement represented as

$Ag \mid AgCl_{(s)}, 0.1 M HCl \mid glass \mid unknown\ pH\ solution \mid KCl_{(satd)}, Hg_2Cl_{2(s)} \mid Hg$

(v) The emf the cell is measured.

(vi) The emf of the cell is given by,

$$E_{cell} = E_G - E_{SCE}$$

E_G – Potential of glass electrode

E_{SCE} – Potential of SCE.

Then, $\quad E_G = E_{cell} + E_{SCE}$

The pH of the solution is determined using the equation,

$$E_G = E_G^\circ + 0.059\ pH \text{ at } 25°C$$

Calibration of glass electrode :

The different gas electrodes have different E_G° values for glass electrodes are determined called calibration of glass electrode. For this purpose standard buffer solution is used. The cell potential is measured with standard buffer solution of known pH and E_G° is found.

$$E_G = E_G^\circ + 0.059\ pH$$

$$E_G^\circ = E_G - 0.059\ pH$$

Using E_G° value, the pH of solution can be evaluated.

Instrumentation :

pH meter : The potentiometer is useful for the measurement of emt of a cell having resistant less than 10^3 ohm. When a glass electrode is used in a cell, the resistance increases to 100 to 500 Mohm. Then the current in the circuit for 0.1 mV range corresponds to 2×10^{-12} to 2×10^{-13} amp. This current is so small that it cannot be detected even by sensitive galvanometer. For this current amplification is required. The electronic instrument generally used for pH measurement is called pH meter. There are two types of pH meter.

1. Potentiometric pH meter :

(i) The instrument is same as potentiometer except that ordinary galvanometer is replaced by electronic circuit that amplifies the current in the cell circuit of the order of 10^{10}. The milliammeter can be used as null point detector.

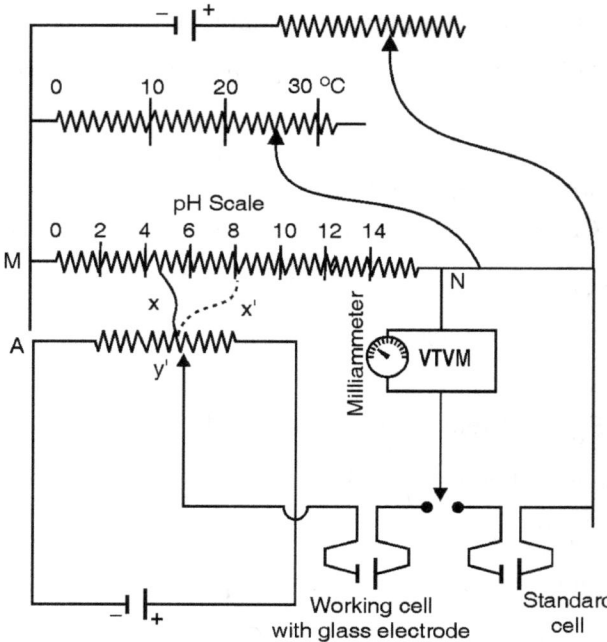

Fig. 2.3 : Schematic diagram of potentiometric pH meter

(ii) Fig. 2.3 shows the schematic diagram of potentiometric pH meter. The VTVM (Vaccum tube volt meter) is a device to amplify current with milliammeter to detect current is placed in circuit.

(iii) It consists of slide wire MN calibrated in both millivolt and pH units.

(iv) The resistance R_T parallel to MN is calibrated in degree celcius which must be adjusted to the temperature of solution before standardization.

(v) The DPDT (Double pole double through) switch S_w can connect either standard cell or cell with unknown pH solution.

(vi) The switch S_w is moved to position D so that Weston standard cell is in circuit.

(vii) Then the resistance R_1 is adjusted to position Y until deflection is zero.

(viii) Now the standard buffer solution of known pH is taken in a cell. The S_w switch is moved to position C. The cell with standard buffer solution, glass electrode and SCE is in circuit. Now the potentiometer MN is a adjusted to position of known pH of buffer solution.

Now potentiometer AB is adjusted to position Y' until balance is obtained. This accounts the variation of $\overset{\circ}{E_a}$ for different glass electrode.

(ix) Now the cell contains solution of unknown pH. Then the position X' is obtained on potentiometer MN where no deflection is obtained. The pH corresponding to X' is unknown pH.

2. **Director Reading pH meter :**

  (i) The direct reading pH meters are based on negative feedback principle.

  (ii) The emt of the cell consisting of glass and SCE and pH solution is impressed across high resistance and direct current flowing, through resistance is fed to amplifier circuit for amplification.

  (iii) The amplified current is recorded on milliammeter. The scale of milliammeter is directly calibrated in pH and millivolts.

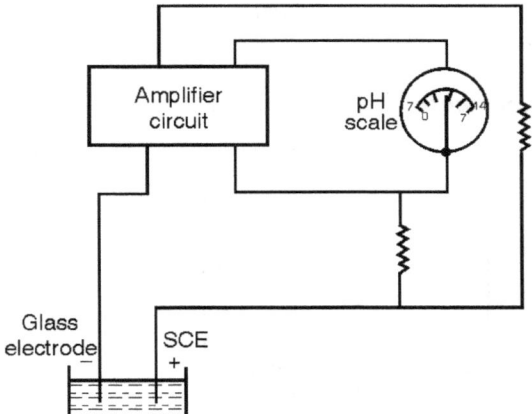

Fig. 2.4(a) Schematic diagram of direct reading pH meter.

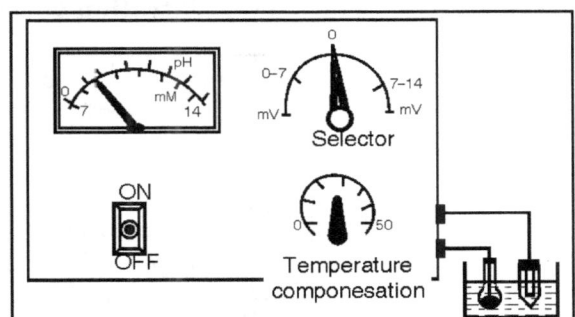

Fig. 2.4(b) Different controls of pH meter

  (iv) The front panel of pH meter is shown in the Fig. 2.4(b). The scale has 0–7 and 7 to 14 range which can be selected by selector knob.

  (v) The cell with standard buffer solution is connected and set buffer knob is adjusted so that buffer knob reads known pH.

  (vi) Now the cell contains solution of unknown pH. The pH of the solution is directly read on pH meter.

2.3.3 Applications of pHmetry :

There are many applications of pHmetry in different fields of science and technology.

(I) Acid–base titrations can be performed easily using pH meter. Weak acids, dibasic or tribasic acids and mixture of acids can be titrated. Arrangement for pH titration is shown in the Fig. 2.5 (a).

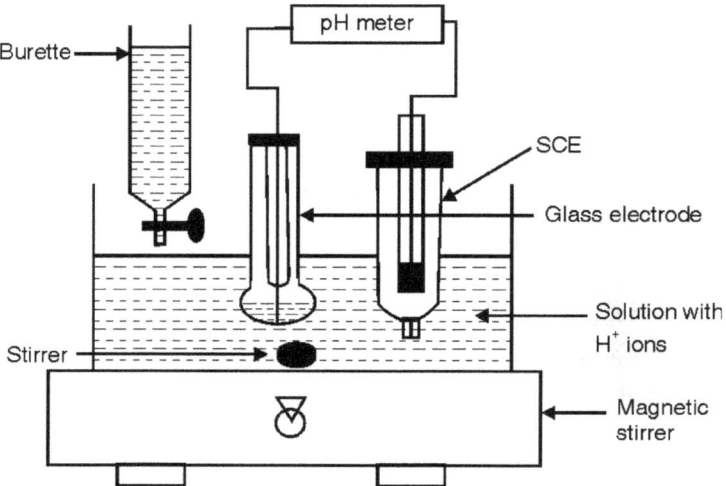

Fig. 2.5 (a) : Titration curves for acetic acid vs NaOH.

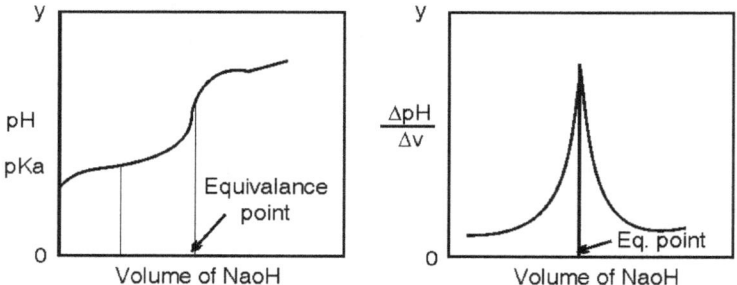

Fig. 2.5 (b) : Titration curves for acetic acid vs NaOH.

(a) When acetic acid is titrated with NaOH. The pH of solution increases as NaOH is added to acetic acid. Midpoint of steepy rising portion gives equivalence point. The plot of pH vs volume of titrant (NaOH) for weak acid acetic acid is showin in Fig. 2.5 (b). The plot of $\Delta PH/\Delta V$ gives equivalent point as the peak.

(b) The tribasic acid can be titrated with NaOH. The equivalence point for each step of neutralisation can be located.

(i) $H_3PO_4 + NaOH \longrightarrow NaH_2PO_4 + H_2O$ (ii) $NaH_2PO_3 + NaOH \longrightarrow NaHPO_4 + H_2O$

(iii) $Na_2HPO_4 + H_2O \longrightarrow Na_3PO_4 + H_2O$

The first and second neutralization steps are clearly shown. The third neutralization point cannot be relized because the solution becomes very alkaline (high pH). Therefore at the point X $CaCl_2$ solution is added in excess. $CaCl_2$ reacts with Na_2HPO_4 and HCl is produced which is equivalent to acid (H) present in Na_2HPO_4 and pH is lowered upto point Y.

$2Na_2HPO_4 + HCl \longrightarrow Ca_3(PO_4)_2 + 2NaCl + 2HCl$

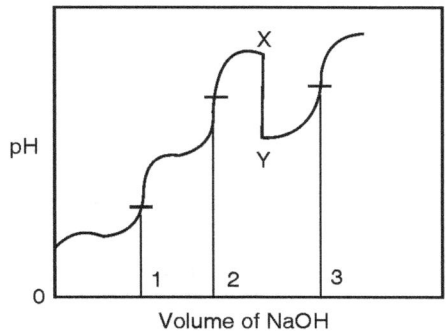

Fig. 2.6 : Titration curve for H_3PO_4 vs NaOH.

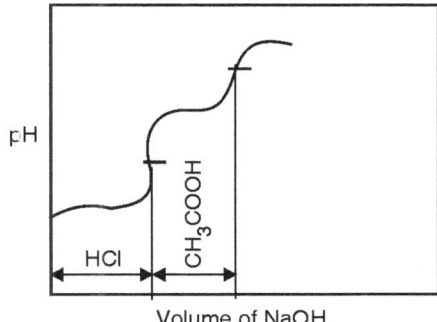

Fig. 2.7 : Titration curve for mixture (HCl + CH_3COOH) of acids vs NaOH.

Further titration of solution with NaOH gives third neutralization point. (see Fig. 2.6)

(c) Pka of weak acids can be determined from the plot of pH vs volume of NaOH. The pH corresponding to half the equivalence point is Pka value of the acid. (see Fig. 2.5 a)

(d) Mixture of acids (HCl + acetic acid) can be titrated to obtain amount of each in the mixture. seperate cures are obtained for two acids. (see Fig. 2.7)

(II) pH of blood : The pH of the blood sample is required for diagnosis. Generally venous blood is taken for pH measurement but for special applications arterial blood may be required. The arterial blood had pH 7.31 to 7.45 for all ages and and sexes at body temperature (37°C)

The pH of blood buffer system changes with temperature. The pH of blood at body temperature is different than at room temperature. Therefore pH of blood should be measured at 37°C and sample should not be exposed to atmosphere.

The standard buffer solution is calibrated at 37°C. The sample should be kept in anaerobic conditions to prevent loss or absorption of CO_2. The sample should be equilibrated to 37°C and pH measurement done within 15 minutes after the sample is collected. The glass electrode should be washed with saline solution after each measurement to prevent coating of glass electrode.

(III) pH of soil sample : pH of soil is most important parameter for the proper growth of plants.

The soil sample is placed in distilled water for definite period. The supernant liquid is removed and used for pH measurement.

(IV) pH in nonaqueous solvents : The measurement of pH in nonaqueous solvent is not very accurate and referred to as apparent pH. The standardization with aquous solution and measurement of pH in nonaqueous solvent has little significance in terms of H^+ activity because unknown liquid junction potential is large depending on the solvent.

2.4 Spectrometry :

2.4.1 Introduction :

Spectroscopy deals with interaction of electromagnetic radiations with matter. In analytical chemistry, X–rays microwave, infra–red, visible, ultraviolet and radio frequency regions of electromagnetic spectrum are widely used. In modern age it is impossible to think of a chemistry lab without spectroscopic units. These methods are simple, rapid, less expensive, less polluting, accurate, reliable and even a person from non–chemistry background can perform.

Electromagnetic radiation and its interactions :

The spectrometric methods of analysis depends on the absorption of electromagnetic radiation from the source and amount of radiation absorbed is related to the concentration of analyte. This method based on absorption of light is called **absorption spectrometry.**

Electromagnetic radiation and its characterization :

(i) Electromagnetic radiation consists of energy associated with electric and magnetic fields resulting from acceleration of electric charge.

(ii) The electric and magnetic fields require no supporting medium and can be propagated through space or vacuum are at right angles to each other and to the direction of propagation.

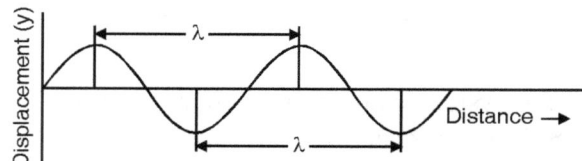

Fig. 2.8 : Electromagnetic radiation as simple harmonic wave

(iii) The electromagnetic radiation possesses properties of both waves and discrete particles which are termed as photons.

(iv) It is considered a simple harmonic wave propagated from a source and travelling in a straight line.

Characteristic Properties of Electromagnetic Radiation :

(i) Wavelength (λ) : Wavelength is defined as the distance travelled during a complete cycle. It is distance between two successive maxima or minima. (See Fig. 2.1). It is represented by λ.

(ii) Frequency (υ) : Frequency is defined as the number of vibrations per second. It is represented by υ.

(iii) Wave number ($\bar{\upsilon}$) : Wave number is the number of waves in unit length. It is reciprocal of wavelength.

$$\bar{\upsilon} = \frac{1}{\lambda}$$

Relations between wavelength, frequency and wave number and energy :

(i) $\quad$ Wavelength $= \dfrac{\text{Velocity of light in cms}^{-1}}{\text{frequency in s}^{-1} \text{ or Hz}}$

$$\lambda = \frac{C}{\upsilon}$$

(ii) $\quad$ Wave number $= \dfrac{1}{\text{Wavelength}}$

$$\bar{\upsilon} = \frac{1}{\lambda}$$

(iii) $\quad \bar{\upsilon} = \dfrac{1}{\lambda} = \dfrac{c}{\upsilon}$

(iv) $\quad \upsilon = \dfrac{c}{\lambda} \qquad\qquad E = h\upsilon$

or $\quad E = \dfrac{hc}{\lambda} \qquad\qquad$ or $\qquad E = h \cdot c \cdot \bar{\upsilon}$

It is Clear from above equations that greater the frequency or shorter the wave length greater is the energy and vice a versa. Thus ultraviolet has higher energy than visible.

Different units of wavelength :

Wavelength is expressed in different units. The unit is chosen for particular range of electromagnetic radiation such that it does not involve large power of ten.

Table 2.3

No.	Unit	Symbol	Value	Region
1.	Centimeter	cm	—	Radio frequency
2.	Meter	m	10^2 cm	Radio frequency
3.	Angstrom	A°	10^{-8} cm $= 10^{-10}$ m	X rays
4.	Nanometer	nm	10^{-9} m = 10 A°	Ultraviolet visible
5.	Micron or Micro–meter	µm	10^{-6} m	Infrared and microwave
6.	Millimicron	mµ	10^{-3} µ $= 10^{-9}$ m = nm	Ultraviolet and visible
7.	Picometer	pm	10^{-12} m	γ–ray

Electromagnetic Spectrum :

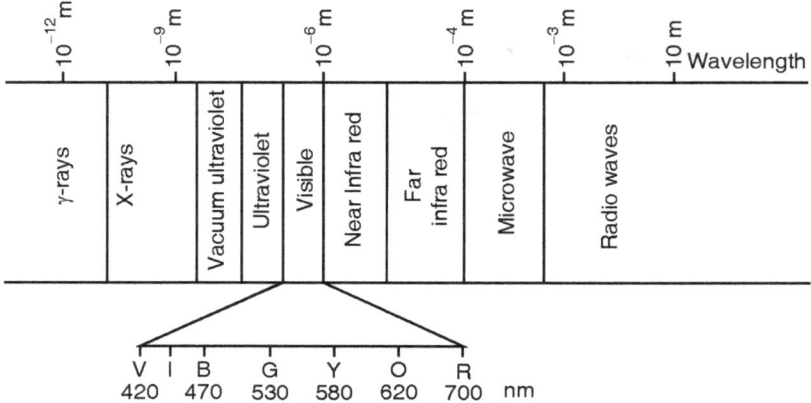

Fig. 2.9 : Electromagnetic spectrum with extended visible region

The electromagnetic spectrum is the range of frequencies over which the electromagnetic radiations are propagated as shown in Fig. 2.9. The spectrum is split into different region according to wavelength. The ultraviolet and visible regions are most important in spectrometry. The near ultraviolet region which extends from 200 – 380 nm to 780 nm which can be seen by human eye. The infrared region extents from 0.75 µm to 300 µm.

Principle of Spectrometry :

Absorption of radiation by matter :

When electromagnetic radiation passes through a layer of solid, liquid or gas certain frequencies or wavelength may be selectivity removed by absorption (180 – 850 nm). The electromagnetic energy is transferred to the atoms or molecules of the sample. In spectrophotometry absorption of light in the UV and visible region is considered. When white light which contains whole spectrum of visible region is passed through the sample, it will absorb certain of the wavelengths and radiation of unabsorbed wavelength is transmitted.

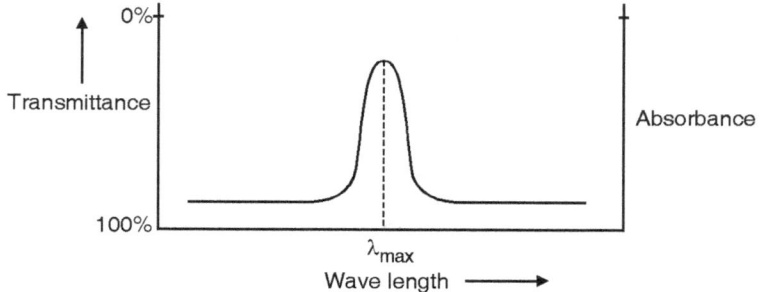

Fig. 2.10 : Absorption of radiation by the substance

For example, $CuSO_4$ solution appears blue because it absorbs 580 – 595 wavelength of yellow colour and transmits the wavelength 435 – 492 corresponds to blue colour.

In spectrophotometry absorption in UV (180 – 400 nm) and visible (400 – 800 nm) region by inorganic and organic substances. The absorption of radiant energy result into displacement of valence electrons. Absorbing species involve n, π and σ electrons.

The coloured inorganic substances absorb in the visible region. The metal complexes are intense coloured inorganic compounds due to charge transfer transitions and shows high absorption in visible region. When inorganic complexes are formed with organic ligands undergo $\pi \rightarrow \pi^*$ [C = O (ketone) $\rightarrow$ C$^+$ — O$^-$] and n $\rightarrow \pi^*$ [C = O (ketone) $\rightarrow$ C$^+$ = C$^-$] transitions and show intense absorption.

The unsaturated organic compounds undergo $\pi \rightarrow \pi^*$ or $\pi \rightarrow \sigma^*$ transition by absorption in UV region. The oganic compounds with atoms likes Cl, N, S, O have unpaired p electrons in addition to σ electrons. The unpaired p electrons are promoted to antibonding σ orbital (n $\rightarrow \sigma^*$ transition by absorption of UV radiation.

2.4.2 Fundamental Laws of Spectrometry :

Firstly, some important terms are considered

[A] Intensity or radiant power (I) :

Energy transferred per unit time is called intensity or power. It is represented by symbol I. The intensity of incident beam is I_0 and that of transmitted beam is I_t. Intensity is detected by photocell.

[B] Transmittance (T) :

Transmittance is the fraction of intensity of incident light transmitted by the sample. It is the ratio of intensity of transmitted beam by a sample to the intensity of incident beam upon the sample.

$$T = \frac{I_t}{I_0}$$

It is expressed in % $\quad\quad \%T = \frac{I_t}{I_0} \times 100$

[C] Absorbance (A) :

Old name of absorbance is optical density. Absorbance is the logarithm to base 10 of reciprocal of transmittance.

It can also be defined as logarithm to base 10 of ratio of intensity of incident beam to the intensity of transmitted beam by a sample.

$$A = \log_{10} \frac{1}{T} \quad , \quad A = \log_{10} \frac{I_0}{I_t}$$

[D] Path length (b) :

It is the thickness of the cell.

Consider a beam of monochromatic wavelength of intensity I_0, incident upon a homogenous medium of thickness b. The part of incident beam is absorbed by the medium and I is the intensity of the transmitted beam.

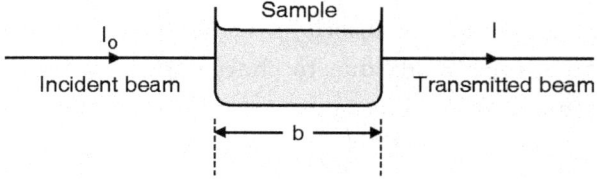

Fig. 2.11 : Absorption of light by the sample

1. Lambert's Law :

When a beam of monochromatic light passes through the transparent medium, the rate of decrease of intensity with respect to thickness of medium is directly proportional to the intensity of incident light

i.e.
$$-\frac{dI}{db} = I$$

$$-\frac{dI}{db} = K_1 I$$

$$-\frac{dI}{I} = K_1 \, db$$

where K_1 is is the constant of proportionality.

$$-\int_{I_0}^{I} \frac{dI}{I} = K_1 \int_0^b db$$

$$[-\ln I]_{I_0}^{I} = K_1 b$$

$$-\ln I + \ln I_0 = K_1 b$$

$$\ln \frac{I_0}{I} = K_1 b$$

$$2.303 \log \frac{I_0}{I} = K_1 b$$

$$\log \frac{I_0}{I} = K_2 b$$

or
$$I = I_0 e^{-k_2 b} \qquad \ldots(1)$$

where
$$K_2 = \frac{K_1}{2.303}$$

From Equation (1), the Lambert's law can be stated as the intensity of transmitted beam decreases exponentially as the absorbing thickness of the medium increases arithmetically at a fixed concentration.

2. Beer's Law :

The law states that when a beam of monochromatic light passes through a transparent medium, the rate of decrease of intensity with concentration is proportional to intensity of incident radiation.

Mathematically, we can write,

$$-\frac{dI}{dc} = K_3 I$$

$$-\frac{dI}{I} = K_3 \, dC$$

$$-\int_{I_0}^{I} \frac{dI}{I} = K_3 \int_{0}^{c} dC$$

$$[-\ln I]_{I_0}^{I} = K_3 [C]_{0}^{c}$$

$$-\ln I + \ln I_0 = K_3 C$$

$$\ln \frac{I_0}{I} = K_3 C$$

$$2.303 \log \frac{I_0}{I} = K_3 C$$

$$\log \frac{I_0}{I} = \frac{K_3}{2.303} C = K_4 C$$

where $\quad K_4 = \dfrac{K_3}{2.303} \quad$ or $\quad I = I_0 \, e^{-K_4 C} \quad$ ...(2)

From the equation (2), the Beer's law can be stated as the intensity of transmitted light decreases exponentially as the concentration of medium increases mathematically when path length is constant.

3. Beer–Lambert Law :

Combining equations (1) and (2), we can write,

$$I = I_0 \, e^{-abc}$$

$$\log \frac{I_0}{I} = abc \quad \text{or} \quad A = abc$$

where a is called absorptivity

When concentration is expressed in mole L^{-1} and path length in cm, a is replaced ϵ.

$$\boxed{A = \epsilon bc} \quad \text{...(3)}$$

Where ϵ is called as molar extinction coefficient or molar absorptivity. Equation (3) is fundamental equation of spectrophotometry and called as Beer–Lambert law.

Definition of Molar Extinction Coefficient (Molar Absorptivity):

When $C = 1$ mol L^{-1} and $b = 1$ cm then

$$A = \epsilon$$

Then molar extinction coefficient (molar absorptivity) is defined as the absorbance of the solution when its concentration is 1 mol L^{-1} and path length is 1 cm.

Absorbance and concentration (Determination of ϵ):

When absorbance is plotted against concentration in mol L^{-1} a straight line passing through origin is obtained. The slope of the line is equal to molar extinction coefficient.

When path length b is constant, absorbance is directly proportional to concentration

$$A \propto C$$

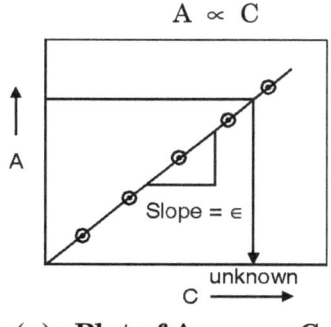
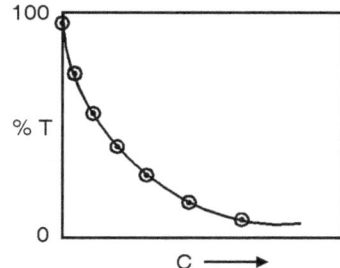

(a) : Plot of A versus C **(b) : Plot of %T versus C**

Fig. 2.12

Also $\quad C \propto \log \dfrac{I_0}{I} \propto \log \dfrac{1}{T}$

The plot of %T versus concentration is exponential in nature as shown in the Fig. 2.5.

Additivity of Absorbances:

The Beer's law indicates that absorbance at any particular wavelength is directly proportional to the number of absorbing species. When the solution contains more that one type of absorbing species which do not interact with each other then total absorbance A is equal to sum of the absorbances of different species.

$$A = A_1 + A_2 + A_3 + \ldots$$

where A_1, A_2, A_3, etc are the absorbances of different absorbing species present in the solution.

2.4.3 Instrumentation
(Basic Component of Single Beam Spectrophotometer)

The instrument absorption spectrophotometer is used for measuring absorbance of solution in both UV and visible region. There are five basic components of spectrophotometer. The block diagram of the spectrophotometer is shown in the Fig. 2.13.

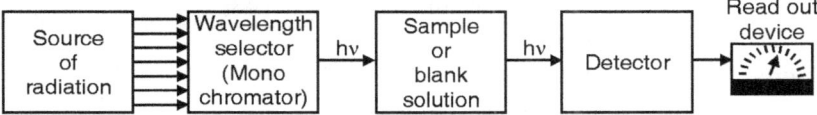

Fig. 2.13 : Block diagram of colorimeter and spectrophotometer

1. Radiation source :

A stable continuous source of radiant energy covering the region of spectrum is used.

(a) Tungsten filament incandescent lamp : This source of radiation is generally employed in the visible region. It provides continuously broad spectrum over a wavelength range of 325 mm to 2500 nm and therefore useful for near UV, visible and near IR regions. The voltage control is required for stable radiation because energy output of the lamp varies as per fourth power of voltage. Battery may be used for this purpose. The tungsten lamps have different shapes and sizes.

(b) Hydrogen or Deuterium lamp : It is low pressure hydrogen or deuterium discharge tube. It provides continuous spectrum in the range 160 nm – 375 nm. Quartz cells must be used when this source is used as glass absorbs strongly below 350 nm.

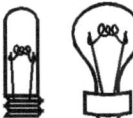

Fig. 2.14 : Tungsten lamp

2. Monochromators (Wavelength selector) :

For spectrophotometer, radiation consisting of limited narrow, continuous group of wavelength or band is required. The device which controls the wavelength of incoming radiation is called monochromator. The device consists of slits, mirrors, lens and dispersing device, filter or prism or diffraction grating. Slits, jaws are made from metal in the shape of knife edge and can be moved.

(A) Slits : There are two types of slits. The entrance slit and exit slit. The entrance slit is variable in width and used to control the incoming light and restrict unwanted radiation. The radiation after dispersion from prism or grating goes through exit slit and travel through the sample.

(B) Mirrors : They are used to extent the path length inside the instrument or change the direction of the beam.

(C) Lens : They are used to focus the light.

(D) Dispersing device :

(a) Filters : These are simplest and inexpensive devices producing narrow band. Filter are of two types

(i) **Absorption filters :** These consists of coloured glass plate or coloured gelatin placed between two glass plates. These are used in visible region. The coloured glass filters are generally used in colorimeter. Each filter has peak transmittance and band pass width which is 35–50 nm.

(ii) **Interference filters :** It consist of glass plate, inner surface of which is coated with semitransparent metal film. The space between two metal films is occupied by dielectric material like CaF_2 or MgF_2 or quartz. The thickness of dielectric material is controlled carefully which determines the wavelength of transmitted radiation. When a beam of radiation is incident on the filter, fraction of radiation passes through metal film and exhibit constructive interference for which wavelength the filter is designed. For other wavelengths destructive interference result and rejected.

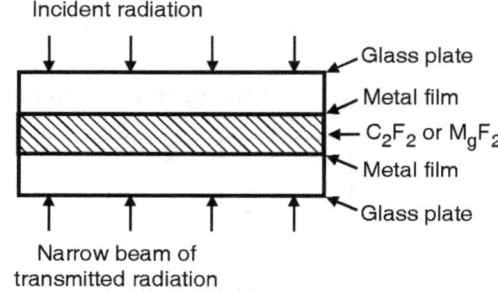

Fig. 2.15 : Interference filter

The band pass width is higher in case of filters. Therefore filters are not considered as a real monochromator.

(b) Prisms : A prism is a triangular shaped piece of glass or quartz or fused silica. The function of the prism is to resolve the radiation from the source into its component wavelengths and to provide for the isolation of radiation to very narrow band width.

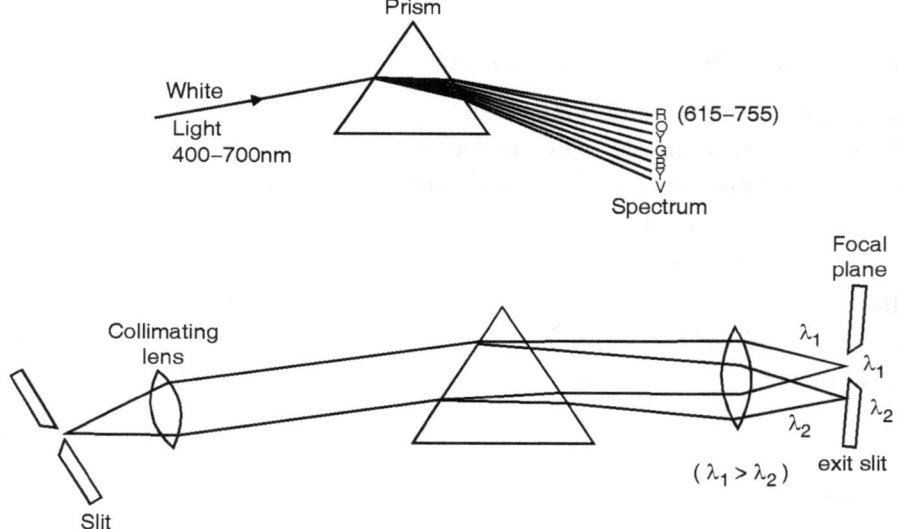

Fig. 2.16 : Dispersion by prism

The light is admitted through the entrance slit and then through collimated lens. Then it enters the prism and gets dispersed by refraction. Any desired portion f the resulting spectrum can be made to pass through the exit slit by rotation of the prism as shown in the Fig. 2.9. Glass prism is used for visible and quartz prism is used for UV region.

(c) **Diffraction grating :** The function of diffraction grating is to get a mochromatic beam of narrower band width. There are two types of gratings

- **Transmission grating (echellete grating) :** Grating is prepared by carefully ruling or etching a large number of parallel and equidistant grooves upon a highly polished surface like glass or transparent material with a drilling engine. The grating for UV and visible region contains 6000 to 12000 grooves per cm. The grooves act as scattering centres for radiation incident on it. From each groove radiation is diffracted over a range of angles. In certain direction constructive interference takes place as shown in Fig. 2.10.

- **Reflection grating :** Reflection gratings are prepared by ruling Closely spaced equidistance grooves on a polished metal strip or thin metallic film deposited on a glass strip. Reflection grating is used in most of the spectrograph. The mounting method of grating is shown in Fig. 2.10.

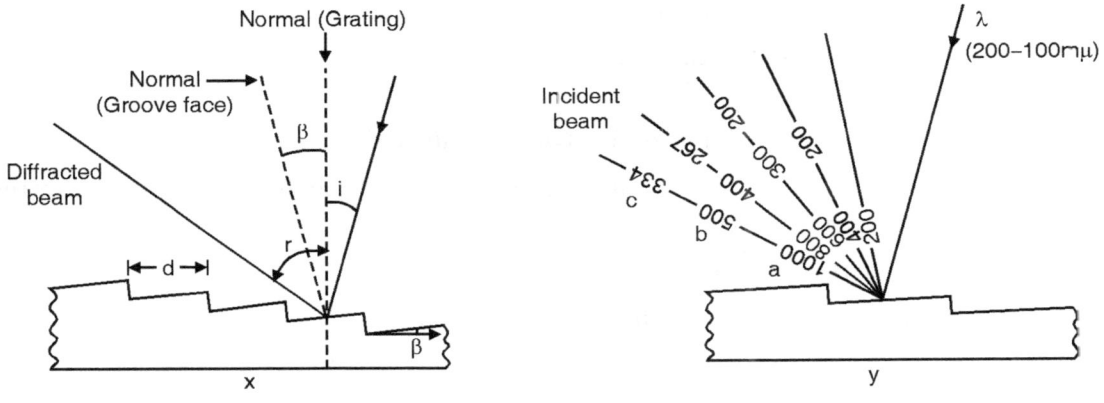

(a) : **Dispersion by grating**   (b) : **Mounting of grating**

Fig. 2.17

3. Sample container or cell :

The solution of absorbing substance of solvent (blank) is place in the path of radiation in a cell or cuvette. The cell walls should be transparent to the radiation of wavelength used. The cylindrical glass cells are generally used in the visible region. The cells made up of quartz and fused silica are used in both UV and visible region. Generally rectangular cells are used with 1 cm path length. In spectrophotometer, two matched cells having identical path length and transmission of radiation. Longer or shorter path length cells are also available.

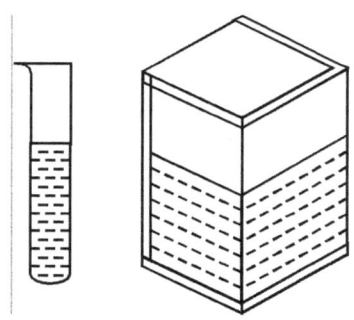

Fig. 2.18 : Different types of cells

4. Detectors :

Detector is the device that changes the radiant energy into electrical energy providing electrical signal. The intensity of absorbed or transmitted radiation is measured by the detector. Two main types of detectors are used :

(a) Phototube (Photo emissive tube) : These are used in UV and visible regions.

- It consists of large semicylindrical photoemissive cathode and a small concentric anode enClosed in an evacuated glass bulb.
- The cathode is coated with photoemissive material such as potassium or silver or cesium oxide.
- A high voltage (90 V) is impressed between anode and cathode.
- When the light (photons) is incident on the cathode through window photo electrons are emitted which are proportional to intensity of radiation.
- All the electrons emitted on anode causing flow of current.
- The current is fed to meter calibrated in absorbance.

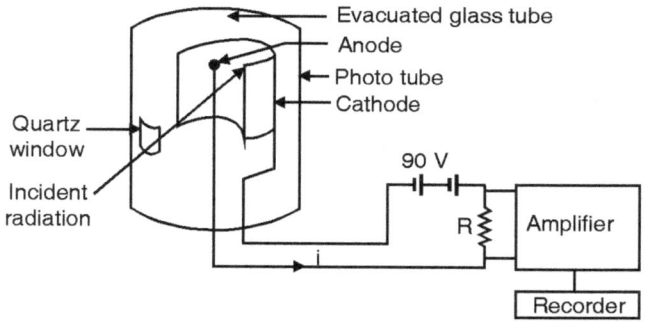

Fig. 2.19 (a) : Phototube

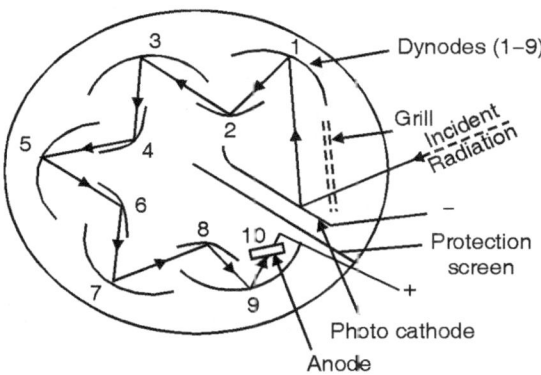

Fig. 2.19 (b) : Photomultiplier tube

(b) **Photomultiplier tube :** This device is extremely sensitive and fast in response. It is useful to measure low intensity of radiation. It is useful in both UV and visible region.

- It consists of photocathode which is coated with photoemissive material and number (1 – 9) of dynodes and a anode enclosed in a evacuated glass tube.
- The surface of each dynode is coated with copper–beryllium or cesium–antimony which emits several electrons (3 – 6) for each electron striking on its surface. Each dynode is at a more positive potential (90 V) than previous dynode.
- When the radiation strikes the cathode surface it ejects electrons. These primary electrons are accelerated towards first dynode and strike it. The first dynode is 90 V more positive than cathode.
- Each primary electron upon striking the surface of first dynode causes the emission of several electrons. These secondary electrons are accelerated towards second dynode and causes the emission several electrons.
- The process is continued for all nine dynodes.
- At the end of the process, nearly 10^6 electrons have been formed for each primary electron produced.
- All these electrons are collected on the anode and discharged and current is produced.
- The measured current is proportional to the intensity of incident radiation.
- The current is amplified and fed to meter.

5. Read out Device :

The current from detector is amplified and fed to read out device. The read out device is meter directly calibrated in absorbance and transmittance. It may be digital in modern instrument complete spectrum can be scanned.

Single Beam Spectrophotometer :

The single beam spectrophotometer gives good results in visible region and are less expensive. The schematic diagram of single beam spectrophotometer is shown in the Fig. 2.20.

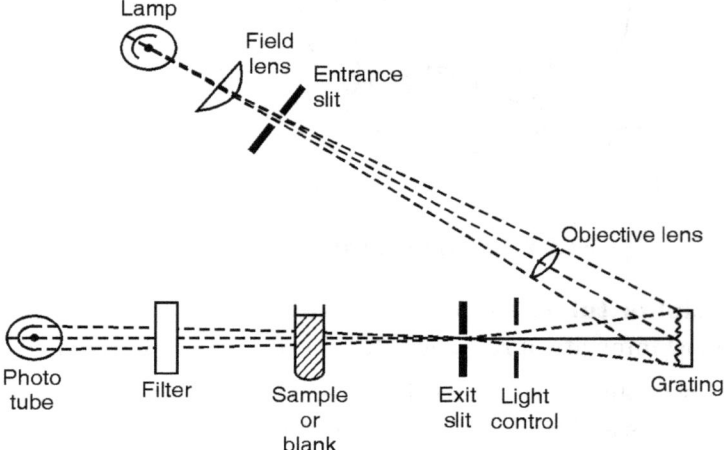

Fig. 2.20 (a) : Schematic diagram of single beam spectrophotometer

Construction :

- It consists of light source which is tungsten filament lamp operated on stabilized power supply provides spectrum in UV and visible region.
- To get monochromatic light diffraction grating is used. It has 6000 grooves per cm and dispersed radiation from 330 to 950 nm and band width is 20 nm. The grating can be rotated turning the wavelength cam, radiation of desired wavelength pass through slit.
- The sample cell is glass tube of 1 cm path length.
- It has blue sensitive phototube that can be used in visible region. The range can be extended from 625 nm to 950 nm using red filter and replacing blue phototube by red phototube.
- The instrument has an arrangement ocCluder or shutter which is placed in front of detector when cell is removed to prevent expose of phototube by radiation.
- The readout device is a meter calibrated in both absorbance and transmittance.

Working :

- The instrument in switch on.
- The desired wavelength is adjusted with help of wavelength control knob.

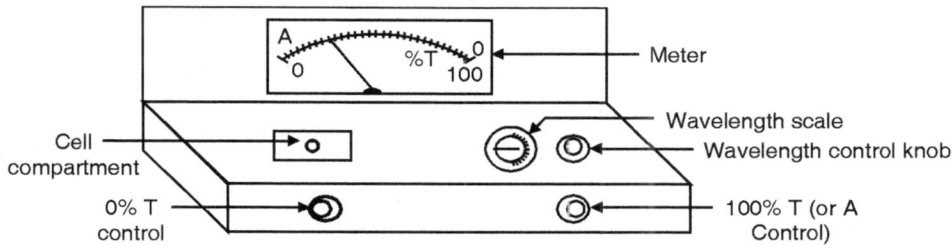

Fig. 2.20 (b) : Different controls of spectrophotometer

- Then zero of the scale is adjusted with help of zero setting knob.
- The cell is filled with blank solution and placed in the cell compartment.
- Now the radiation from tungsten lamp is converted to desired wavelength by monochromator and fall on the blank.
- With help of 100% T control, 100% transmission is adjusted.
- Now blank is removed and sample solution is filled in the tube and placed in cell compartment.
- The absorbance reading is recorded on scale.
- The procedure is repeated to known solutions and unknown solution.
- Plot of absorbance verses concentration gives straight line passing through origin. From this curve concentration of unknown can be determined as shown in Fig. 2.20 (a).

Deviation from beer's law :

When the absorbance is directly proportional to concentration of the absorbing species, Beer's law is said to be obeyed. Then the plot of A versus C is a straight line passing through origin called calibration curve i.e. when $C = 0, A = 0$.

However when a plot of measured absorbance versus concentration do not give a straight line but is concave either upward side (curvex, A is larger than expected) or downwards (curve y which indicate positive and negative deviations respectively) as shown in Fig. 2.21. Then Beer's law is not obeyed. There are three types of deviations.

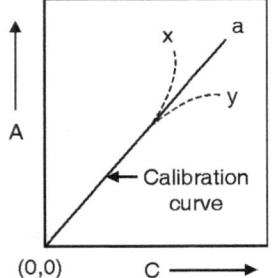

Fig. 2.21 : Deviation from Beer's law

(i) Real Deviation :

The Beer's law is obeyed for dilute solutions (10^{-2} M to 10^{-6} M) only. It is not obeyed at higher concentration (> 0.1 M) and deviations are observed. At higher concentration molecules come Close and do not behave independently. The line obtained is like line x. This is real limitation of Beer's law.

(ii) Chemical Deviation :

Any reaction that can change the concentration of the absorbing species can cause deviation. When absorbing species undergo dissociation, association, complexation reaction and reaction with solvents then number of species can increase or decrease and deviation is observed. Factors like pH, temperature, pressure etc. affect the calibration curve.

(iii) Instrumental Deviations :

The instrumental deviations are due to errors in instruments.

(i) If stable power supply is not provided to light source, intensity of radiation given out by source changes which changes detector response and hence A.

(ii) The Beer's law is strictly obeyed only for monochromatic light. If the purity of monochromatic light is not maintained by the instrument deviations are observed.

(iii) Stray light arises due to reflections from cell walls and cavity of the cell compartment with in instrument. When stray light strikes the detector without passing through sample, deviations are observed.

(iv) If the thickness of the cell is not uniform it affects the analysis.

Applications :

1. Quantitative analysis : The unknown concentration of coloured substances as low as 10^{-7} M can be estimated. For colourless solutions complexing agents are used to give colour to the solution and then estimated. A calibration curve is constructed by measuring absorbance of known concentration solutions. The absorbance of unknown solution is determined. The unknown concentration is determined using absorbance of unknown solution as shown in the Fig. 2.22.

It is applicable to inorganic and organic substances.

2. Simultaneous determination of two or three cations in the solution : The absorbance in an additive property. Measuring the absorbance of the mixture A_1 and A_2 at two absorption maxima T_1 and T_2 of two species X and Y. The molar absorptivities of species in the mixture are determined from known concentration solutions, then

$$C_x = \frac{(\epsilon_y)_{\lambda_1} A_1 - (\epsilon_y)_{\lambda_1} A_2}{(\epsilon_x)_{\lambda_1} (\epsilon_y)_{\lambda_2} - (\epsilon_y)_1 (\epsilon_x)_2}$$

$$C_y = \frac{(\epsilon_x)_{\lambda_1} A_2 - (\epsilon_x)_{\lambda_2} A_1}{(\epsilon_x)_1 (\epsilon_y)_2 - (\epsilon_y)_1 (\epsilon_x)_2}$$

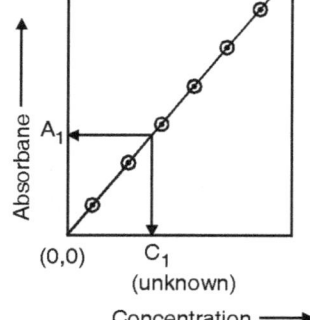

Fig. 2.22 : Determination of unknown concentration

pKa of indicator, instability constant of complexes can be determined by spectrophotometric analysis.

3. Qualitative analysis : (Determination of structure of organic compound) :
Compounds of similar structure have analogous absorption spectra. By comparing the spectra it is possible to find structure of organic compounds.

2.5 Chromatography :

2.5.1 Introduction :

Chromatography is most important analytical tool. It is useful to separate the components of the mixture and provide both quantitative and quantitative information of components. The word chromatography was used by Russian chemist Tswette. Two nobel prizes have been awarded to scientists who worked in the field of chromatography. The first noble prize was awarded to Swedish scientist Tiselins for his research on electrophoresis and adsorption. The English scientist Martin and Synge were awarded noble prize in 1952 for their research on gas chromatography. Gas chromatography is now most popular and advanced technique of analysis.

Chromatography :

Chromatography is a physical process of separation.

Definition : It is most widely used technique of separation. Chromatography consists of group of techniques of chemical analysis of separation of the components in the pure form from the small amount of mixture.

Process of chromatography :

- Chromatographic separation is based upon the distribution of components of the mixture in two different phases.
- One of the phases is fixed called stationary phase. Stationary phase may be either liquid or gas. The other phase is moving called mobile phase. The mobile phase may be either solid or liquid.
- The stationary phase is usually fixed on paper or plate or packed in column and moving phase moving through it.
- The distribution of components in two phases is based on difference in absorption coefficient or partion coefficient or ion exchange abilities or size of solute molecules of the various components in two different phase.
- The components are made to travel through stationary phase at different rates under the influence of a mobile phase so that separation occurs.

2.5.2 Types of Chromatography :

There are two different ways to Classification of chromatography

1. Based on different principles involved in chromatographic separation. There are four different principles.
2. Based on the nature of mobile and stationary phases

1. **Separation based on different principles :**

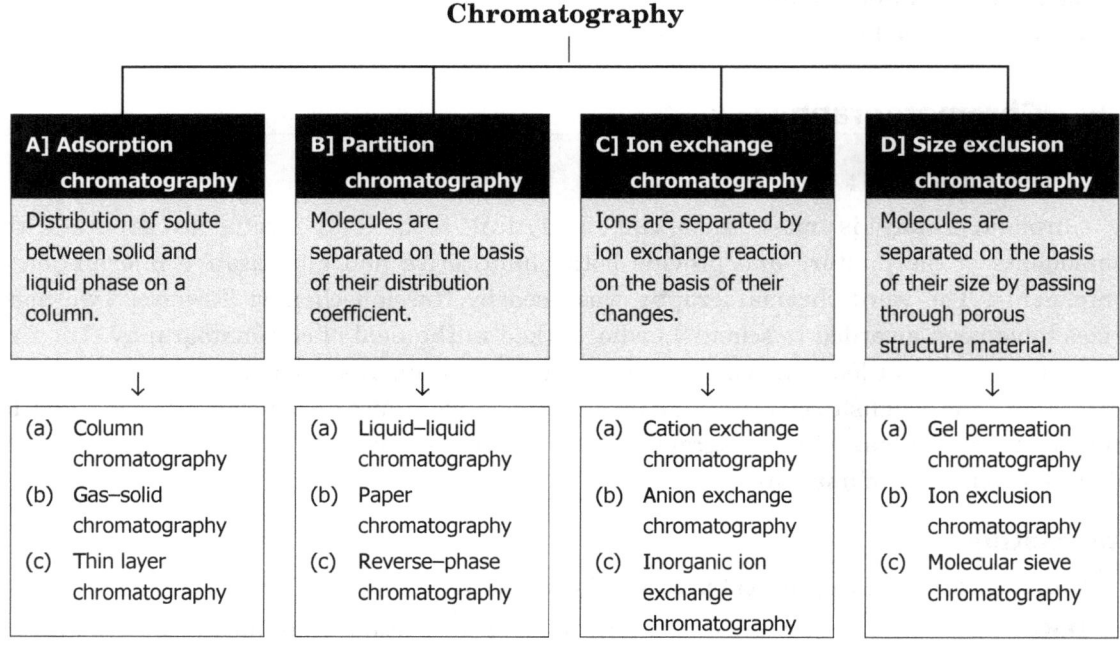

(A) Adsorption charmatography :

Principle : This technique of chromatography is based on the principle of difference in adsorbility of the solute present in the given sample on absorbent (stationery phase).

The solute having stronger adsorption removed slowly in mobile phase while solute having weaker adsorption removed fast in the mobile phase.

Technique : The difference absorbents are used in this technique such as silica (SiO_2), alumina (Al_2O_3), magnesium silicate, cellulose, graphite etc. The silica is most widely used adsorbent. The absorbent is applied on a flat glass plate or it may be filled in the column. The adsorbent has adsorption sites and polar solute can be adsorbed on it through hydrogen bonding. The non polar solutes are also adsorbed by physical adsorption through van der Waal's force of attraction.

The mixture of solutes is placed on the stationary phase and mobile phase (elute) is allowed to flow through it. The competition between adsorption of solute on stationary phase and desorption of solute by mobile phase takes place. The stationary phase tries to retain the solute on it while mobile phase tries to take the solute with it. This process continuously takes place. The adsorptivities of solutes in mixture are different in stationary phases.

This difference in adsorptivities of solute separate the solutes in different bonds over the stationary phase.

Sub–Types or examples of adsorption chromatography :

1. **Column chromatography :** Stationery phase – Solid. It is in the form of column (alumina, magnesium silicate etc.)
   Mobile phase – Liquid.
2. **Gas–Solid Chromatography (GSC) :** Stationery phase – Solid
   Mobile phase – Gas
3. **Thin Layer Chromatography (TLC) :** Stationery phase – Solid. It is in the form of thin layer on plate (silica gel, alumina, cellulose, kieselgutrr powder).
   Mobile phase – Liquid. (Benzene, cyClohexane, chloroform, diethyl ether acetone or mixture of two or three solvents)

(B) Partion chromatography :

Principle :

Distribution coefficient :

When small quantity of solute is shaken with two immiscible liquids or solvents A and B, solute gets distributed or dissolved in two liquids. The concentration of solute in two liquids is proportional to the solubilities of solute in two liquids. Then the distribution coefficient, K_d is given by,

$$K_d = \frac{C_A}{C_B}$$

Where C_A = Concentration of solute in liquid A

C_B = Concentration of solute in liquid B

Higher the value of K_d higher is the solubility of solute in liquid A than in liquid B. Lower the value of K_d smaller the solubility of solute in liquid A than in liquid B.

Example :

Distribution of solute iodine (I_2) in two solvents carbontetrachloride (CCl_4) and water (H_2O)

$$K_{d\,(I_2)} = \frac{C_{CCl_4}}{C_{H_2O}}$$

Technique : Consider a stationery phase as a liquid supported on solid material (like paper) and another liquid which is immiscible with first liquid is a mobile phase. The mixture of two component is applied on the stationery phase. Then the two components move on stationery phase with different speed in the direction of flow of mobile phase.

The first component having higher solubility in stationery liquid moves slowly along with mobile phase and second component having more solubility in mobile phase moves faster along with mobile phase and separation of two components take place.

Hence the difference in the partition coefficients of two solutes in two immiscible liquids (stationery and mobile phases) helps to separate two components from mixture.

Sub types or examples of partion chromatography :

1. **Paper chromatography :**

   Stationery phase – liquid supported on paper (solid) – polar (water)

   Mobile phase – liquid – non polar (n–hexane, $CHCl_3$, CCl_4, benzene)

2. **Reverse phase partion chromatography :**

   Stationery phase – liquid – non polar (squalane, cyanoethyl silicone)

   Mobile phase – liquid – polar (water and water – alcohol mixtures)

3. **Ion exchange chromatography :**

Principle :
Ion exchange resins :

The ion exchangers consist of beads make up of polystyrene polymer, cross linked with diviny benzene (DVB). The cross linked polymer is called resin having free phenyl group attached to a chain which can be treated to add group like SO_3^{2-}, COO^-, HPO_2^-, $N^+(CH_3)_3$, $-N^+(CH_3)_2$, CH_2-CH_2OH etc. The ions of the exchanger is called mobile ion and ion in the solution is called counter ion. The resins are mainly two types, cation exchanger and anion exchanger depending on functional group.

Cation exchanger : $R_2 SO_3^- H^+$

Anion exchanger : $R_2 N^+ R_3 OH^-$

Ion exchange reaction :

Cation exchange reaction : $\underset{\text{solid}}{R^- - H^+} + \underset{\text{solution}}{M^+} \longrightarrow R^- M^+ + H^+$

Anion exchange reaction : $\underset{\text{solid}}{R^+ - OH^-} + \underset{\text{solution}}{N^-} \longrightarrow R^+ N^- + OH^-$

The cations and anions have different ion exchange abilities for ion exchange resin. The separation of two or more cations or anions in a mixture is based on this different ion exchange abilities of the ions for ion exchange resins.

Technique : The ion exchange resin in H^+ or OH^- form is packed in a column. The mixture of cations or anions is poured on the column of resin when cation or anions of higher valency and higher ionic weight retain on the resin while other cations or anions run faster down a column along with mobile phase.

Sub type or examples of ion exchange chromatography :

1. **In organic ion exchange chromatography :**

   Stationery phase – solid – inorganic ion exchanger

   Mobile phase – liquid

2. **Cation exchange chromatography :**

   Stationery phase–solid–cation ion exchanger

   Mobile phase – liquid

3. **Anion exchange chromatography :**

   Stationery phase–solid–anion ion exchanger

   Mobile phase – liquid

(D) Size exclusion chromatography :

Principle :

The separation of the solute is based on the size and geometry (shape) of the molecules of solute. The stationery phase used in this type of chromatography is a porous material of same pore size. The mixture solutes along with mobile phase through stationery phase. The separation of molecules depends upon the penetration of solute molecules into interior of gel particles. While passing through porous structure of stationery phase. Smaller size particles are trapped and strongly retained by gel depending on their size and available pore size distribution. On the other hand larger size particles cannot penetrate the gel network and run down along with the mobile phase.

Technique :

The stationery phase in the form of porous gel like sepadex is filled in the column. The mixture to be separated like organic, inorganic and biochemical substance along with mobile phase is passed through column. Smaller size particles are retained while large size particles run down with mobile phase.

Sub Type or Examples of Size Exclusion Chromatography :

(a) Gel permeation chromatography.

(b) Ion exclusion chromatography.

(c) Molecular sieve chromatography.

[II] Separation based on nature of mobile and stationery phases :

Depending on the nature of mobile phases and stationery phases the chromatography is Classified as follows :

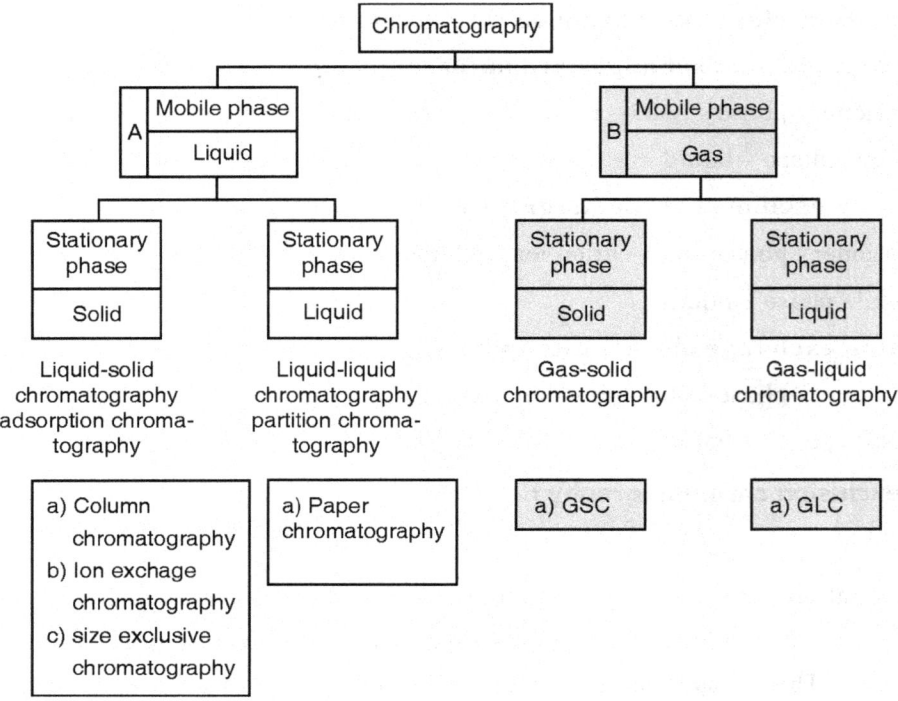

2.5.3 Gas Liquid Chromatography (GLC) :

Gas chromatography :

Gas chromatography is one of the most widely used and powerful analytical tool available for separations. It is particularly used for separation organic substances. Gas chromatography is the method of separation of a mixture in vapour form into its constituents using a gas as mobile phase. Very complex mixtures can be separated using this technique.

Types of gas chromatography :

The gas chromatography can be divided into two types on the basis of stationery phase.

Type I : Gas–liquid chromatography (GLC) :

When the mobile phase is a gas and stationery phase is liquid the technique is called gas–liquid (GLC) chromatography.

Type II : Gas–solid chromatography (GSC) :

When the mobile phase is a gas and stationery phase is solid the technique is called as gas–solid (GSC) chromatography.

Gas–liquid chromatography (GLC) :

Principle :

Mobile phase : In this technique the mobile phase is a gas. It is called carrier gas. The gases like N_2, H_2, He and CO_2 may be used as carrier gas. A high density gas gives best efficiency but low density gas gives faster speed. The choice of the gas depends upon the detector used.

Stationery phase : In this technique stationery phase is non volatile liquid, which is coated on solid support in a column. The liquids like silicone oils, squatone, apieson, grease etc. are used. By changing the liquid phase the different separation can be carried out.

Sample : The sample should be in gaseous state. The solid samples dissolved in volatile solvent and liquid samples are injected and vaporized at higher temperature. The organic components in the mixture can be separated.

Separation : The separation is based upon relative distribution of sample component between stationery liquid phase and mobile gas phase. As the mixture of components is introduced into the column, the molecules of components are distributed between stationary phase and a mobile phase and dynamic equilibrium is established. As the fresh mobile phase enters the column process of distribution between two phases and fresh dynamic equilibrium is established. This process continues till final equilibrium is established and Clear and Clean separation occurs.

Analysis : The components are automatically detected as it carries out from column at a constant flow rate using variety of detectors. Whose response depends upon composition of vapour. The response of detector is fed to the recorder where chromatogram is recorded.

(i) Chromatogram :

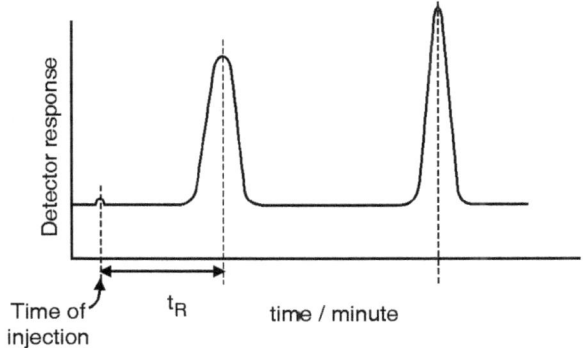

Fig. 2.23 : Chromatogram injection of a sample containing two components

It is the plot of detector response against time as shown in the Fig. 2.23. It consists of series of peaks. Each peak corresponds to individual component detected in the sample.

(ii) Retention time (t_R) :

It is the time required for the component to come out from column after injection of the sample. In other words it is the time in minutes between the time the sample is injected and the time the peak is recorded as shown in the Fig. 2.23.

Retention time is characteristic of each component and represents chromatographic behavior of the component. It is used for the qualitative identification of the components in a mixture. It also depends upon nature of mobile and stationery phase.

The quantitative analysis can be done by measuring the area under the peak. Area of the peak is proportional to the percentage of the component in the mixture.

Instrumentation of Gas Chromatography :

Instrument :

The gas chromatograph consist of

1. A tank of carrier gas
2. A sample injection system (injection part)
3. A separating column
4. Oven
5. Detector
6. Recorder and sample collector

1. Tank of carrier gas :

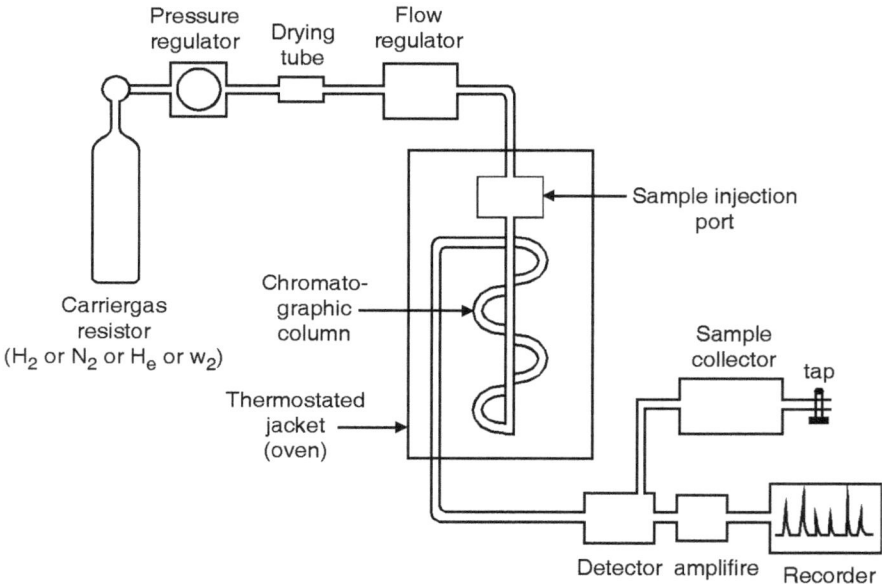

Fig. 2.24 : Diagram of chromatograph

A high pressure gas cylinder containing a chemically inert gas which acts as mobile phase is used. The gas must be cheap, pure and risk free to use. Choice of the gas depends on the detector used. The gas carriers the sample therefore it is called as carrier gas. The carrier gas in either helium, nitrogen, CO_2 and H_2. Generally helium is used as carrier gas when thermal conductivity detector is used. The cylinder is attached with pressure regulator to control the gas flow which must be constant.

2. Sample injection system (Injection port) :

It consists of small chamber having an inlet into the column. The chamber has self sealing silicon rubber septum through column. The carrier gas passes through one side of the port. The gaseous sample can be directly injected into the column with the help of gastight syringe.

Solid samples are first dissolved into small quantity volatile solvent and introduced into the chamber.

Generally 0.1 to 0.5 micro litre of gaseous or liquid samples are used for analysis. The fraction of milligram of solid sample may be used. The injection part is kept at high temperature to promote rapid vaporization of sample.

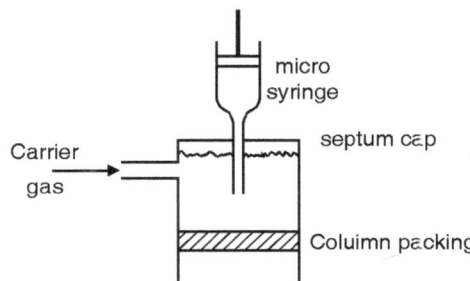

Fig. 2.25 : Arrangement of injection port

3. Chromatographic column :

The column is made up of glass or metal (stainless steel, cm, etc.). The length of the tube is 2–3 meter and internal diameter 2–4 mm. It is in the form spiral will of 3 or 4 turns.

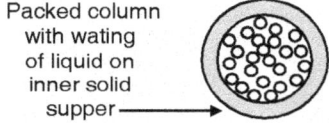 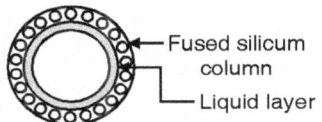

Fig. 2.26 : Chromatographic column design

The liquid is coated on size graded inert support and packed in the column. The solid support material consists of finely divided celite, glass beads, ground fire brick which can hold sufficient amount of liquid. The liquids silicon oils, greases, apieson, squalene polyethylene glycol etc. may be used. At one end of the column carrier gas is passed through an injection port. The component of the sample are carried down the column along with carrier gas.

4. Oven :

The column is enClosed in thermostatically controlled oven so that its temperature is hold constant with in 0.5°C for reproducible conditions. The heating should be rapid to desired temperature. The cooling should be also rapid when required.

5. Detector :

The separated components along with carrier gas at other end of the column is directed fed to detector system. The components are automatically detected into detector system.

There are many types of detectors which gives zero signal to carrier gas alone passing through. We will discuss some important types of detectors.

(a) **Flame ionization detector :**

- It consists of small hydrogen flame burning in excess of air and surrounded by an electrostatic field.
- The vapours of the compound ionize by high temperature of the flame to form ions and electrons.

- The resistance decreases (or conductance increases) between the electrode. There is a drop of voltage of 400 V due to increased current. The increase of current is proportional to concentration of the component. It is amplified and recorded by the detector.

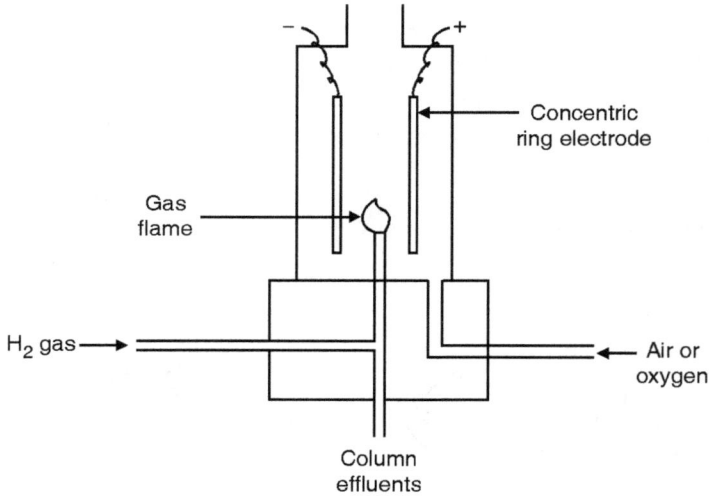

Fig. 2.28 : Arrangement of flame ionization detector

(b) Thermal conductivity detector :

- It detects the difference in conductivity between carrier gas and carrier gas with sample.
- The detector consists of heated filament which is heated by d.c. supply placed in the stream of emerging gas. The filament is placed within cavity in a brass block.
- Heat lost from filament to brass block is constant when carrier gas flowing but when even small amount of organic vapour of component is flowing decrease the thermal conductivity.

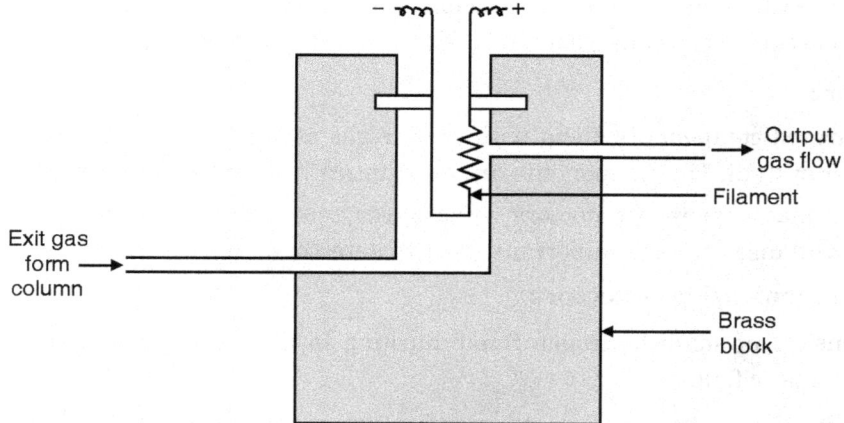

Fig. 2.29 : Arrangement of thermal conductivity detector

- Filament retains heat, temperature rises and electrical conductance increases which is detected and recorded.

6. Recorder and sample collector :

The electrical analog output of detector is applied and fed to the chart recorder or digital signal. The data is stored in computer system. The chromatogram is continuously recorded. The Clear and Clear components are collected separately from sample collector.

Working procedure of chromatograph :

(i) The desired temperature of the oven is maintained.

(ii) The column is filled with appropriate liquid with proper solid support.

(iii) The carrier gas is passed through the column, detector and recorder under standard conditions of recorder. It gives base line for polarogram in the recorder.

(iv) The sample in injected in the part at the little higher temperature than oven along with carrier gas under same conditions.

(v) When carrier gas with sample pass through the column separation of component occurs giving Clear and Clean components which are detected by recorder and chromatogram is obtained giving retention time of each component.

(vi) The components of mixture are collected in sample collector.

Applications :

1. Qualitative analysis :

Under identical conditions of experiment, the retention time is characteristic of different components which help in identification of compounds in the sample.

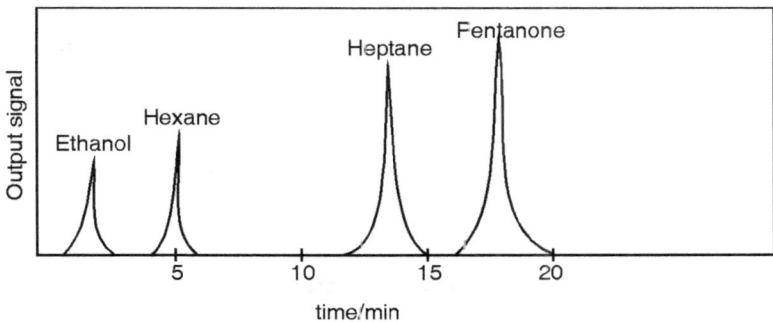

Fig. 2.30 : **Chromatogram of different organic compounds**

2. Quantitative analysis :

The area under the peak is proportional to the concentration of the components. Therefore % composition of different components can be quantitatively determined.

Advantages of GLC :

- GLC is fast and convenient method for analysis of organic compounds.
- GLC is applicable to solid, liquid and gas samples.
- The sensitivity and resolution of GLC is very high.
- The technique is applicable to complex mixtures.
- GLS is useful for both qualitative and quantitative analysis.

Disadvantages of GLC :

- The GLC technique is not applicable to inorganic substances because inorganic substances cannot be vaporized to oven temperature.

Exercise

Long Answer Questions

1. What is electromagnetic radiation ? Give characteristics of electromagnetic radiation. Define the terms wavelength frequency and wave number. Give the relation between them.
2. State and derive the Lambert's and Beer's laws.
3. Explain basic components of a spectrophotometer giving its schematic diagram.
4. Give the construction of single beam spectrophotometer giving its diagram. Give the working of spectrophotometer.
5. Explain the construction of pH meter giving schematic diagram.
6. Give the applications of pHmetry.
7. Give the mechanism of glass electrode.
8. Discuss measurement of pH of the solution.
9. How are the chromatographic technique Classified ? Discuss the principles of different chromatographic techniques.
10. What is gas chromatography ? What are the types of gas chromatography ? Give the principle of GLC.
11. Give the schematic diagram of gas chromatograph. Explain different components of gas chromatograph.

Short Answer Questions

1. Define pH and operational defination of pH.
2. Give the construction of glass electrode.
3. Write a note on electromagnetic radiation.
4. Give the principle of spectrometry.
5. State Lambert's law. Derive the equation for Lambert's law.
6. State Beer's law. Derive the equation for Beer's law.
7. Derive the equation for Beer–Lambert law. How is it verified ?

8. Discuss the deviations from Beer's law.
9. Explain the applications of spectrophotometric analysis.
10. Give the advantages, disadvantages and mentainence of glass electrode.
13. Define the term chromatography ? What is the process of chromatography ?
14. Give the Classification of chromatographic techniques.
15. Discuss the adsorption chromatography.
16. Explain principle and technique of the partition chromatography.
17. Give the principle and technique of ion exchange chromatography and size exclusion chromatography.
18. Discuss different detectors used in gas chromatography.
19. Explain the working of gas chromatograph.
20. Explain the chromatographic column used in gas chromatograph.
21. What sample injection system is used in gas chromatograph?
22. Discuss the applications of gas chromatographic technique.

University Questions

1. Write short notes on :
   (a) Lambert Law (b) Beer – Lambert's law
   (c) Advantages of instrumental methosd over non–instrumental methods.
2. Explain the working of single beam spectrophotometer with suitable diagram. How it can be used to determine concentration of unknown solution?
3. Explain the components of single beam spectrophotometer and their functions.
4. State and explain beer's law. How It can be used to determine concentration of unknown sample ?

Unit 3

Advanced Materials

- Polymers
  - Introduction
- Plastics
  - Classification of Plastics : Thermosoftening and thermosetting plastics
  - Industrially important plastics (i) Phenol formaldehyde (ii) Ureaformaldehyde (iii) Eposy Resin
  - Conducting Polymer
  - Biodegradable Plastic
- Nanomaterial
  - Introduction
  - Synthesis
  - Applications
- Composite materials
  - Introduction
  - Constituents
  - Types of composite
  - Advantages
  - Fiber reinforced plastics (FRP)
  - Glass reinforce plastics (GRP)
- Excercise

3.1 Polymer:

3.1.1 Introduction :

The term 'Polymer' is derived from the two words 'Polys' and 'meros'. Polys means many and meros means units. The polymers occur in the nature in the form of starch, silk, wood, cotton, cellulose, proteins etc. Since ancient time man started using these natural polymers. Another important natural polymer, rubber was known to man since hundreds of years. In eighteen century it was used for the production of foot wears, rain coats and tyres. In recent years many polymers were investigated by different reactions and used. There are different types of polymers having variety of applications in every field of science, technology, domestic and industry. We will consider in this chapter details of polymers, rubber and plastics.

Polymer – Important Terms:

Definition :

Polymer is a large molecule of high molecular weight formed by linking large number of small molecules known as monomer.

Monomer :

A molecule having two or more functional groups which is repeating unit in the formation of polymer.

Examples :

(i) Ethylene : $CH_2 = CH_2$
(ii) Ethylene glycol : $HO-(CH_2)_2-OH$
(iii) Adipic acid : $HOOC-(CH_2)_4-COOH$
(iv) Vinyl chloride : $CH_2 = CH-Cl$

Degree of polymerization (D_p) :

Degree of polymerization is defined as the actual number of monomer units present in the polymer chain. Degree of polymerization may be high or low. When degree of polymerization is high, the polymer is called 'high polymer' with high molecular weight and when degree of polymerization is low is called 'oligo polymer'. In case of high polymers repeating units may be 100 or more. If degree of polymerization is known exactly, the molecular weight of the polymer can be calculated exactly as follows

$$M = D_p \times M_w$$

Where,
M = Molecular weight of the polymer
D_p = Degree of polymerization
M_w = Molecular weight of monomer

The average molecular weight of polymers may range from 10000 to 100000. In some cases it may be millions.

Examples of polymer :

(i) $n\ CH_2 = CH_2 \xrightarrow{\text{Polymerisation}} [-CH_2-CH_2-]_n$

(ii) $n\ CH_2 = CH-Cl \xrightarrow{\text{Polymerisation}} \left[-CH_2-CH(Cl)- \right]_n$

Classification of Polymers :

The polymers can be classified by various ways because

- Polymers includes large number of materials.
- Polymers have different properties.
- Polymers have different structure.
- Polymers behave in different manner.

(I) Classification based on occurrence of polymer

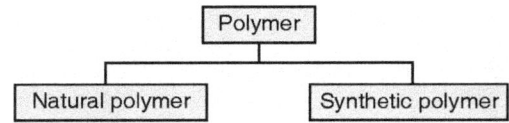

[A] Natural polymer :

The natural polymers occur in nature. They are also called as biological polymers.

Examples :

(i) Proteins and enzymes are natural polymers present in the body of man and animal.

(ii) Rubber, cotton, etc. starch obtained from plants.

(iii) Silk and wool obtained from animals.

[B] Synthetic polymers :

These are man made polymers. These polymers are synthesized from low molecular weight substances i.e. monomers. They can be manufactured as per the need and their molecular weight can be controlled. Different reactions such as addition and condensation reactions can be used for their synthesis.

Example :

(i) Polypropylene is obtained from propylene by simple addition reaction.

$$n\ CH_2 - CH = CH_2 \xrightarrow[\text{Catalyst}]{\text{Polymerisation}} [-CH_2 - CH - CH_2 -]_n$$

Propylene → Polypropylene

(ii) Polyester used for the manufacture of fibres is synthesized as –

$$CH_3O - \overset{O}{\overset{\|}{C}} - \underset{\text{di methyl tetraphthalate}}{\bigcirc} - \overset{O}{\overset{\|}{C}} - O\ CH_3 + 2\ HO - \underset{\text{ethlene glycol}}{CH_2 - CH_2\ OH} \xrightarrow{\Delta}$$

$$HO-CH_2-CH_2-\overset{O}{\underset{\|}{C}}-\underset{}{\bigcirc}-\overset{O}{\underset{\|}{C}}-C\,CH_2-CH_2\,OH + 2\,CH_3OH$$

$$\downarrow \Delta$$

$$\left[-O-CH_2-CH_2-O-\overset{O}{\underset{\|}{C}}-\underset{}{\bigcirc}-\overset{O}{\underset{\|}{C}}-\right]_n$$

Polyester (Polyethene phthalate)

(II) Classification based on structure of polymer :

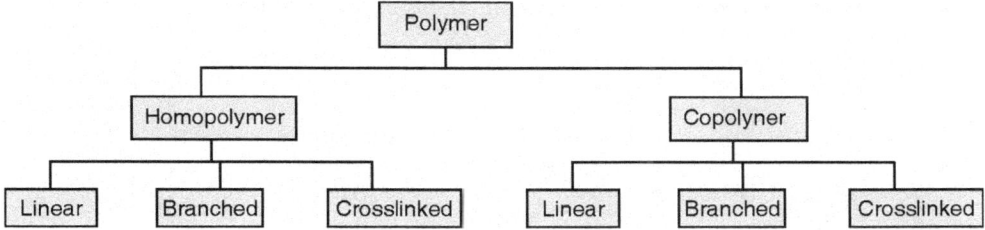

[A] Homopolymer :

When polymer consists of identical repeating units monomer of same chemical substance. It is further classified as

(i) **Linear Homopolymer :** Polymer has linear structure as, ▬▬▬▬
Where X is the monomer unit.

(ii) **Branched Homopolymer :** Polymer has branched structure as,

```
..-X-X-X-X-....
       |
       X
       |
       X
       |
       X
       :
```

(iii) **Cross linked Homopolymer :** Polymer has cross linked structure as,

```
    -X-X-X
     |     \
     X      X
     |       \
     X-X-X-
    / /
   X  X
  /  /
 X   X
```

[B] Copolymer or mixed polymer :

When the polymer consists of two or more types of different monomer units of different chemical structure are called copolymers.

(i) Linear copolymer : One unit attaches to another as

Where X and Y are monomer units.

Block Linear polymer : In this units of one type form a block and then block of other type as shown below is called **block copolymer.**

(ii) Branched copolymer : The branched copolymer is shown below :

```
- X - Y - X - Y - X -
    |       |
    X       X
    |       |
    Y       Y
    |       |
```

Graft copolymer : Branched copolymer with one type of monomer X is linear and other type Y is branched is called **graft copolymer**.

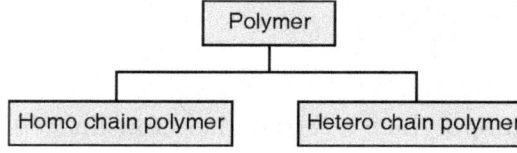

(iii) Cross linked copolymer : The cross linked copolymer is as,

```
        A     A     A
       /     /     /
      B     B     B
     /     /     /
  - A - B - A - B - A - B -
    |
    B
    |
    A - B - A - B - A
```

(III) Classification based on types of atoms present in main chain :

```
         Polymer
        /       \
Homo chain   Hetero chain
 polymer       polymer
```

[E] Homochain polymer :

In this type of polymer main chain contains same type of element as shown below only carbon and sulphur atoms are present in the main chain.

$$...... - C - C - C - C - C - C - ......$$
$$...... - S - S - S - S - S - S - ......$$

[F] Heterochain polymer :

In this type of polymer the main chain consists of two or more different atoms as shown below. Two atoms carbon and oxygen are present.

$$...... - C - C - C - O - C - C - C - O ......$$

(IV) Classification based on chemical composition :

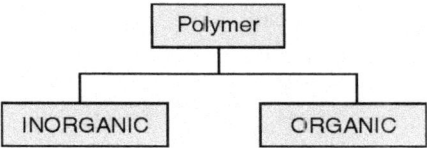

[A] Inorganic polymers :

These polymers do not have carbon atoms in the chain. The chain is composed of atoms of inorganic nature largely from IV – VI groups of periodic table such as Mg, Si, B, P, O, etc. The atoms are attached with one another by covalent bonds and weaker inter molecular forces act between the chains. The common examples of inorganic polymers are polysitane, polygermane, boracole, hydrogen borides, polyselicic acid, polyphosphates, polystibnates etc.

(i) Hydrogen boride 　　H　　H 　＼／＼／＼／ 　B　　B　　B 　／＼／＼／＼ 　　H　　H	(ii) Polysilane 　　H　H　H　H 　　|　|　|　| 　– Si – Si – Si – Si – 　　|　|　|　| 　　H　H　H　H
(iii) Borazole 　　　H 　　　N 　　／　＼ 　HB　　BH 　|　　　| 　HN　　NH 　　＼　／ 　　　B 　　　H	(iv) Polyphosphoric acid 　　O　　　O　　　O 　　||　　||　　|| – P – O – P – O – P – O – 　|　　　|　　　| 　OH　　OH　　OH
(v) Polystibnates 　OMe　OMe　OMe 　|　　|　　| – Sb – O – Sb – O – Sb – O – 　||　　||　　|| 　O　　O　　O	(vi) Polyselicic acid 　　　　| 　　　　O 　　　　| – Si – O – Si – O – Si – OH – 　|　　　|　　　| 　OH　　O　　　O 　　　　|　　　| 　　　– Si – O – Si – 　　　　|　　　| 　　　　OH　　OH

[B] Organic polymers :

Organic polymers have carbon as main constituent of backbone chain. This may also contains S, N and O attached in the backbone chain. Organic polymer may contains other atoms like hydrogen, oxygen, nitrogen, sulphur, Cl, Br, I.

Examples :

(i) Polypropylene : $[-CH_2 - CH - CH_2-]_n$

(ii) Polyvinyl alcohol : $[-CH_2 - \underset{|}{\overset{OH}{CH}} -]_n$

(iii) Polyurethane : $\cdots - \overset{O}{\underset{||}{C}} - \underset{|}{\overset{H}{N}} - (CH_2)_a - \underset{|}{\overset{H}{N}} - \overset{O}{\underset{||}{C}} - (CH_2)_b - O - \cdots$

3.2 Plastics :

Plastics and Resins are polymers of high molecular weight. Words Plastic and Resin are used synonymous. They are widely used in industry and have many useful applications in day–to–day life.

Resins :

Resins are amporphous, semi–solid organic substances. Resins are soluble in organic solvents and oils but insoluble in water. This is basic binding material of plastic which is the major part of it. Resins undergo condensation reaction during moulding.

Plastic :

Plastics are synthetic organic substances of high molecular weight which can be moulded into different stable shapes when heat and pressure is applied to it in presence of catalyst.

Plastics are new materials of construction available. Plastics have tremendous applications in industries due to their different properties.

Properties of Plastics :

- They are easily fabricated / manufactured at commercial level economically.
- They have low specific gravities and light in weight.
- They are insoluable in most of the common solvent.
- They have low thermal conductivity and are excellent insulators.
- Some plastics have high refractive index and are transperant. Ex. Polystyrene
- Many plastics can be coloured in different shades using a suitable dyes and pigments.
- Plastics can be used in combination with metals and solve many design problems.
- Many plastics have higher strength than metals and have wear resistance.

Applications and uses of plastics :

- Plastic parts of accurate dimensions and complicated shapes can be manufactured easily in low cost by moulding.
- Large number of moulding materials, fancy articles can be manufactured like toys, combs, bottle caps, parts of machines and vehicles, electrical instruments, optical instrument, telephones, panels for instruments.
- Plastics are used to manufacture different articles in different colours and shades and decorative purposes.
- Plastics reduces the vibration and noise of machines and reduce the sound pollution.
- Wear resistance plastics are used to prepare gears, bearing etc.
- Plastics can be used in conjunction with metals and reduce the design problems during manufacture of machines parts.
- Non metallic bearing can be made having long life which can be lubricated with greese and water. These water lubricated bearing are mainly used in food industry which avoid contamination of oil. Bearings are also used in rolling mills for the manufacture of steel.
- Plastics are used in the preparation of screens for aircrafts and automobiles since they have good clarity and high strength.
- Plastics in the form of granules or flakes or powder are supplied by manufacturers. The required articles are manufactured by pressure moulding or introducing softened plastics in a die to form sheets, tubes, rods and desired shapes. Liquid plastics are used to impregnate material like cloth, glass, wood, paper.
- Plastics in the form of foam are helpful in packaging, insulation, cushioning etc.

Drawbacks of plastics :

- Some plastics are poor weather resistant and their plastic properties deteriorate. The dimensions of plastic also change.
- The plastics cannot be used at higher temperatures.
- Some plastics are inflammable.
- Thermosetting plastics may shrink.
- Some plastics are soft, less strength and less elasticity.
- The plastics parts cannot be repaired.

3.2.1 Classification of Plastics :

Plastics are mainly classified as

(1) Thermoplastics / Thermosoftening plastics

(2) Thermosetting plastics

(1) Thermosoftening Plastics :

Thermoplastic resins are polymers which softens on application of heat and get hard or stiff on cooling. The phenomenan is reversible. These are the polymers which can be reutilized by recycling many times from one shape to another by application of heat.

These are long chain polymers which are linear having negligible cross links. The van der walls forces of attraction exists between linear polymer chains. Van der Waals forces of attraction become weaker and linear chain slide over one another on heating and plastic became soft. On the other hand on cooling van der walls forces become prominent and plastic become hard and rigid. Thus hardening and softening processes are temporary and molecular weight remains same during this process. Hardening and softening process also give good mouldability to the plastic. Thermoplastic resins have lower molecular weight and are less brittle. They are soluble in organic solvents.

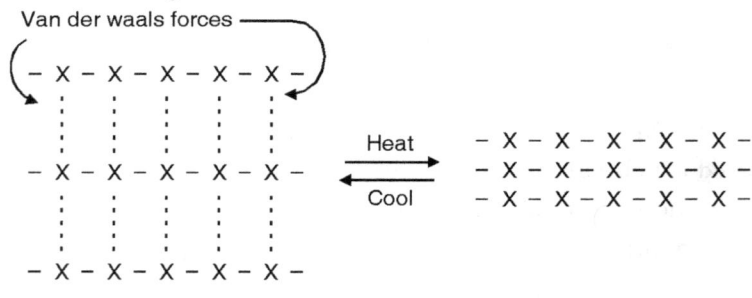

X – Monomer for polymerization

Van der Waals forces in thermoplastics

Examples of thermoplastics :

(i) Polystylene (ii) Polyvinyl chloride (PVC)

(iii) Teflon etc.

(2) Thermosetting plastics

Thermosetting plastics are polymers of high molecular weights which on application of heat are converted into permanently hard and infusible product. The infusible structure in due to the formation of cross link structure on heating. The thermoplastics once set and become hard cannot be moulded even by heating or applying pressure. Thus this is permanent property. On prolong heating degradation occurs.

Thermosetting plastics are formed by condensation reaction and have three dimensional network structure. There are covalent bonds between long chain molecules as shown.

Thermosetting plastics are insoluble in organic solvent due to strong covalent bond. They are more stronger, harder and stronger than thermoplastics.

```
 |   |   |   |   |
-X - X - X - X - X -
 |   |   |   |   |
-X - X - X - X - X -
 |   |   |   |   |
-X - X - X - X - X -
 |   |   |   |   |
-X - X - X - X - X -
 |   |   |   |   |
-X - X - X - X - X -
 |   |   |   |   |
```

X – Monomer for polymerization

Cross–linked structure of thermosetting plastic

Examples of Thermosetting Plastics :

(i) Backelite (ii) Polyesters

(iii) Silicones etc.

Table 3.2 : Points of distinction between thermoplastics and thermosetting plastics :

	Thermoplastics		Thermosetting plastics
1.	Formed by addition polymerization reaction.	1.	Formed by condensation polymerization reaction.
2.	Thermoplastics are polymers with comparatively of smaller molecular weight.	2.	Thermosetting plastics are polymers of higher molecular weight.
3.	They have long chain structure bonded with weak van der waals forces.	3.	They have three dimensional structure with strong covalent bonds.
4.	They have negligible cross lnking.	4.	They have three dimensional cross link.
5.	They soften readily on heating or applying pressure due to presence of weak van der waals forces and can be remoulded or reused.	5.	They cannot be soften on heating due to presence of strong covalent bond and cannot be remoulded or reused.
6.	They are soluble in organic solvents.	6.	They are insoluble in organic solvents.
7.	They are weak, soft and less brittle.	7.	They are strong, hard and more brittle.
8.	Examples : Polystyrene, PVC and Teflon.	8.	Examples : Backelite, polyesters and silicones.

3.2.2 Industrially Important Plastics :

(I) Backelite (Phenol Formaldehyde) :

Backland first synthesized and patented in USA hence the resin is named 'Bakelite'. It is the oldest thermosetting resin.

Preparation :

It is prepared by condensation reaction in presence of acid or alkali catalyst between phenol and formaldehyde to form addition compound, a monomer. A monomer is prepared as follows :

(i) Phenol + Formaldehyde → Monomethylol Phenol

(ii) Monomethylol Phenol + Formaldehyde → Dimethylol Phenol

(iii) Dimethylol Phenol + Formaldehyde → Trimethylol phenol (monomer)

(iv) Trimethylol phenol —Polymerization→ Backelite

Properties :

- Backelite is a moulding resin.
- Backelite sets to rigid, infusible and hard mass which is resistant tc high temperature, scratch and cold water flow.
- Backelite has good dielectric properties.
- It excellent adhesive and bonding properties.
- Backelite has good machinability.
- Backelite is flammability resistant.
- Properties of backelite are improved by adding fillers like asbestos, wood flours, rags etc. The cost is also reduced.

Uses :

- Backelite is used to prepare missile nose cone since it withstand high temperature.
- It is used to prepare parts of automobiles, television and electrical instruments.
- It is used to produce laminates, for printed circuits, wall coverings and deformation purpose.
- It is used in point and varnishes.
- It has – OH functional group therefore used to prepare in exchange resin fcr water treatment.
- It is used to prepare sand paper, abrasive wheels, brake linings etc.

(II) Urea Formaldehyde

Urea formaldhyde is commercially important polymer. It is amino resin.

Preparations : Urea formaldehyde is prepared by combining chemically of urea and formaldehyde in basic medium at 50°C. During the reaction first monomethylol urea and dimethylol urea are formed.

$$O=C(NH_2)_2 + 2\,HCHO \longrightarrow$$

$$O=C\begin{pmatrix} N(H)-CH_2OH \\ NH_2 \end{pmatrix} + O=C\begin{pmatrix} N(H)-CH_2OH \\ N(H)-CH_2OH \end{pmatrix}$$

Monomethylol urea   Dimethylol urea

When methylol derivates are compounded with filler, plasticisers, pigments and catalysts and then cured by applying heat and pressure. The long chain is formed during the curing process.

$$\begin{matrix} H-N-CH_2OH \\ | \\ C=O \\ | \\ H-N-CH_2OH \end{matrix} \;+\; \begin{matrix} H-N-CH_2OH \\ | \\ C=O \\ | \\ H-N-CH_2OH \end{matrix} \;+\; \begin{matrix} H-N-CH_2OH \\ | \\ C=O \\ | \\ H-N-CH_2OH \end{matrix}$$

dimethylol urea

$$\longrightarrow \begin{matrix} -N-CH_2-N-CH_2-N-CH_2- \\ | \quad\quad | \quad\quad | \\ C=O \quad C=O \quad C=O \\ | \quad\quad | \quad\quad | \\ -N-CH_2-N-CH_2-N-CH_2- \end{matrix}$$

Urea formaldehyde resin (Cross–linked Polyer)

Properties :

(i) It has good tensile strength and electrical insulation.

(ii) It has good resistance to abrasion and chemicals.

(iii) It has better hardness and heat resistance.

(iv) It gives clear white products.

Uses :

(i) It is used as adhesive for plywood and furniture.

(ii) It is used for moulding and as a laminating adhesive.

(iii) It is used to cover wood to prevent it from cracking.

(iv) It is used for cosmetic container closers and store hardware.

(v) It is used for electrical insulation.

(III) Epoxy resin :

Epoxy resins are surface coating material and commonly used. Epoxy resins are polyesters and have great recognition in industries. The name 'Epoxy' is derived from the starting material epichlorohydrin and epoxide group $\underset{O}{CH_2 \underset{\diagdown \; \diagup}{\quad} CH_2}-$ present in molecular strcture before cross linking.

Preparation of epoxy resin :

Two compounds required for the preparation of epoxy resin are (i) Epichlorohydrin and (ii) Diphenylol propane called as Bis–phenol A. These compounds are synthesized in three steps as follows :

(i) Epichlorohydrin :

It is prepared by heating propylene and chlorine at 400°C when allylchloride is formed. Allychloride is treated with water and chlorine at 300°C when glycerol dichlorohydrin is formed which decomposes to give Epichlorohydrin. The reactions are represented as,

Reaction :

$$CH_3-CH_2=CH + Cl_2 \xrightarrow{400°C} CH_2-CH-CH_2Cl + HCl$$

Propylene → Allyl Chloride

$$CH_2-CH-CH_2Cl + H_2O + Cl_2 \xrightarrow{300°C} Cl-CH_2-CHOH-CH_2-Cl$$

Glycerol Dichlorohydrin

$$Cl-CH_2-CHOH-CH_2-Cl \longrightarrow H_2C-CH-CH_2Cl \text{ (with epoxide O)}$$

Epichlorohydrin

(ii) Diphenylol prppane (Bis–Phenol A) :

It is synthesized by heating acetone and phenol at 50°C in presence of NaOH.

$$(CH_3)_2C=O + 2\ C_6H_5OH \xrightarrow[NaOH]{50°C} HO-C_6H_4-C(CH_3)_2-C_6H_4-OH$$

Acetone → Diphenylol propane (Bis - phenol A)

Synthesis : The two compounds Epichlorohydrin Epichlorohydrin and Bis–Phenol A when heated at 60°C in presence of NaOH when condensation occurs to form epoxy resin of high molecular weight. The reactive epoxide and hydroxide groups give three dimensional cross linked structure.

Reaction :

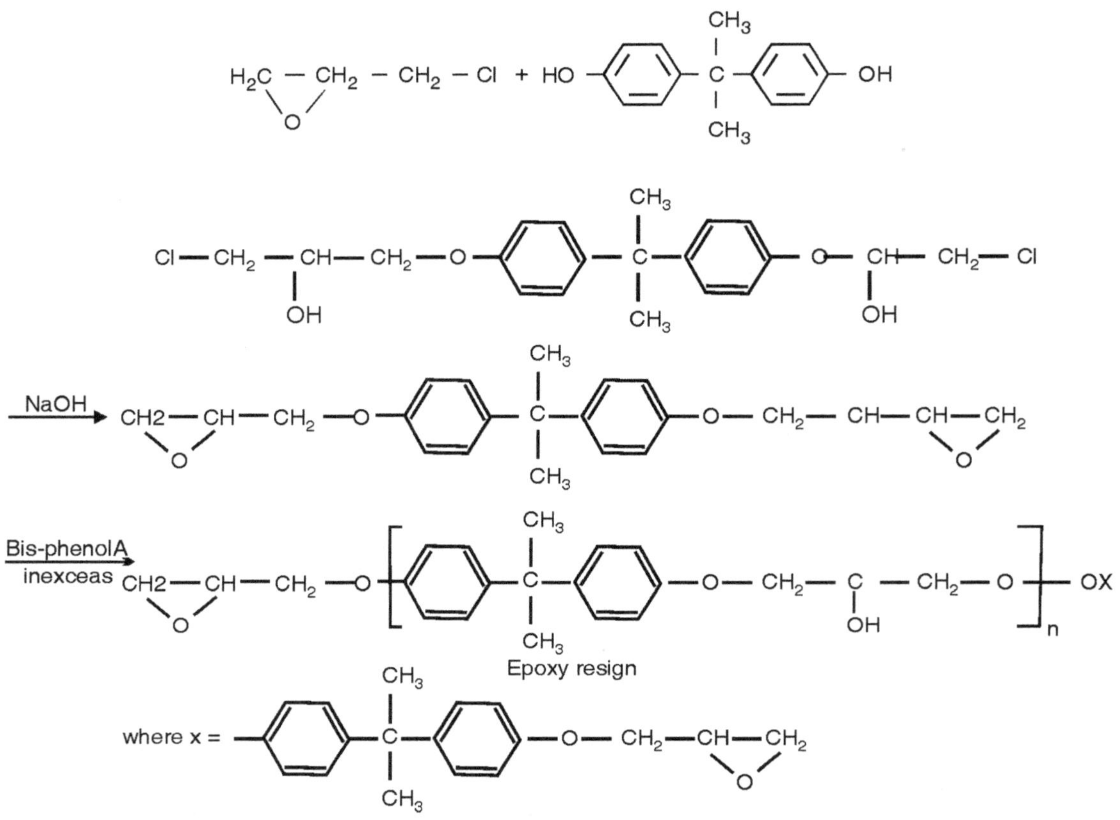

$$H_2C-CH_2-CH_2-Cl + HO-C_6H_4-C(CH_3)_2-C_6H_4-OH$$

(epichlorohydrin + Bisphenol A)

Intermediate:
$$Cl-CH_2-CH(OH)-CH_2-O-C_6H_4-C(CH_3)_2-C_6H_4-O-CH(OH)-CH_2-Cl$$

$\xrightarrow{NaOH}$

$$CH_2-CH(O)-CH_2-O-C_6H_4-C(CH_3)_2-C_6H_4-O-CH_2-CH-CH-CH_2$$
(epoxide)

$\xrightarrow{\text{Bis-phenol A increase}}$

$$CH_2-CH(O)-CH_2-O-[-C_6H_4-C(CH_3)_2-C_6H_4-O-CH_2-C(OH)-CH_2-O-]_n-OX$$

Epoxy resign

where X =

$$-C_6H_4-C(CH_3)_2-C_6H_4-O-CH_2-CH-CH_2(O)$$

Here n varies from 1 to 20. Molecular weight range from 350 to 8000.

Type of Epoxy Resins :

Epoxy resins are of two types :

1. Liquid epoxy resin :

When the molecular weight is low upto 350 the resin is mobile and easily flowing liquid.

2. Solid epoxy resin :

When molecular weight is high upto 8000 the epoxy resin is solid having melting point 145 to 155°C.

Properties :

- Epoxy resins show chemical inertness.
- Epoxy resins show high resistance to water, acids, alkalies, organic solvents and many chemicals.
- Epoxy resins are flexible because of widely spaced reactive groups.

- Epoxy resins are tough and heat resistant due to cross-linking present in the structure.
- They have excellent adhesive property due to polar nature.
- Epoxy compounds are dissolved in some solvent to form solution.
- When metallic surface is dipped in this solution, a thin film leaves behind which on baking gets hardened.

Applications :
- Epoxy resins are best surface coating material. They give flexibility, toughness and resistance to chemicals to the surface like metals, wood, paper, leather etc.
- Epoxy resins are used to prepare glass-fibre reinforced articles by moulding and lamination technique. These articles formed have good strength, electrical insulating properties and chemical resistance. Liquid resins are more useful for this purpose than solid resins.
- Epoxy resins are useful as adhesives and applied on cotton, rayon, fabrics to make them crease resistive and non-shrinking.
- Epoxy resins are surface and patching material for roads.
- They are useful for the preparation of adhesive, foams industrial flooring, glass fibre boards.
- Epoxy resins are used as laminating and casting materials for electrical equipments and stabilizes for PVC resins.
- Araldite, M-seal, Feviseal etc. are some of the commercial adhesive.

3.2.3 Conducting Polymer

It is observed that most of the polymers do not conduct electricity, on the other hand they are excellent insulators. In recent years, the polymers that can conduct electricity to certain extent have been prepared. These specially prepared polymers are called conducting polymers. The conductivity of these conducting polymers lies between semi conductors like Si, Ge (10^{-5} to 10^2 ohm cm^{-2}) and good conductors like metals Fe, Cu (>10^5 ohm cm^{-2}). The insulators (Nylon, glass etc.) have very low conductivity (10^{-18} to 10^{-18} ohm cm^{-2}). The conductive polymers are polyacetylene, polyphenylene, polypyrrol, polythiophene etc.

Types of Conducting Polymers :

(A) Intrinsic Conductors : The polymers which are inherently conductor i.e. they conduct electricity of their own are called intrinsic conductors.

The system with alternate double bond is called conjugated system. If alternate double bond is present in the polymer chain, the polymer conducts electricity of it own. Out of the two double bonds, one is strong σ (sigma) bond and other is a weak π (Pi) bond.

In the conjugated system, overlapping of conjugated π bond electrons over the entire back bone takes place. This results in the formation of valence bond (VB) and conduction bond (CB) which extent over entire molecule. The bond gap is significant therefore thermal or photo excitation is essential for the process of conduction. In other words, the excitation of π electrons present in VB is done by supplying heat or exposing to light, the polymer conducts electricity.

Examples of intrinsic polymer

(a) Conjugated trans polyacetelene :

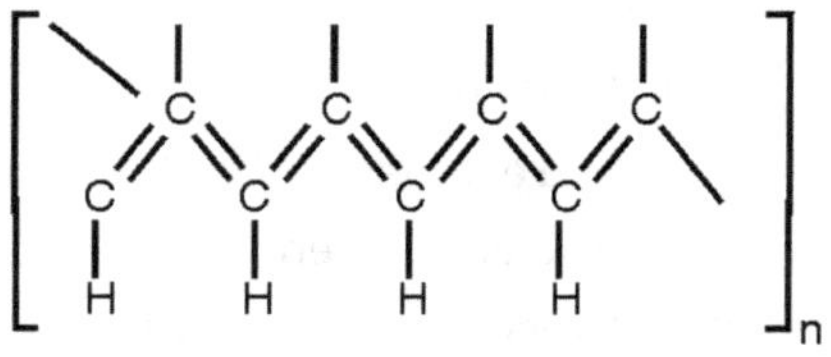

(b) Polypyrole

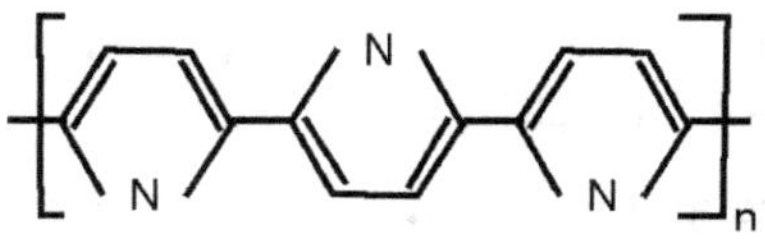

(c) Polyphenelene

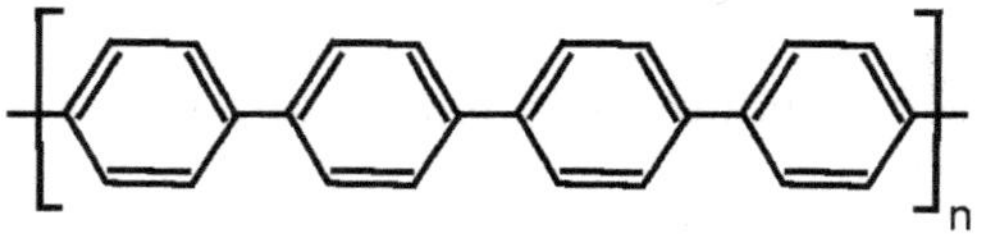

(d) Polyaniline :

(i) Leo Emeraldine

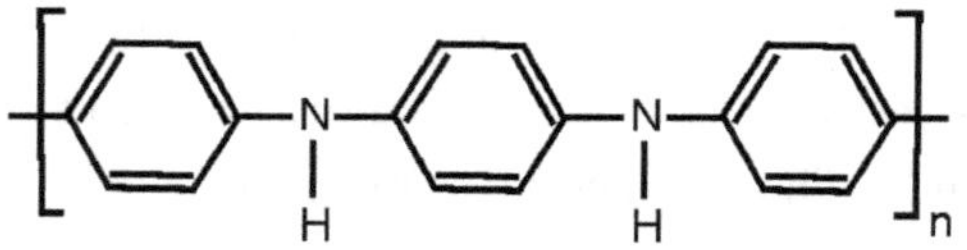

(ii) Emeraldine

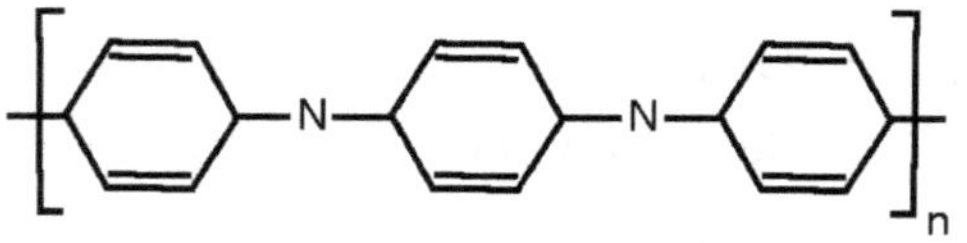

(B) Extrinsic Conductors : Some polymers are made conducting by addition of suitable substance to the polymer. The process of addition of external acceptor substance to polymer with electron donors or to make it conductive is called doping. The conducting polymers prepared by doping is called extrinsic conductors.

There are two types of doping.

(a) P–type doping (Oxidative doping) : A suitable oxidising agent take halogen are dopped to conjugated chains. It extracts a pair of π electrons from the chain and convert it into +vely charged on called polyron. Recombination of radial yield two +ve carriers which are mobile on each chain. Thus delocalization of +ve charges are carriers. The polymer chain has lost π electrons to halogen molecule therefore called oxidative doping.

Example : Polyacetylene + I_2

$$— CH = CH – CH = CH – CH = CH – CH = CH — + I_2$$
$$\downarrow$$
$$- CH = CH - CH = CH - CH = CH - \overset{+}{CH} - CH . I_2^-$$

(b) N – type doping (Reductive doping) : A suitable reducing agent like alkali metal atoms (Na, K and Li) are added to conjugated polymer chain which donate pair of electrons to polymer chain leads to the formation of polyrons and bi polyrons (–vely charged anions) in two steps. This results the conducting polymer due to a delocalization of π electrons. The polymer chain accepts the electrons from Na atom hence called reductive doping.

Example : Polyacelene +Na

$$— CH = CH – CH = CH – CH = CH – CH = CH — + \ddot{\ddot{Na}}$$
$$\downarrow$$
$$- CH = CH - CH = CH - CH = CH - \overset{-}{CH} - CH - . Na^+$$

Properties :

(i) Conducting polymers are flexible.

(ii) Conducting polymers are light in weight.

(iii) Conducting polymers are easy to fabricate as compared to other materials.

Applications :

(i) They are used in Fuel cells.

(ii) They are used in conductive paints.

(iii) They are used in electrochromic displays.

(iv) They are used in sensors.

(v) They are used to manufacture polymeric batteries (light weight, non leakage, high reliability, flexible, high energy density and ultra thin film form)

(vi) They are used as cathode and solid electrolyte in batteries for automobiles.

3.2.4 Biodegradable of Plastic :

Biodegradation is the process that involves almost complete decomposition of polymer under the attack of micro–organisms or fungi over a period of few months.

(i) Degradation by miro–organisms : This is the slow process of polymer degradation. The bacteria those occur in nature like psendomas, bacilli, protozoa, fungi attack on polymer and break C–C bond of polymer chain and break it.

(ii) Degradation of Enzyme : The enzymers are natural catalysts. They speed up the process of degradation of polymer. The natural polymer like starch is converted into maltose (simple sugar) by $\propto$ – amylose.

(iii) Degradation by Environment Constituents : The miosture, oxygen, ozone etc. are the constitutents of atmosphere. These constituents attack the sigma bonds of polymer chain and break into smaller chains. Finally low molecular weight compounds like N_2, NH_3, CO_2, CO, CH_4 are obtained. The process is slow.

(iv) Degradation which depends on nature of polymer : The condensation polymers containing functional group like $-NH_2$, $-COOH$ undergo degradation easily. Such polymeric groups have tendency to absorb moisture and swell and then decompose.

Biodegradable Polymers :

Natural polymers undergo degradation easily. The synthetic polymers do not undergo degradation easily. The life of polymer may range from few hundred years to millions of years. Polymers can be degraded by thermal, mechanical means, ultrasonic waves, light energy radiation and oidation. These processes give degradations products whichh are harmful to environment. Therefore these methods cannot be used for degradation of polymers.

The polymers such as poly propelene, PET, polystyrene, PVC are immune to attack by enzyme which is responsible for biological oxidation process. Therefore there is need for biodegradable polymer material used as disposable plastic packaging material.

(i) Aliphatic polyesters are biodegradable. It is believed that biodegradation of aliphatic polysters proceeds by attack of ester group by non specific enzyme produced by ground microflora combined with hydrolytic attack. Products of degradation are quickly metabolized by micro– organisms. Thus naturally occuring polyester poly β– hydroxy alkanonate is biodegradable. It is used as disposable plastic packaging material.

$$[O - \overset{O}{\underset{\|}{C}} - CH_2 - \overset{\overset{CH_2}{|}\overset{(CH_2)_n}{|}}{CH}]$$

Poly β hydroxy alkanoate

(ii) Poly β– hydroxy butyrate (PHB) : This is used in the manufacture of shampoo bottles.

(iii) The self condensation or lactic and produces polydactic acid abbriviated as PLA. It produced by fermentation of potato waste. PLA is biodegradable.

$$\left[O - \underset{\underset{CH_3}{|}}{\overset{\overset{O}{\|}}{C}} - CH \right]_n$$

PLA is used in drug delivery stems, wound clips. PLA is also used in agriculture as time released coatings for fertilizers and pesticides. It is also used for heat and moisture retention and to control weed growth between rows of crops.

PLA breaks down in environment to lactic acid which is metabolized.

Cellulose and its derivaties are biodegradable.

3.3 Nano Material :

3.3.1 Introduction :

The word nano has been derived by 'Greek nanos' or 'Latin nanus' meaning dwarf. Thus nano science pertians to the study of tiny objects in the size range of 1 to 100 nanometer. Nanotechnology entails the manipulation of matter at nanoscale paving the way of finding new properties, phenomenon and their applications. In recent times rapid advances in new synthetic techniques have mode manipoulation of matter at nanoscale in reality.

The development of nanotechnology is largely dependent on the availability of cost effective and accessible methods to manufacture nanostructures. Scientists in all fields such as physics, chemistry, biology, engineering are working in this area and all have a role to play in its development. In 1974, Taniguchi used the word nanotechnology.

Nano Particle :

A nanometer (nm) is 10^{-9} meter. This can be written as $10^{-6} \times 10^{-3}$ meter i.e. 10^{-6} millimeter. (One millionth of a millimeter). Also nanometer can be written as 10^{-3} micron (one thousandth of a millionth). The nanostructures are the smallest solid things in the range of 1 to 100 nm.

An atom or small molecule (vapour form) is smaller than a nanometer in size (hydrogen atom – 0.1 nm). The size of the human hair is 75000 nm. They do not fall in the catagory of nano particle.

Properties of nanoparticles :

The properties of nanoparticle are size dependent when it is below 100 nm. The shape of nanostructures also decides the properties of the material. The desired property of the material can be obtained by choosing differnt size and shape.

These properties can be used in different applications in various fields of science and technology.

(i) When nanostructures are build by starting with individual atoms small number of atoms are placed in the manner which is different from the arrangement in the bulk form. They are not just the fragment of bulk material. The nanostructures are affected by pressure and temperature.

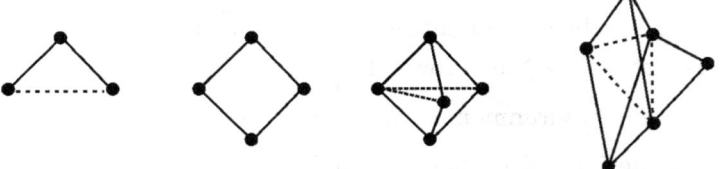

Stable structures of silicon with different atoms.

(ii) The mechanical properties of nanostructures such as harness, ductility, elasticity depends on the composition and number of bonds between atoms. The mechanical properties change if impurities are present in material and crystalline forms are imperfect.

The mechanical properties also depends on nature of nanostructures. Young's modulus of polycrystalline form is 4100 Nmm^{-2} which reduces to 3900 Nmm^{-2} in use of metallic nanocrystals. The hardness of nanomaterial decreases linearly with increase in particle size. The density of nanocrystalline pellet is found to be low as some pore are left during compression to form pellets.

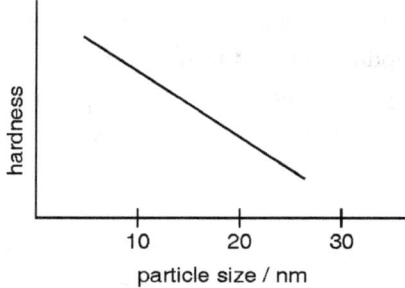

(iii) Some nanostructures show ferromagnetism which are not ferromagnetic in bulk form. This happens because nanoparticles have large surface to volume ratio and at the surface symmetry constant and lattic constant changes.

The data storage capacity of the nanomaterial is higher. Nanomagnetic material is formed by reducing one of the magnetic components of magnetic material.

(iv) The nanomaterial has higher resistivity as compared to polycrystalline material. The moving electrons are scattered to grain boundaries resulting into higher resistivity. Nanomaterial has higher number of grain boundaries than polycrystalline material.

The nanomaterial has high current density and high heat conductivity. It posses super conductivity under certain conditions.

(v) When nanoparticles of metals like gold, cobalt, nickel are incorporated in glass form stained glasses which show different colours. The colour appears due to different sized nano particles. Now gold particles impart intense red colour.

Synthesis of nano particles :

The process by which the nano particles are obtained is calles synthesis. The synthesis is also called as nano fabrication. When one starts with bulk material and cut down it to nano scale is called top down nano fabrication. On the other hand starting with individual atom and building upto a nanoparticle is called bottom up nano fabrication.

There are large number of different techniques available to synthesis various types of nanomaterial in different forms like powder, thinfilm colloids, cluster.

There are different methods of synthesis of nano particles. The most important technique of synthesis include,

(i) Physical method.
(ii) Chemical methods.
(iii) Biological methods.
(iv) Hybrid methods

(I) Physical Method :

(A) Some physical methods are discussed here. Mechanical method (High energy ball milling) : This is the simples method of making nanoparticle. The nano particles some metals and alloys are produced in the powdered form. In this method material flakes of particle of size < 50 μM are reduced to nanoparticle therefore it is top down nano fabrication.

Technique :

(i) There are different types of mills useful to produce nanoparticles are planetary ball mill, vibratory mill, and rod mill.

(ii) One or more containers are used to prepare nano particles and container size depends upon quality of material used.

(iii) The planatary ball mill consists of a container in which hardened steel or tungsten carbide balls and flakes of bulk material are placed in the ration 2:1. The container should be half filled only. Efficiency of milling is reduced if balls and material are more than half filled. If the large balls are put into container, increases the impact energy on collision and gives small grain size but produces larger defects in particle size.

(iv) After addition of balls and material the container is tightly closed with lid.

(v) The container is rotated at very high speed around the central axis.

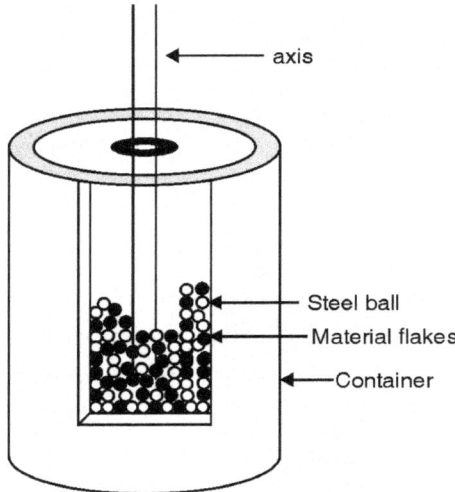

Fig. 3.1 : Mechanical Method

(vi) The material is forced to the walls and pressed against the walls due to centrifugal force but due to spinning action of container, the material is forced to other region of container.

(vii) Controlling the speed of rotation a fine powder of uniform size of few nm to few tens of nm can be obtained.

(B) Vapour Method :

In this technique, there is arrangement to carry physical evaporation of the material and compressing the powder in pellet form. The schematic diagram of the method is shown in the Fig. 3.2

(i) It consists of Chamber in which crucibles are placed which contain the material to be evaorated. The metals or metal oxides of material with high vapour pressure are evaporated from crucible. The density of the vapour of particle size < 5 nm near the crucible is high. The size of particles may increase by interaction of particles with each other. Therefore an inert gas is forced near the crucible to remove the particles away from it.

(ii) There is an arrangement of cold finger. It is a tube cooled by water or nitrogen as shown in the Fig. 3.2 The evaporated particles moves up and condense on cold finger. While moving from source to cold finger particle size grows and hence the distance between source and cold finger will decide the particle size.

If clusters are formed on inert gas atoms, on reaching the cold finger gas atoms leave the particle and escape to the gas phase. If reactive gases like O_2, N_2, H_2 are used, they form oxide, nitride or hydride particles. The size, shape and phase of particle depends upon the gas pressure inside the chamber.

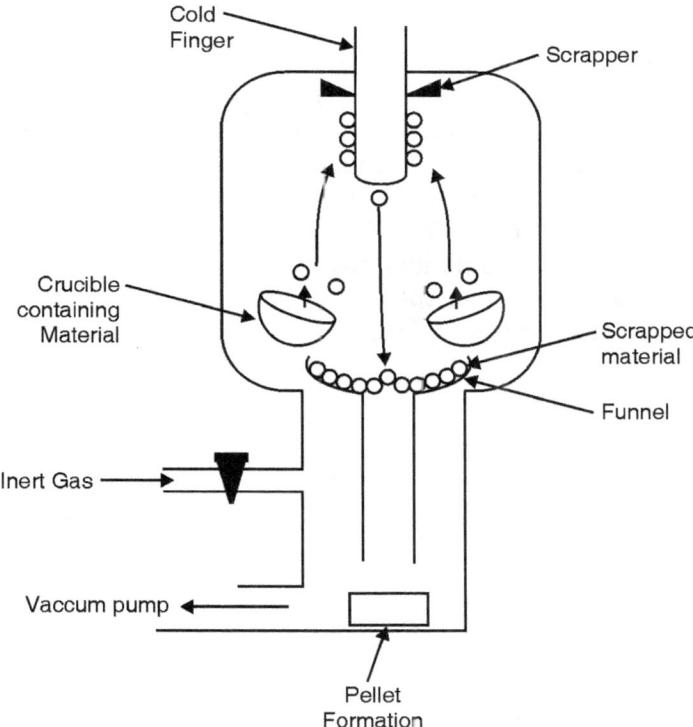

Fig. 3.2 : Vapour Method

(iii) The particles condensed on cold finger are scrapped by scrapper.

(iv) The scrapped particles are collected in funnel and pellelts are formed.

(v) The above procedure is repeated several times to collect required quantity.

(II) Chemical Method :

(i) In chemical method, nano particles are synthesized in the form of collids. Colloids are filtered and dried to obtain the powder form. By electrodeposition, thin film of colloids can be obtained.

(ii) The chemical methods have advantages over other methods.

(a) Less expensive and simple method.

(b) Synthesized at low temperature.

(c) Doping is possible during synthesis.

(d) Colloids is the form of powder, film, rod, fibre, plates, spheres can be obtained.

(e) Synthesis gives large quantity of product.

(f) Particles in liquid form can be easily converted to powder form.

Colloids as nano material :

A substance present in solution in colloidal state is called colloid. Colloidal state is a system of particles in a dispersion medium. The particle aquires surface charge in the medium. The coulomb force acting on them stabizes. Colloids have +ve or -ve charge. The common examples of colloids are starch, albumin, colloidal metals etc. The solvent is termed as dispersion medium and the dissolved substances the dispersed phase. The size of dispersed phase range < 100 nm. Several types of colloid solution are possible depending upon wheather the dispersion medium and dispered phase are liquid and solid (suspensoid), liquid and liquid (emulsoid), gas and solid etc. The small size of dispersed phase prevent them from being filtered easily and settle rapidly. The nano materials are subclass of colloids.

Technique :

(i) In this method colloids are used for self assembly of neutral particles on a neutral base.

(ii) The colloidal solution dissolved in ethanol is taken in a beaker and a glass plate is inserted in it as show in the Fig. 3.3

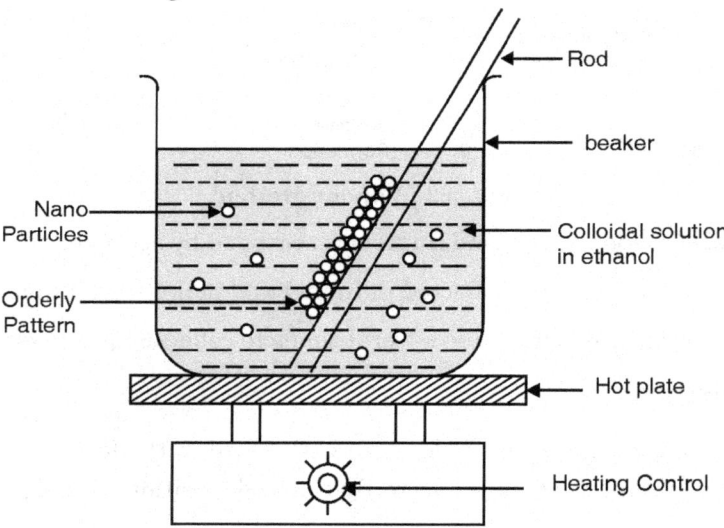

Fig. 3.3 : Chemical Method

(iii) The beaker is placed on a heating plate.

(iv) The solution heated slowly. The temperature rise and ethanol evaporates and liquid surface moves down.

(v) During this process, nano particles present in colloidal solution assemble themselves on a glass plate called self assembly.

(vi) As the process of evaporation continues the liquid surface moves down, more and more nano particles floating stick to the plate forming orderly arranged pattern.

(vii) The number of layers can be added by repeating process.

Synthesis of Colloids By Chemical Root Technique :

(i) The simple arrangement of preparation of nano particles by colloidal method is shown in the Fig. 3.4

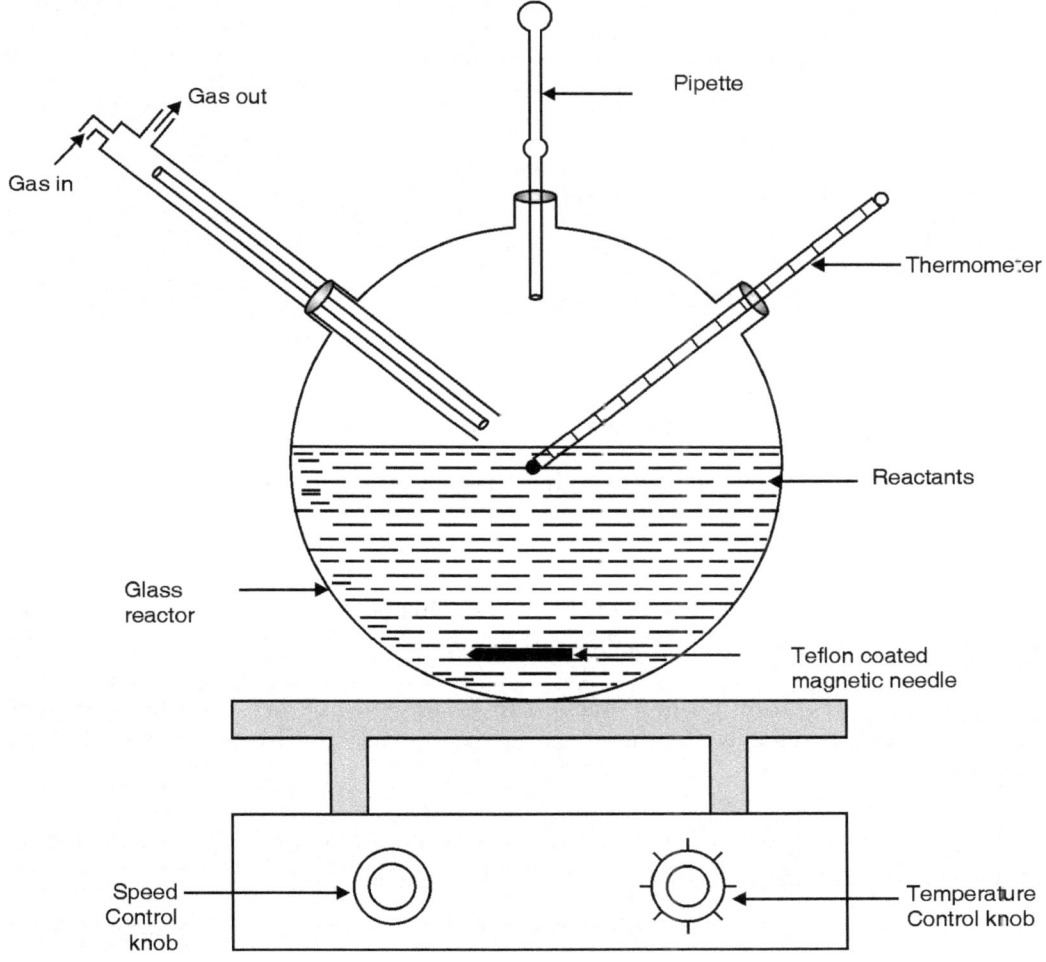

Fig. 3.4 : Chemical root technique

(ii) It consists of glass reactor of appropriate size placed on magnetic stirrer with heating arrangement. The reactants are placed in the reactor. The reactor has provision for thermometer to record temperature of reaction mixture, pipette to add reactants and gas inlet and outlet. The reaction takes place in glass reactor.

(iii) The temperature of the reactor is controlled by temperature control and for proper mixing of reactant teflon coated magnetic needle roated with magnetic stirrer is used.

(iv) The reaction is carried out in an inert atomospher by passing argon or nitrogen gas to avoid unwanted oxidation of the nano particles.

(v) The product (nano particles) formed in the reactor can be removed after suitable time interval.

Growth of Nano Particles :

In a bottom up fabrication method the particles of nearly same size can be obtained by controlling different steps. The growth of nano particles can be understood by Lamer Diagram.

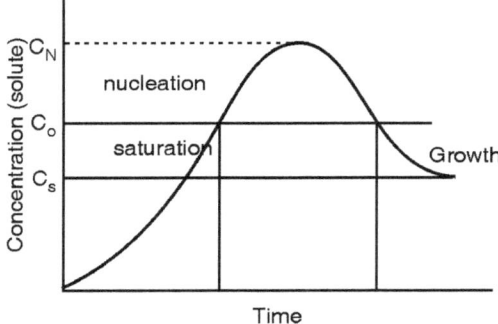

Fig. 3.5 : Lamer diagram

(i) As the concentration of reactant increases and reach certain value C_o at which formation of nuclei begin. (See Fig.)

(ii) The increase in concentration is continued which increases the nucleation upto the concentration C_N situated at the peak of the curve. This point indicates the supersaturation. C_N represents the maximum rate of nucler formation.

(iii) After supersaturation no new nuclei can be formed and crystal growth reduces the concentration which reaches to C_o, the minimum of nucleation. This gives an equilibrium at concentration C_s.

(iv) If new nuclei are formed during the growth, the growth will be in different stages. This results in the formation of different sized nano particles.

(v) Larger particle are move stable because they love lower surface energy. The larger particles grow at the expense of smaller particles called Ostwald's ripening.

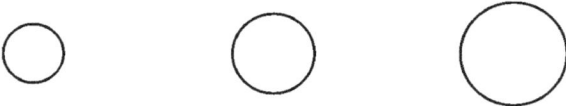

Fig. 3.6 Ripening

(vi) Aggregation of particles has been found in some cases becausee it lowers surface energy. Thus Ostwald's ripening and aggregation are competing with each other.

Fig. 3.7 Aggregation

Synthesis of Metal Nano Particles by Colloidal Route :

(i) The colloidal nano particles of metal can be systhsized by the process of reduction of metal oxide or metal acid.

(ii) The synthesis of highly stable gold nano particle is as follows :

The reduction of $HAuCl_4$ (Chloroayric acid) takes place when $Na_3C_6H_5O_7$ (trisodium citrate) react with it in aqueous medium. The reaction can be written as,

$$HAuCl_4 + Na_3C_6H_5O_7 \longrightarrow Au^{3+} + C_6H_5O_7^{-3} + HCl + 3\,NaCl$$

The gold nano particles are formed by the process of nucleation and condensation. The growth of gold particle in bigger size occurs when more Au^+ ions condense on surface. These atoms of gold are stabilized by –vely charged citrate ions. This can be represented diagramatically as,

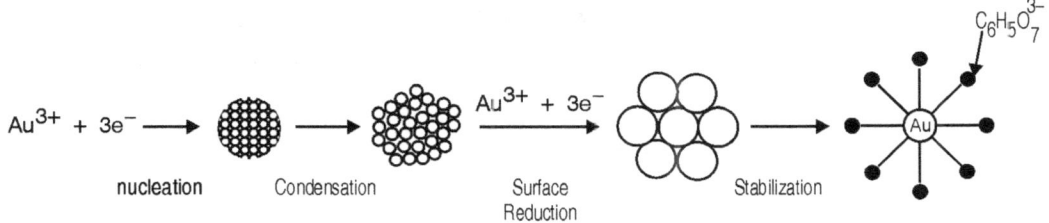

Fig. 3.8 : Nano particle of gold formation

(iii) Gold nano particles of different size exibit different colours. (Intensered, magenta)

(iv) The stabilizer thiol may be used as capping to stabilize the gold nano particle. The nano particle of silver and copper can be synthesized controlling the different factors.

(III) Biological Methods

The nano particles are prepared using biological material like plant extract, enzymes, DNA, membranes, viruses and microorganisms like bacteria. The biological methods of preparation of nano particles are ecofriendly and called green synthesis. There are three biological methods of prepartion of nano particle.

(A) Method based on the uses of microorganism like bacteria, yeast and fungi.

(B) Method based on the use of plant extracts or enzymes.

(C) Method based on the use of membranes, viruses and DNA.

(A) Method Using Micro Organism : In this method metal comes in contact with micro organisms and interact with cells to form nano particles. The interaction of cell metal is very complex.

Some bacteria found in silver mines are capable of accumulating silver inside or outside the cell walls.

Fungi (fusarium oxysporum) is used to obtain silver and gold nano particles extracellularly.

Lactobasillus converts low concentration metal ions into nano particles.

(B) Method Using Plant Extracts :

Plant extracts may be used for the preparation of nano particles. This method has limited scope. The leaves of geranium or alfalfa plant may be used to synthesize gold nano particles.

(C) Method Using Viruses and DNA :

The inorganic nano material are synthesized by DNA, enzymes and membrane.

(IV) Hybrid Methods :

(A) Chemical Vapour Deposition Method : This is a hybrid method. In this method chemical in vapour phase are used and obtained coating of different organic and inorganic material.

The method is advantagous because of :

(i) It has simple arrangement of working

(ii) It has simple processing and

(iii) It is cheap method.

The different types of chemical vapour deposition are possible by changing factors like gas pressure, temperature and arrangement. Metallic organic chemical vapour decomposition, vapour phase epitoxy, plasm enhaced chemical vapour deposition are the examples of CVD.

Technique :

(i) The substrate is kept at high temperature in the range of 300 – 1200°C.

(ii) The reactant gas or its vapour is transported to the substrate.

(iii) The reactants craks different products which diffuses on the surface. The chemical reaction occurs and grows to form film of desired material (nano particles)

(iv) The by products of reaction are formed on the substrate are removed and transported to gasous phase.

(v) The substrate is heated either by hot wall or cold wall set up. In hot wall set up, heaters are fitted out side chamber above and below. Cold wall is preferred because in hot wall set up deposition of nano particle may occur on reactor wall along with substrate and reaction may occures in gas phase.

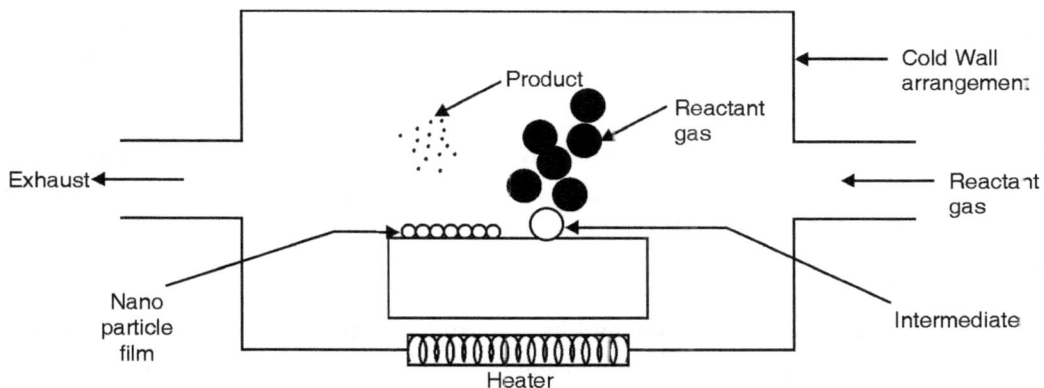

Fig. 3.9 Hybrid method (Cold wall setup)

(vi) The growth rate and film quality depends on substrate temperature reaction is faster. The gas pressure 0.1 to 1 torr is generally preferred.

(vii) If A and B are two types of atoms and molecules, both are absorbed on the surface of substrate and interact to form product AB. When one species is absorbed in excess of other, the growth depends on available adsorption sites for A and B (hangmuir Hinshelwood mechanism)

In other type, one species absorbed on the substrate and other species from phase reacts with it. There is no sharing sites (Elay – Riedel mechanism)

Applications :

Presently, nano science nano technology is a field of frontline research and is being driven by number of developments, ideas and technical advances. Nano technology by its very nature is an interdisciplinary area and chemists, physicists, biologists and engineers all have role to play in its development. Nano technology is a tool for improving the quality of human life.

(A) Field of Electronics :

(i) One of the ultimate goal in nanotechnology is to build electronic devices using individual molecules and this branch is popularly term as molecular electronics. Molecular electronics is being proposed as an alternative to the silicon based micro electronics. It is anticipated that the Si technology is likely to face the scaling limit in near future. The size of transistors goes down to 20 nm or below it.

(ii) New devices like SET (Single electron transistors), MTJ (Magnetic Tunnel Junction), spin valves are built using nano technology. These devices are cheap, small and faster. These are charge and spin based devices. The spin based devices are called spin tronic. Spin valve devices are used in PC to read disk which enables to increase data storage capacity of hard disks. Earlier devices were only charged based devices. Using an external magnetic field spin transport can be controlled. Spin can be easily destroyed by scattering from collisions with other charges, inpurities. The spin based device developd are spin RTD, spin LED and spin FET.

(iii) The nano particle coating on screen on monitors and TV improves the picture quality and resolution. Nano technology is useful to design smaller and faster micro processors, nonvolatile memory and good quality monitors.

(B) Field of Energy :

(i) The conventional energy sources like coal and oil will exhaust in 100 years and they damage the environment. The non conventional source of energy is solar energy. The solar energy can be converted to electrical energy using solar cells which are inconvinent to use. It requires large surface area and has low efficiency. Therefore efforts are taken to construct solar cells of small size and higher efficiency using nano technology

(ii) Hydrogen is ideal fuel and versatile energy carrier. It is easy to produce, environmentally compatible, and conveniently transported. The hydrogen storage materials hold hydrogen 2 to 4% of their weight. More recently, researchers evidenced keen interest in hydrogen storage methods aroused by the discovery of high hydrogen absorption capacity in carbon nanotubes and low diamensional carbon materials. If large scale carbon nanotubes are made possible, storing and trnasportation problem of hydrogen gas will be solved.

(iii) Researchers are attempting to prepare recharable batteries which should not be frequently replaced or rechard by replacing their electrode material on the basis of nano technology.

(C) Automobile Industries :

(a) The weight of the car can be reduced using thinner and light weight tyres of the wheel. Thinner and light weight tyres can be manufactured using nano particles consuming less rubber. This will reduce the price of the car and will consume less fuel.

(b) The nano tube combosites have better mechanical strength than steel. Steel is used to prepare the body of the car. Therefore attempts are made to replace steel by nano tube composites to obtain strong and non deformable car.

(c) Nano tube paints gives smooth and thin layer of paint on car and gives attractive look.

(D) Defence and Space :

(a) The aerogels (nano material) have low density (0.01 to 0.8 gcm^{-3}) poor unductivity and nano sized poroes. The scientists are trying to replace conventional material by nano material. The low weight space suit and jacket can be made using aerogel.

(b) Low weight and high efficiency battries and solar cells can be prepared using nano material for defence and space programmes.

(E) Medical Field :

(a) The scientists are tring to prepare biological system to fully understand how they work using nano technology.

e.g. digestive process, how virus interact in the body etc.

(b) Nano particles are useful in the process detection of cancer and tumer and its control.

(c) The drug filled nano capsules can be guided towards desired part of the body. The drug can be delivered in controlled manner (fast or slow). The opening of the capsule can be controlled externally. This is useful particularly to treat dibetic patients.

(d) The scientist are developing tests which are simple and fast to perform for the detection of enzymes, DNA, viruses, proteins and antibodies.

(e) Porous silicon and carbon nano tubes based sensors can be used in medical field.

(F) Field of Environment :

(a) Highly sensitive nano particle–based sensor are useful in detection of metal ions, toxic ions, pesticides, water purification system which are related to environment.

(b) Industrial pollution is minimised by the efficient production of nano particles at low temperature.

(c) The hydrogen fuel storage and oil filters using nano material can reduce the emission of gases through automobiles.

(G) Textile Industry :

(a) The products of nano technology are used to prepare special threads and dyes. The beautiful cloths of smooth texture and pleasant look can be prepared using nano particle based materials. The cloth produced will be wrinckle free and will not require frequent washing and ironing.

(b) Use of silver nanoparticles in washing machines will make the cloths germ free.

(H) Cosmetics :

(a) The sunscreen lotions containing nanoparticles of zinc oxide and titanium oxides of uniform size absorb ultra violet radiation and protects skin from tanning.

(b) The creams and gels containing nanoparticle based colours and dyes are harmless to skin and hair.

(c) Nano particle based make up creams do not have gap between them and gives smooth appearance and beautiful look.

3.4 Composite Materials :

Introduction :

Manytimes it is difficult to obtain suitable engineering material for particular application. In such situations readymade engineering material is required. such materials can be formed by blending, casting, rolling, sandwitching of different chemicals or materials called composites.

Definition of Composite :

A material system consisting of a mixture of two or more constituents which are mutually insoluble, differing in form and composition and forming distinct phases with improved properties is called as composite.

3.4.1 Constituents of Composite :

Composite are physical mixture of polymer matrix and reinforcing agents. For enhancing the properties of polymer such as mechanical strength, diamensional stability, some reinforced materials are added to the polymer matrix.

The addition of external material to the polymer matrix is called reinforcement and polymer matrix formed after reinforcement is called polymer composites. The polymer is called substrate or matrix and reinforced material is called as dispered phase.

Change in properties of polymer after forming composite (Properties of composite)

(i) The stiffness is increased without the disadvantages of brittleness.

(ii) The flexibility of polymer decreases after reinforcement as compared to original polymer matrix.

(iii) The material with ability to withstand extreme variation of temperature can be achieved.

(iv) Material with desired coefficient of thermal expansion can be achieved.

(v) Material with corrosion resistanced can be achieved by reinforcement.

(vi) Addition of metal and metal oxides to polymer material increases the thermal and electrical conductivity.

(vii) Polymer composites have higher glass transition temperature (T_g) and melting point t_m as compared to original polymer matrix.

(viii) Reinforcement of cheaper material in matrix, lowers the cost of composites.

3.4.2 Types of Composites :

There are three types of composites :

(a) Particulate Composites : This type of composites are made by dispering particles of varying size and shape of one material in a matrix of other material.

Examples :

(i) **Cermets :** Metals are dispersed in ceramics.

Used in cutting tools.

(ii) **Tugsten – thoria :** Tungesten is dispersed in thoria.

Used for lamp filament.

(iii) **Concrete :** Aggregate in cement.

Used in civil constructions such as building, bridge etc.

(b) Layered Composites : This type of composites are made by bonding thin layers of two materials together. There are many familiar application.

Examples :

(i) **Plywood :** Thin layers of wood with alternate layers having different orientation are glued together by adhesive.

(ii) **Copper bottom vessels :** Copper metal is layered on stainless steel or brass.

(iii) **Non Stick Cookwares :** Tephlon is coated on steel.

Used for cooking utensils.

(c) Fibre Reinforced Composites : This type of composite contains three components.

(i) **Filament**

(ii) **Polymer Matrix :** This is encapsuling agent for filament.

(iii) **Bonding Agents :** This binds filament or fibre to polymer matrix. Many a times polymer serves as matrix and bonding agent.

Examples :

(i) Acid Storage Tank

(ii) Boat Hulls

(iii) Space Craft

3.4.3 Properties and Applications of Fibre Reinforced Plastic (FRP) and Glass Reinforced Plastic (GRP) :

(I) Fibre Reinforce Plastic or FRP :

Fibre Reinforce Plastic (FRP) is manufactured by inforcing a fibre material of a very high strength in a plastic or resin matrix and curing it with heat and pressure.

Fibre Material :

Different types of fibre materials are used which are natural and synthetic. Natural fibres include asbestos, sisal cotton etc. and synthetic fibres are carbon, graphite, glass, boron, alumina polyamide beryllia etc. The fibre used depends on described properties of final prouct. The fibres or reinforcement may be woven fabrics or short chopped fibres. The glass fibre is widely used in industry.

Resin Material :

The resin matrices such as phenolic, silicone, epoxy, polysters, melaxine, vinyl derivatives, polyamide, polyesters, are generally used for the preparation of FRP. Matrices have low cost and therefore widely used in industry. For FRP with high temperature resistance phenolic resins and for good mechanical properties epoxy resins are used. Silicon resins give excellent thermal and electrical properties to FRP.

Properties of FRP :

- FRP has higher strength and stiffness.
- FRP has higher toughness, impact resistance and shock resistance.
- FRP has low thermal expansion and electrical conductivity.
- FRP has higher corrosion and oxidation resistance.
- FRP can be easily fabricated and it is cheap.
- FRP maintains strength at higher temperature.

Uses of FRP :

- FRP is used in space craft and supersonic planes.
- FRP is used to prepare speed boats, race car body, acid storage tanks.

Manufacturing Techniques :

FRP are manufactured by different processing techniques. The following techniques have been used.

(1) Hand lay up technique
(2) Spray up technique
(3) Injection moulding technique
(4) Matched metal die mould
(5) Continuous lamination
(6) Centrifugal casting
(7) Pultrusion and
(8) Filament winding.

(1) Matched die moulding technique :

This technique is cheap and efficient and useful to manufacture parts having high strength. It consists of female and male parts of the mould which is filled with resin and fibre and pressed at a pressure of 300 psi and temperature set at about 125°C.

(2) Continuous lamination technique :

This technique is useful to produce wrinkled panels, glazing articles of big size continuously on rolls. This is economical technique. The mats of required fibre are produced and impregnated with appropriate resin and passed through laminating rolls between sheets to control the thickness and resin content in FRP. The curing of FRP sheets occurs in heating zone.

(3) Pultrusion :

The articles of different shapes like oval, tapered, rectangular, round can be produced with the help of this techniques. The mat of fabric and continuous strand of fibre are combined and mixed with appropriate resin are pulled through a hot steel die of appropriate shape.

II Glass fibre reinforced plastic or grp :

In the manufacture of GRP, glass fibre is most popular and extensively used in industry. It has following useful properties.

(i) Glass fibre is finer than silk and cotton thread and can be woven into mats.
(ii) Glass fibre has high tensile strength.
(iii) Glass fibre has low dielectric constant and coefficient of thermal expansion.
(iv) It is non–flammable.
(v) It is chemical resistive and corrosion resistive.
(vi) The cost of production is low as compared to other fibres.

When the fibre used is glass fibre the plastic formed is called glass inforced plastic (GRP). The borosilicate glass (E–glass) is generally used for this purpose. The glass fibre are spur as single glass filament of size $2.5 - 5 \times 10^{-3}$ cm diameter. In thermoplastic, glass content is about $20 - 40\%$ and in thermosetting plastics glass content is $\sim 80\%$.

Properties of GRP :

- The tensile strength is high about 5×10^5 psi. S–glass has higher strength but are costly.
- The GRP is lighter, tough and elastic.
- The GRP is chemical and corrosion resistive.
- The GRP is cheaper.

Uses of GRP :

- GRP is used to prepare air filters which removes dust from air.
- GRP prepared from S–glass is used to manufacture insulation material for pipe. It also provides insulation against electricity, heat and sound.
- GRP is used to prepare air craft parts, speed boats, fishing rods, acid storage tanks, long pole for pole–vault, race car bodies etc.

Exercise

Long Answer Questions

1. Define polymer and monomer. Classify the polymers on the basis of structure. Give the example of each type.
2. Define compsite. Give the constituents of composite.
3. What are the different types of composite?
4. Define plastic. What are the properties of plastic ? Give applications and uses of plastic.
5. Give the classification of plastic. Discuss each type of plastic with examples.
6. Discuss the preparation reaction, properties and uses of urea aldehyde..
7. Explain the preparation, properties and uses of backelite.
8. Discuss the preparation, properties and uses of conducting polymer.
9. Discuss the preparation, properties and uses of epoxyresin
10. What is Fibre Reinforce Plastic (FRP). Give the properties of FRP. Discuss manufacturing techniques of FRP.
11. What are the useful properties of glass fibre ? What is glass reinforce plastic (GRP) ? Give the properties and uses of GRP.
12. What is epoxy resin? Discuss different methods of preparation of epoxy resin.
13. Discuss properties and uses of epoxy resin.
14. Define nano particle discuss 4 properties of nano particles.
15. Discuss two important methods of synthesis.

Short Answer Questions

1. Explain the term thermosetting plastic.
2. Explain the term thermosetting plastic.
3. Distinguish between thermoplastic and thermosetting plastic.
4. Write short note on backelite.
5. Discuss biodegradation nad bidegradable plastic.
6. Give the properties and uses of phenol formaldehyde/urea formaldehyde.
7. Write a note on conducting polymers.
8. Write a short note on fibre reinforce plastic.
9. Discuss manufacturing techniques of FRP.
10. Explain preparation, properties and uses of epoxy resin.
11. Discuss the applications of nano particle in the field of electronics/ energy/ automobile/ space/ medical/ environment/ textile/ cosmetics.

University Questions

1. Give preparation proportions and applications of phenol formcaldehyde resin.
2. Distinguish between thermosoftening plastics and thermosetting platics.
3. **Write notes on :**
   (a) Thermoplastics and thermosetting polymer.
   (b) Thermosoftening and thermosetting polymer.
   (c) Thermosetting polymer

Section – II

Unit 4

Fuels

- Introduction
- Classification
- Calorific Value
  - Definition
  - Unit (Calorie, Kcal, Joule, kJoule)
- Characteristics of Good fuels.
- Comparison between Solid, Liquid and Gaseous Fuels
- Types of Calorific Value (high and low)
- Calculation of Calorific Value by Dulong's formula.
- Determination of Calorific Value by Bomb Calorimeter Method
- Determination of Calorific Value by Boy's Calorimeter Method
- Numerical Problems on Calorific value.
- Fuel Cells
  - Classification
  - Limitations
  - Advantages
  - Applications
- Excercise

4.1 Introduction :

In modern age, energy has become basic requirement for industry, agriculture, transport, domestic purposes etc. The energy consumption is increasing day by day. Industrial progress is measured in terms of per capita energy consumption. For the production of energy we require fuels. Coal (carbon) has been used as fuel since many centuries. The combustion of coal (reaction with oxygen) gives heat and light (energy). Crude oil and natural gas are also important sources of fuels. With more need of energy different energy sources have been investigated. In this nuclear energy is most important for which fuels used are radioactive substances. In this chapter we will consider details about fuels.

Fuels :

Definition of Fuel :

(A) Fuel is defined as any combustible substance containing carbon as main constituent which on burning in air produces large amount of heat (energy) which can be commercially used for domestic and industrial purposes.

(B) More general definition of fuel : Fuel is defined as any combustible substance which is available in bulk which on combustion produces large amount of heat which can be used for various purposes.

Explanation and Importance of fuel :

- The main constituent of fuels is carbon along with other elements like hydrogen, oxygen, nitrogen and sulphur. Fuels include any material such as wood, coal, petrol, diesel, oils etc. having main constituent as carbon.
- Fuels like crude oil, natural gas and coal are called fossil fuels found in earth crust.
- Combustion is the main reaction to obtain heat from fuel. Combustion is the reaction of the substance with oxygen. The fuel reacts with atmospheric oxygen with evolution of heat at very fast rate along with other products. The product include gases like carbon dioxide, sulphur dioxide, water vapour etc. and ash as well as other materials.

  Combustion reaction :

  $C + O_2 \longrightarrow CO_2 + \text{heat}$

  $\text{Fuel} + O_2 \text{ (air)} \longrightarrow \text{heat} + \text{by product}$

- Nuclear energy is obtained from fission reaction. Nuclear energy is obtained from nuclear fuels like ^{235}U, ^{239}Pu, ^{233}U etc. When thermal neutrons are bombarded on nuclear fuel nuclear energy is liberated. Very small amount of nuclear fuel can produce tremendous amount of energy. One kg of Plutonium–239 liberates energy which is equivalent to about 2000 – 2500 tons of good quality coal. Nuclear fuels are not true fuels as energy is not obtained by combustion reaction.
- Fuels like fossil fuels and vegetable oils which produce heat on burning are called as chemical fuels. Chemical fuels are the most important source of heat energy and mainly used for heating purposes. They have also other functions such as generating electricity and mechanical energy. Petrol and diesel are used to generate (a) mechanical energy in automobiles and (b) electricity in generators. In the manufacture of metals coke is used in furnace as reducing agent as well as heating agent.
- The coal and crude oil which are natural fuels are consumed at a very fast rate and will last only for few decades. Therefore new sources of energy are needed. The wind energy, solar energy, tidal energy, geo–thermal energy, wave energy will be used in future.

4.2 Classification of Fuels :

Classification of fuels is based on two factors

1. Occurrence of fuels ; 2. Physical State (solid, liquid and gas) of fuels

1. Classification based on occurrance

(A) Primary and natural fuels :

These fuels are found in nature and can be utilized as they are obtained from nature.

Examples : (a) coal (b) wood (c) natural gas (d) peat (e) ignite etc.

(B) Secondary or artificial fuels :

These fuels are prepared artificially by processing primary fuels.

Examples :

1. Charcoal obtained by partial combustion of wood.
2. Petrol and diesel derived from by fractional distillation of crude oil.
3. Alcohol obtained by fermentation of sugar.
4. Biogas obtained from dung.

(2) Classification based on physical state of fuel

(C) Solid fuel :

Fuels are in solid state.

Examples : (1) coal (2) wood (3) charcoal etc.

(D) Liquid fuel :

Fuels are in liquid state.

Examples : (1) Crude oil (2) vegetable oil (3) petrol (d) diesel.

(E) Gaseous fuel :

Fuels are in gaseous state.

Examples : (1) natural gas (2) LPG (3) Biogas etc.

Classification of fuels based on both factors is summarised in Table 4.1 with example of each type.

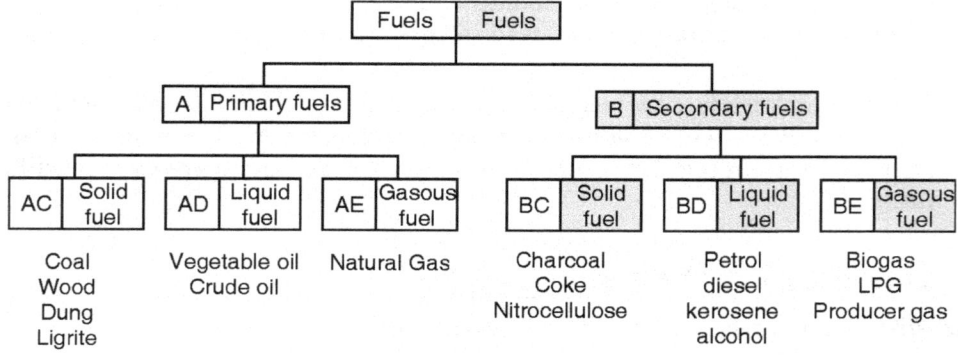

4.3 Characteristics of Fuels :

The important characteristics of fuel are as follows :

4.3.1 Ignition Temperature or Kindling Temperature :

Definition :

Ignition temperature is defined as the minimum temperature at which fuel ignite or catches fire and continues to burn without addition of further heat.

It is also called as kindling temperature.

Explanation :

- Fuels exist in air practically indefinitely if not heated to ignition temperature.
- Ignition temperature is not definite for particular fuel. It is influenced by many factors.
- Ignition temperature of solid and liquids depends on,
  (a) Nature of fuel   (b) Fineness of fuel   (c) Extent of exposed surface
- The ignition temperature of gaseous fuel depends on
  (a) Pressure – As the pressure is increased usually ignition temperature decreases.
  (b) Size and shape of the vessel – As the ratio of surface of the vessel to volume of vessel increases the ignition temperature increases.
  (c) Ratio of gaseous fuel to air.
  (d) Environment of combustion.
  (e) Presence of catalyst.

4.3.2 Calorific Value :

Definition :

Calorific value is defined as the total quantity of heat liberated by complete combustion of a unit mass or volume of a fuel.

Explanation :

(a) Calorific value is a characteristic property of a fuel which is different for different fuels.

(b) Calorific value has a unit in terms of heat expressed in different units.

(c) It gives the efficiency of a fuel to produce heat on combustion.

(d) Calorific value of gaseous fuel refers to one atmospheric pressure and at 15°C.

Units of Calorific Value :

1. **C.G.S. units :** In this system, heat is expressed in terms of calorie. Calorie is the amount of heat required to raise the temperature of 1 g of water through one degree celsius.

The unit of mass is gram and unit of volume is cm^3. C.G.S. units of calorific value is **calorie per gram (cal g^{-1})** for solid and liquid fuels.

1.A. unit is **calorie per cm^3 (cal cm^{-3})** for gaseous fuel.

2. M.K.S. units : In this system, heat is expressed as kilocalorie. Kilocalorie is the amount heat required to raise the temperature of 1 kg of water through one degree celsius.

The unit of mass is kilogram and unit of volume is m^3. M.K.S. unit of calorific value is kilocalorie per kilogram (kcal kg^{-1}) for solid and liquid fuels.

2.A. unit is kilocalorie per meter^3 (kcal m^{-3}) for gaseous fuel.

3. S.I. units : In this system heat is expressed in Joule. 1 cal = 4.184 Joule unit of mass is kg and units of volume is m^3. S.I. units of calorific value is **Joule per kilogram (J kg^{-1})** and kJ kg^{-1} for solid and liquid fuel and **Joule per meter^3 (Jm^{-3})** and kJ m^{-3} for gaseous fuel.

Table 4.2 summarises the units of calorific value in different system.

Table 4.2 : Units of calorific value

No.	System	Units of calorific value	
		Solid and liquid fuels	**Gaseous Fuels**
1.	C.G.S.	Calorie per gram – cal g^{-1}	Calorie per milliliter – cal cm^{-3}
2.	M.K.S.	Kilocalorie per kilogram–kcal kg^{-1}	Kilocalorie per meter^3 – kcal m^{-3}
3.	S.I.	Joule per kilogram – J kg^{-1} and kJkg^{-1}	Joule per meter^3 – Jm^{-3} and kJm^{-3}

Interconvertion of calorific value in different units :

$$1 \text{ kcal kg}^{-1} = 4,186.8 \text{ J kg}^{-1}$$

Higher or gross calorific value :

Most of the fuels contain hydrogen along with carbon. The carbon atoms are bonded with hydrogen atoms. During combustion of fuel hydrogen atoms combine with oxygen atom and form water molecules which are vaporized during combustion. In the measurement of calorific value if the products of combustion are cooled to room temperature (15°C) then the heat is liberated called latent heat of condensation also should be considered. The total heat liberated is higher and hence gives higher calorific value.

Definition :

Higher or gross calorific value is defined as the total amount of heat produced by complete combustion of a unit mass or volume of a fuel in air and products of combustion are cooled to room temperature (15°C).

Units of higher calorific value :

(i) k cal kg^{-1} or kcal m^{-3} (ii) J kg^{-1} or J m^{-3} (iii) cal g^{-1} or cal cm^{-3}

Low or Net calorific value :

In practice, when fuel undergoes combustion water fromed is evaporated cannot be condensed but escape along with gaseous products fromed. Practically, it is not possible to condense the vapour at room temperature and use its latent heat. Therefore less heat is available from fuel and calorific value is lower called low or net calorific value.

Definition :

It is defined as the net heat produced when 1 gram or cm^3 of fuel is burnt completely and product of combustion are not condensed but allowed to escape.

Units of low calorific value :

(i) k cal kg^{-1} or kcal m^{-3} (ii) J kg^{-1} or J m^{-3} (iii) cal g^{-1} or cal cal cm^{-3}

Heat lost due to escape of water vapour :

Combustion of hydrogen reaction :

$$H_2 + O_2 \rightarrow H_2O$$
$$2g\ H_2 \equiv 18\ g\ of\ H_2O$$
$$1\ g\ H_2 = 9\ g\ of\ H_2O$$

Latent heat of vapour = 587 cal g^{-1}

Heat lost due to escape of water vapour

= Latent heat of condensation of water vapour

$$= \frac{9 \times (\%H)\ in\ fuel \times 587}{100}$$

∴ Net calorific value = Gross calorific value

– Latent heat of condensation of water vapour

$$= Gross\ calorific\ value - \left(\frac{9 \times (\%H\ in\ fuel) \times 587}{100}\right)$$

Calorific value at constant pressure :

The calorific value at constant pressure depends on the increase or decrease in number of gaseous molecules formed given by the equation,

$$(calorific\ value)_p = (calorific\ value)_v - (\Delta n)\ RT$$

Where, $(calorific\ value)_v$ – Calorific value at constant volume obtained from bomb calorimeter

Δn – Increase or decrease in number of gas molecules formed

R – Gas constant

T – Absolute temperature

4.4 Characteristics of Good Fuel :

There are different types of fuels. A fuel which is most suitable for our purpose is a good fuel. The good fuel should have following characteristics.

(a) High calorific value : For good fuel, calorific value should be high. Heat liberated and temperature attained depends on calorific value.

(b) Low cost : A good fuel should be available in bulk and should have cheap rate.

(c) Low moisture content : A good fuel should contain very small percentage of moisture. Moisture reduces the calorific value of the fuel.

(d) Moderate ignition temperature : If ignition temperature is low as in case of gases, there is risk in storing and transporting the fuel. If the ignition temperature is high as in case of solids, it is difficult to start the combustion when temperature is low in winter season. The fuels which have moderate ignition temperature like liquids are preferable fuels.

(e) Harmless combustion product : A good fuel should not evolve or as low as possible poisonous gases (CO, SO_2, H_2S) and harmful polluting substances to protect the environment.

(f) Low non–combustible matter : Non combustible matter are converted into ash which is spread into atmosphere and harmful to environment. It also decreases the calorific value therefore a fuel should have low non–combustible matter.

(g) High flexibility : A fuel with higher flexibility can be controlled easily to obtain heat at desired rate and are cheap.

(h) Risk free and cheap transportation : Transportation of a good fuel should be risk free and cheap. Gaseous fuels are dangerous to transport because of possibility of explosion and requires more care. A liquid fuel can be easily transported through pipes. A solid fuel can be transported easily but laborious.

(i) Uniform size : Size of a good fuel should be uniform.

4.5 Comparison between Solid, Liquid and Gaseous Fuels :

Comparison between solid, liquid and gaseous fuel is necessary for the selection of a fuel for definite purpose. Different properties are compared of these fuel in Table 4.3.

Table 4.3 : Comparison of solid, liquid and gaseous fuels

No.	Property or criteria of fuel	Solid fuel	Liquid fuel	Gaseous fuel
1.	Calorific value	Low	Higher	Higher
2.	Relative cost	Cheaper	Costly	More costly
3.	Space of storage	Large	Less than solid special tank necessary	Depends on pressure

No.	Property or criteria of fuel	Solid fuel	Liquid fuel	Gaseous fuel
4.	Transportation	Easy but laborious	Easy through pipe otherwise more care is necessary	More care is necessary as highly inflammable and if hazardous
5.	Specific gravity	Highest	Medium	Lowest
6.	Moisture content	Moisture present	Moisture absent	Moisture absent
7.	Smoke produced	Considerably high	Low	No smoke produced
8.	Ash produced	High	No ash produced	No ash produced
9.	Ignition temperature	High I.T.	Low I.T.	Lowest I.T.
10.	Flexibility	High flexibility	No flexibility	No flexibility
11.	Use in internal combustion engines	Cannot be used	Used conveniently	Used conveniently
12.	Solid products of combustion	Leaves ash, clinker, cinder etc.	No solid products	No solid products
13.	Rate of combustion	Cannot be controlled	Can be controlled	Can be controlled

4.6 Determination of Calorific Value :

(I) Calculation of theoretical calorific value by Dulong's formula :

Theoretical value of gross calorific value can be determined knowing percentage of carbon, hydrogen, oxygen and sulphur elements in the fuel sample. Dulong formula gives the theoretical gross calorific value. Dulong formula is as follows :

Theoretical Gross Calorific Value $= \dfrac{1}{100}\left[8080\,C + 34500\left(H - \dfrac{O}{8}\right) + 2240\,S \right]$ kcal kg^{-1}

Where,   C – % carbon

H – % hydrogen

O – % oxygen

S – % sulphur

8080 – Calorific value of carbon in kcal kg^{-1}

(Heat liberated in kcal when 1 kg of carbon is burnt)

34500 – Calorific value of hydrogen in kcal kg^{-1}

2240 – Calorific value of sulphur in kcal kg^{-1}

4.6.1 Determination of Calorific Value by Bomb Calorimeter Method :

The bomb calorimeter is useful to determine calorific value of solid fuel as well as non volatile liquid fuel.

Principle of Method :

The known quantity of solid or non-volatile liquid is combusted completely and the amount of heat produced is allowed to be absorbed by the known quantity of water leading to rise in temperature of water. From rise in temperature of water, calorific value of the fuel can be calculated.

Apparatus :

The schematic diagram of bomb calorimeter is known in the Fig. 4.1.

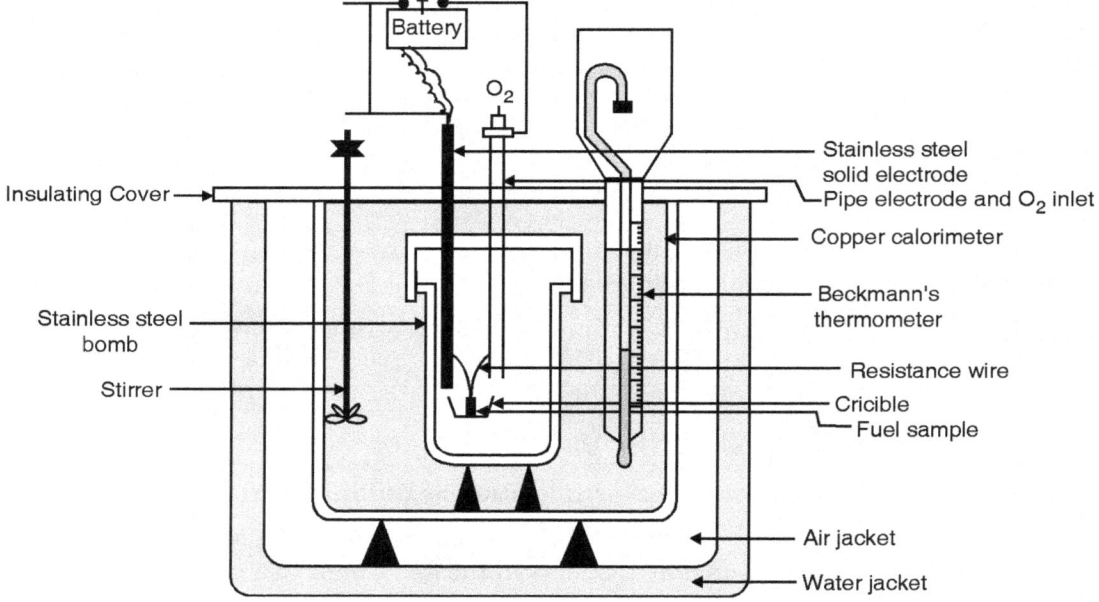

Fig. 4.1 : Arrangement of bomb Calorimeter

(A) Bomb :

(i) It consists of a strong stainless steel cylindrical vessel which is corrosion resistant and withstand high pressure of 50 atmosphere called as bomb.

(ii) The vessel is provided with a lid which can be made gas tight with the help of screw provided.

(iii) Two stainless steel electrodes are fitted through the lid. One electrode is rod type while other electrode is tubular which can act as an oxygen inlet in the vessel. A small ring is attached to this electrode which hold, the crucible containing pallet of fuel.

(iv) Lid is also provided with release valve at the centre.

(v) A thin resistance wire (7.5×10^{-3} cm thick) is tied to electrodes in loop form.

It touches the fuel placed in the crucible.

(B) Calorimeter :
- Calorimeter is stainless steel or copper vessel containing known volume of water.
- It is provided with a stirrer which is electrically operated and stirs the water in calorimeter at a uniform rate.
- It is also provided with Beckmann thermometer which dips in water in calorimeter and measures the temperature of water nearest to 2×10^{-3} °C.
- The bomb is placed in calorimeter containing water during experiment.

(C) Air jacket and water jacket :
- The calorimeter is surrounded by air jacket which is further enclosed with water jacket to prevent losses due to radiation.

(D) Other accessories :
- **Pellet press :** Solid fuel in powder form is converted into pellet form.
- **Capsule :** Capsule of negligible mass may be used to fill the liquid fuel.
- **Oxygen cylinder :** Oxygen cylinder is required with a pressure gauge to fill the oxygen gas in bomb at a pressure of about 25 kg cm^{-2}.
- **D.C. battery :** Six volt D.C. battery is necessary to ignite the fuel.

Experimental procedure :
- About 1 g of finely ground air dried sample of solid fuel is compressed into pellet with the help of pellet press.
- The pellet of the fuel is placed in a weighed crucible. The crucible with pellet is accurately weighed. The weight of pellet is calculated and recorded as x gram.
- Crucible in placed in the ring and thin platinum wire is bent into loop and inserted into the fuel pellet in crucible.
- 10 cm^3 of distilled water is introduced into the bomb. It absorbs H_2SO_4 and HNO_3 formed. The lid of bomb is screwed to make it gas tight.
- The bomb is filled with oxygen at the pressure about 25 kg cm^{-2}.
- The calorimeter is weighed. Sufficient water is added to calorimeter and weighed. The weight of water is calculated and recorded as Wg.
- The calorimeter is then kept in outer air and water jackets on insulating studs.
- The bomb is lowered in calorimeter.
- The stirrer and adjusted Beckmann thermometers are placed in calorimeter and lid of calorimeter is placed in position.
- The stirrer is started.
- After 5 minutes of stirring, record the temperature of water in calorimeter and record the temperature after every minutes for 5 minutes. Mean temperature of water is t_1°C.

- The two electrode in bomb are connected to battery till the fuel is ignited and combustion of fuel occurs. Heat is transferred to water.
- Temperature of water is recorded for every minute till maximum temperature is attained. Recording is continued till attain room temperature. Record the maximum temperature of water $t_2°C$ and time required to cool water from maximum to room temperature, t minute.
- If the fuel contains nitrogen and sulphur elements which are converted to nitrogen pentoxide and sulphur trioxide on combustion in bomb. N_2O_5 and SO_3 dissolve in water and form HNO_3 and H_2SO_4.
- Stirring is stopped and bomb is removed from calorimeter. It is cooled for half an hour. The bomb is washed with water and content is removed in a breaker. Amount of HNO_3 and H_2SO_4 are determined by analytical method.

Calculations of calorific value :

Observations :

1.	Weight of the fuel	$= x_g$
2.	Weight of water in calorimeter	$= W_g$
3.	Initial temperature of water	$= t_1°C$
4.	Final temperature of water	$= t_2°C$
5.	Increase in temperature of water	$= t_2 - t_1$
6.	Water equivalent of calorimeter, stirrer, thermometer, bomb etc.	$= w\ g$
7.	Gross calorific value of fuel sample	$= Q\ cal\ g^{-1}$ or $kcal\ kg^{-1}$
8.	Time required to cool water from maximum to room temperature	$= A$ minute
9.	Specific Heat of water	$= S = 1\ Cal/g/°C$
		$= 4.185\ kJ/kg/K$

Calculations :

(i) Heat liberated by complete combustion of given sample of fuel $= xQ$ cal

(ii) Heat absorbed by water, calorimeter $= (W + w)(t_2 - t_1)$ cal

Heat liberated by fuel = Heat absorbed by calorimeter etc.

$$xQ = (W + w)(t_2 - t_1)$$

Formula : Gross calorific value, $Q = \dfrac{(W + w)(t_2 - t_1)}{x}$ cal g^{-1} or Kcal kg^{-1}

$$Q = \dfrac{[(W + w)\, S]\,(t_2 - t_1)}{x} \text{ kJ kg}^{-1}$$

$$= \dfrac{[(W + w) \times 4.185]\,(t_2 - t_1)}{x} \text{ kJ kg}^{-1}$$

Water equivalent, w can be determined using above formula by combustion of fuel of known gross calorific value in a separate similar experiment.

Net calorific value = Gross calorific value, Q

– Latent heat of water vapour formed during combustion of x_g of fuel sample

= 0.09 × %H × 587

∴ Latent heat of water vapour = 587 Cal g^{-1}

Mass of H$_2$O formed by 1g of fuel = $\dfrac{9 \times \%H}{100}$ = 0.09 × %H

Latent heat of water vapour formed during combustion of xg of fuel sample

N.C.V. = G.C.V. (Q) – (0.09 × H × 587) cal g^{-1}

Corrections for Accurate Result :

(i) Corrections due to acids formation (A) : If the fuel sample contains elements Nitrogen (N) or Sulphur (S) undergo combustion and form acids as follows :

(a) $2 N_2 + 5 O_2 \rightarrow 2N_2 O_5 + 5H_2 O = 4 HNO_3 + \Delta H\ 57.16$ kcal

Heat liberated by one cm^3 of 0.1 N HNO$_3$ = 1.43 cal

(b) $\qquad\qquad\qquad S + O_2 = SO_2$

$\qquad\qquad SO_2 + O_2 + 2H_2 O = 2 H_2 SO_4 + \Delta H\ (144\ kcal)$

Heat liberated by one cm^3 of 0.1 N H$_2$SO$_4$ = 3.6 cal

These two reactions are exothermic and heat is liberated. This additional heat produced is also responsible for rise in temperature of water in calorimeter. Hence it must be considered for correction since it is in closed space of bomb. Heat liberated should be subtracted.

(ii) Correction due to fuse wire (F) : When fuse wire is ignited again additional heat is produced should be considered for correction. The information is given by fuse wire manufacturer.

(iii) Correction due to cotton thread (C) : The cotton thread used for firing the charge should be considered for correction. The weight of dry cotton thread and calorific value of cellulose (4140 cal g^{-1}) gives this correction C.

(iv) Correction due to cooling (t_c) : The time taken for the water in calorimeter to cool from maximum temperature to room temperature is t_c minute then rate of cooling = dt min^{-1}. Then cooling correction = $t_c \cdot$ dt. This correction should be added to observed rise in temperature.

Corrected formula of gross calorific value :

$$\text{Corrected G.V.C.} = \frac{(W + w)[(t_2 - t_1) + t_c]}{x} - (A + F + C)$$

4.6.2 Determination of Calorific Value by Boy's Calorimeter Method :

The Boy's calorimetric method is used to determine calorific value of gaseous and volatile liquid fuels.

Principle of Method :

A sample of gaseous fuel is burnt at a known constant rate in a calorimeter under such conditions that whole amount of heat liberated is absorbed by water flowing at constant rate. The calorific value is determined by knowing the volume of gas burnt, volume of water collected and rise of temperature of water.

Apparatus :

Apparatus used for Boy's calorimeter method is shown in Fig. 4.2.

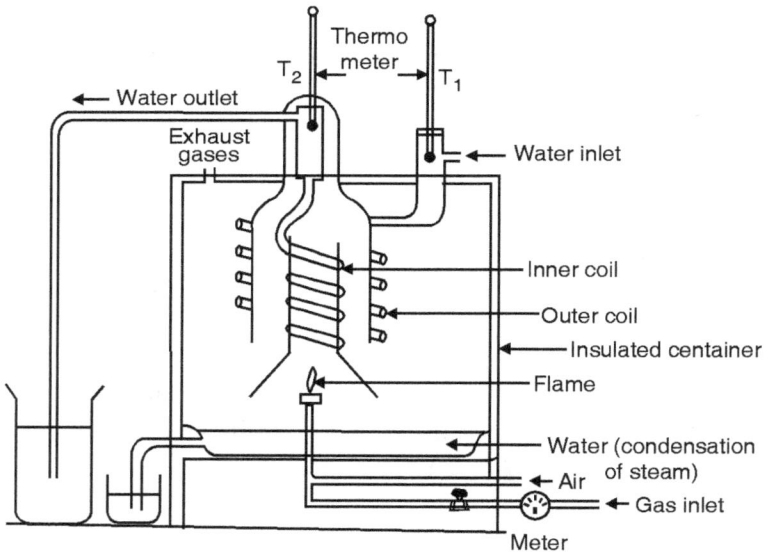

Fig. 4.2 : Arrangement of Boy's calorimeter

(A) Gas Burner Assembly :

(i) It consists of a flat flame gas burner through which known volume of gas is passed at a known pressure measured by pressure meter attached. There is an arrangement of stop cock.

(B) Calorimeter (Combustion Chamber):

- It consists of vessel which is insulated outside.
- The burners are situated at the centre of the vessel covered with chimney or combustion chamber. It has copper tubing coiled inside and outside of it.
- The water enters from the top of outer coil and goes to bottom of chimney and then moves upward through the inner coil to the outlet at the top.
- The cold water is passed at constant rate through the coil. Heat of combustion is completely carried away by the water.
- The temperature of incoming water is recorded by thermometer–1 and temperature of outgoing water is recorded by thermometer–2.
- The water formed during combustion of fuel is condensed and collected at the bottom of the vessel and removed through the tube in a container. The volume of water is measured.
- There is an outlet for exhaust gases.

Experimental procedure :

- Make sure that the apparatus is leak proof.
- Open the gas cock and gaseous fuel enters the burner and lighted. The gas is burnt at the rate of about 4 litre min^{-1}.
- The water is allowed to flow. The rate of flow water is so adjusted that the rise in temperature of water is about 20°C.
- These conditions are allowed to stabilise for about 45 minutes.
- Record the following readings :
  (a) The volume of gas burnt at a given temperature and pressure in time t.
  (b) The amount of water flow though the cooling coils in time t.
  (c) Temperature of inlet water recorded by thermometer–1.
  (d) Temperature of outgoing water recorded by thermometer–2.
  (e) Weight of condensed water from the combustion products collected from bottom trough.
  (f) Atmospheric pressure is recorded from barometer.
  (g) Gas pressure is recorded from manometer.

Calculation of Calorific Value :

Observations :

1. Volume of gas burnt at STP in time t = V m^3
2. Weight of cooling water passed in time t = W kg
3. Temperature of incoming water = t_1°C
4. Temperature of outgoing water = t_2°C

5. Different in temperature = $(t_2 - t_1)°C$
6. Weight of condensed water = m kg
7. Amount of water condensed by burning 1 m³ of gas = $\frac{m}{V}$
8. Latent heat of steam per m³ of gas = 587 kcal

Calculations :

(I) Gross (higher) calorific value :

$$Q = \frac{W(t_2 - t_1)}{V} \text{ kcal kg}^{-1}$$

$$Q = \frac{(W \times S)(t_2 - t_1)}{V} = \text{kJ kg}^{-1}$$

(II) Latent heat of steam per cubic meter of gas = $\frac{m \times 587}{V}$ kcal

(III) Net (low) calorific value N.C.V. = $\left[Q - \left(\frac{m\ 587}{V} \right) \right]$ kcal kg^{-1}

4.7 Numerical Problems :

Example 1 :

In bomb calorimeter method, 0.980 g of solid fuel was completely combusted in excess of oxygen when 900 g of water in calorimeter showed 3.55°C increase in temperature. Determine gross calorific value of fuel. Water equivalent of calorimeter etc. is 140.0 g.

Solution :

Data : x = 0.980 g   W = 900 g
           w = 140 g $t_2 - t_1$ = 3.55°C

Formula : $Q = \frac{(W + w)(t_2 - t_1)}{x}$

$$= \frac{(900 + 140)(3.55)}{0.98} = \frac{1040 \times 3.55}{0.98}$$

Result : Q = 3767.35 cal g^{-1}

Example 2 :

Find the water equivalent of bomb calorimeter assembly. On the basis of following data observed in the experiment

(i) Weight of salicylic acid = 1.22 g
(ii) Weight of water taken in calorimeter = 1500 g
(iii) Rise in temperature of water = 2.73°C
(iv) Cooling correction = 0.015°C

(v)	Fuse wire correction		= 21 cal
(vi)	H_2SO_4 (Acid) produced		= 3.0 cm^3 of 0.1 N H_2SO_4
	(1 cm^3 of 0.1 N $H_2SO_4 \equiv 3.6$ cal)		
(vii)	Gross calorific value of salicylic acid		= 5270 cal g^{-1}

Solution :

Data : $\quad x = 1.22$ g $\qquad\qquad W = 1500$ g

$\qquad\qquad (t_2 - t_1) = 2.43°C \qquad\qquad t_c = 0.015°C$

Corrected $(t_2 - t_1) = (t_2 - t_1) - t_c = 2.73 + 0.015 = 2.745°C$

$\qquad\qquad A = 3 \times 3.6 = 10.8$ cal $\qquad\qquad F = 21$ cal

$$\text{Formula } Q = \left\{ \frac{(W+w)[(t_2 - t_1) + t_c]}{x} \right\} - (A + F)$$

$$w = \left\{ \frac{[Q + (A+F)] \, x}{(t_2 - t_1) + t_c} \right\} - W$$

$$= \left\{ \frac{[5270 + (10.8 + 21)] \, 1.22}{2.745} \right\} - 1500$$

$$= \frac{(5270 + 31.8) \, 1.22}{2.745} - 1500$$

Result : $\quad w = 856.35$

Example 3 :

Compute the gross calorific value and net calorific value of a fuel containing 7% hydrogen from the following data observed in experiment using bomb method.

(i)	Weight of fuel	= 1.05 g
(ii)	Water equivalent of calorimeter etc.	= 825 g
(iii)	Weight of water in calorimeter	= 2.025 kg
(iv)	Initial temperature of water	= 25.12 °C
(v)	Final temperature of water = 27.75 °C	

Solution : Data : $\quad x = 1.05$ g $\qquad\qquad W = 2.025$ kg $= 2025$ g

$\qquad\qquad\qquad w = 825$ g $\qquad\qquad\qquad t_1 = 25.12°C$

$\qquad\qquad\qquad t_2 = 27.75°C \qquad\qquad (t_2 - t_1) = 27.75 - 25.12 = 2.63°C$

$\qquad\qquad\qquad \%H = 7.0\%$

Formula 1 : $$Q = \frac{(W+w)(t_2-t_1)}{x} = \frac{(2025+825)(2.63)}{1.05}$$

Result 1 : $Q = 7138.57$ cal g^{-1}

Formula 2 : N.C.V. $= Q - (0.09 \times \%H \times 587)$

$= 7138.57 - (0.09 \times 7 \times 587) = 7138.57 - 369.81$

Result 2 : N.C.V. $= 6768.76$ cal g^{-1}

Example 4 :

The following data was recorded in Boy's calorimeter experiment

(a) Volume of gas burnet $= V$ $= 0.09 \, m^3$
(b) Weight of water used $= 30.0 \, kg$
(c) Weight of steam condensed $= 0.035 \, kg$
(d) Increase in temperature $= 11 \, °C$
(e) Latent heat of condensation of steam, H $= 587 \, Kcal/kg = 2450 \, kJ/kg^{-1}$
(f) Specific heat of water $= S$ $= 4.185 \, kJ \, kg^{-1} \, K^{-1}$

Find gross and net calorific value of fuel.

Solution :

Formula : Gross calorific value $= Q = \dfrac{(W \times S)(t_2-t_1)}{V}$

$$= \frac{(30 \times 4.185)(11)}{0.09}$$

Result : $Q = 15345.0 \, kJ/m^{-1}$

Formula : Net calorific value $= \left[Q - \left(\dfrac{m \times H}{V}\right)\right]$

$$= \left[15345 - \frac{0.35 \times 2450}{0.09}\right] = 15345 - 952.7$$

Result : Net calorific value $= 14392.3 \, kJ \, m^{-3}$

4.8 Fuel Cells

4.8.1 Introduction

Fuel cell was used as a source of energy in Appolo Moon space craft. About 200kg of fuel sufficient for eleven days was used. The product of combustion is water which was used for drinking purpose by the astronauts.

Definition of Full cell :

An electrochemical cell that converts the chemical energy of fuel directly into electrical energy in a continuous manner is called fuel cell.

Working :

The working of fuel cell is like galvanic cell. The reactants are not integral part of the cell as in galvanic cell. The reactants are continuously supplied from out side at unreactive electrodes. The redox reaction takes place at the electrodes. The cell contains two chemicals one is a fuel which undergoes oxidation and other undergo reduction. The gasous hydrogen is the most commonly used fuel. The other oxidising agent generally used is gasous oxygen or air which undergo reduction reaction. The fuel cell contains an electrolyte between two electrodes. It helps to carry ions from one compartment to other. The redox reaction that occur in fuel cell is responsible for generation of electric current in the cell. The cell do not store energy and hence can not be charged.

4.8.2 Type 1 : Fuel Cells :

(I) H_2/O_2 Cell is called Bacon Fuel Cell :

Construction :

(i) It consists of two electrodes made from porous nickel in the form of compressed powder. The electrodes have large surface area and life about one thousand hours.

(ii) The electrolyte is aqueous solution of potassium hydroxide at high concentration (75% KOH + 25% H_2O) at 200°C. The electrolyte is placed between two electrodes so that electrodes are saturated with it.

(iii) The hydrogen acts as a fuel is passed from left compartment and oxygen or air is passed from right compartment continuously.

(iv) The cell is represented as,

$H_{2(g)} | KOH_{aq} | O_{2(g)}$

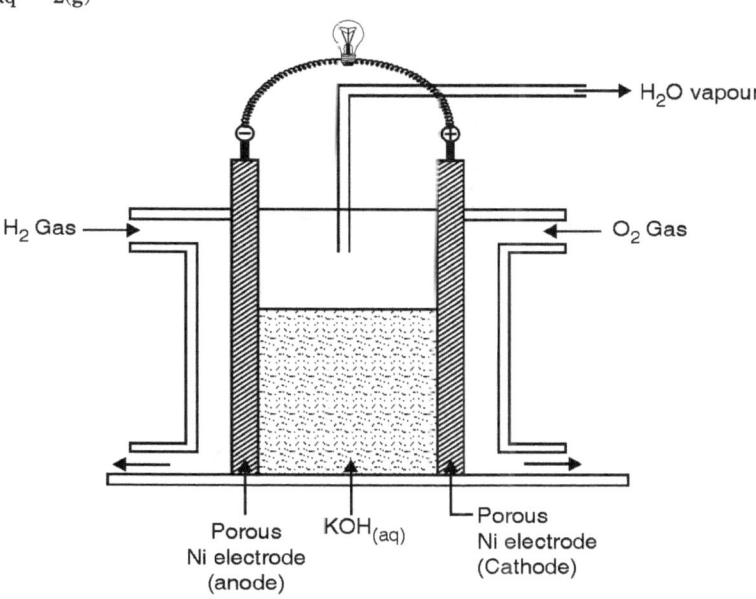

Fig. 4.3 : H_2 - O_2 Fuel Cell

(v) The redox reaction takes place at the electrodes as,

At –ve electrode : $2 H_{2(g)} + 4OH^-_{aq} \longrightarrow 4 H_2O + 4 e^-$

At –ve electrode : $O_{2(g)} + 2 H_2O + 4 e^- \longrightarrow 4OH^-$

The net cell reaction : $2 H_2 + O_2 \longrightarrow 2 H_2O$

(vi) Emf of fuel cell is 1.2 v

(vii) Water vapour is generated in cell

Effiency of Fuel Cell :

For the reaction, $H_{2 (g, 1atm)} + \frac{1}{2} O_{2(g, 1atm)} \longrightarrow H_2O\ (l)$

$\Delta H = -63.32$ kcal, $\Delta G = -56.69$ kcal

The emf of the cell is 1.2 V at 200°C.

Efficiency of the fuel cell is given by,

$$\text{Efficiency} = \frac{-\Delta G}{-\Delta H} = \frac{56.69}{63.32} = 0.83$$

Efficiency = 83.0%

(II) Phospheric Acid Fuel Cell : (PAFC)

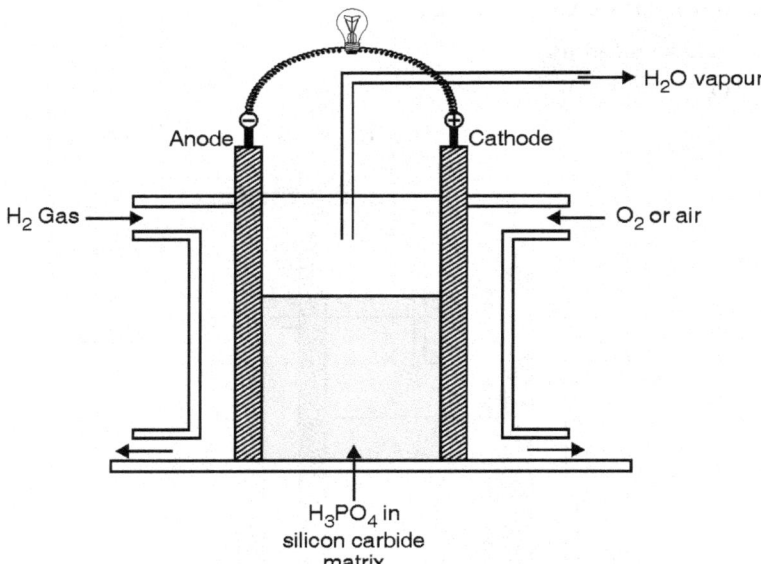

Fig. 4.4 : Phosphoric acid fuel cell

Construction :

(i) It consists of two electrotes which are made up of carbon and coated with finely powdered platinum metal.

(ii) The electrolyte is not liquid phosphoric acid but it is incorporated in the silicon carbide matrix.

(iii) The hydrogen gas acts as fuel and oxygen as oxidising agent which are passed through as shown in the Fig. 4.5.

(iv) The operating temperature is about 200°C and redox reaction that takes with cell is,

At anode : $2 H_2 \longrightarrow 4 H^+ + 4 e^-$

At cathode : $O_2 + 4 H^+ + 4 e^- \longrightarrow 2 H_2O$

Net cell reaction : $2 H_2 + O_2 \longrightarrow 2 H_2O$

(v) The efficiency of the cell is ~ 70%

(vi) The water vapour is generated in the cell.

4.8.3 Type II Fuel Cells :

(I) Polymer Electrolyte Membrane Fuel Cell : (PEMFC)

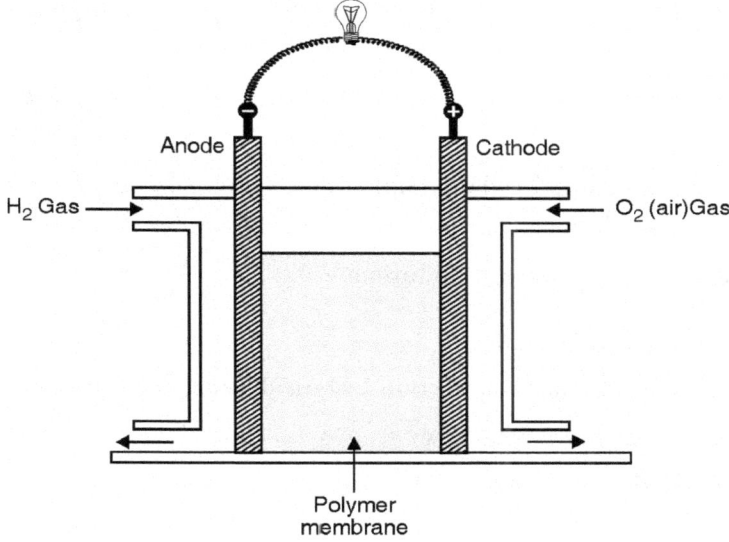

Fig. 4.5 : Polymer Electrolyte Membrane Cell

Construction :

(i) It consists of cathode and anode made up of carbon with finely powdered platinum metal.

(ii) The electrolyte placed between two electrodes is polymer membrane. These memevranes are specific. They permit H^+ ions to pass through it. the membrane does not allow other gases present in the cell to pass through it.

(iii) The hydrogen gas is continuously passed through left compartment acts as fuel and oxygen as is continuously passed through right compartment acts as oxidising agent.

(iv) The redox reaction takes place in the cell. H_2 in presence of Pt catalyst at electrode oxidation reaction takes place.

At –ve electrode : $2 H_2 \longrightarrow 4 H^+ + 4 e^-$

The H^+ ions pass through membrane and reach the cathod and reacts with molecular oxygen and electrons.

At +ve electrode : $4 H^+ + O_2 + 4 e^- \longrightarrow 2 H_2O$

(v) The net cell reaction is,

$2 H_2 + O_2 \longrightarrow 2 H_2O$

4.8.4 Advantages of Fuel Cells :

(i) In the fuel cells the hydrogen and oxygen are continuously supplied hence cells never become dead.

(ii) The cells operate at a temperature of 70–140°C and give the potential ~ 0.9V continuously.

(iii) The efficiency of the fuel cells is approximately 60–80% which is far superior to the thermal power plants which have effeciency not more than 40%.

(iv) The fuel cells do not cause any pollution.

4.8.5 Limitations of Fuel Cells :

(i) Construction of fuel cells arise certain technical, practical and economical difficulties.

(a) The electrolytes used are corrosive.

(b) High cost of catalysts like Ag, Pt, Pd needed for electrode reactions.

(c) Electrode is poisioned by fuel.

(iv) High operating temperatures are difficult to handle.

(v) Handling hydrogen gas at low temperature and high pressure is difficult. It is risky to store, transport and use hydrogen gas.

4.8.6 Applications :

(i) Fuel cells are used where continuous supply of emf is required.

(ii) Fuel cells are used in space ship. The water produced in the cell reaction is the additional water supply for astronuts.

Exercise

Long Answer Questions

1. Explain different types of calorific value of fuel. How is it determined using bomb calorimeter?
2. Define calorific value. How is calorific value determined using Boy's calorimetric method?
3. Distinguish between solid, liquid and gaseous fuels.
4. Discuss the following characteristics of fuel.
   (i) Ignition temperature
   (ii) High and low calorific value
   (iii) Calorific intensity
   (iv) Flexibility of fuel
5. Define calorific value. Give the units of solid, liquid and gaseous fuels. Explain gross calorific value and net calorific value.
6. Explain the construction, working of bomb calorimeter. How is the gross calorific value calculated ?
7. Explain the construction and working of Boy's calorimeter. How is the gross calorific value calculated?

Short answer Questions

1. Explain carbonization of fuel.
2. How is the theoretical calorific value determined by Dulong formula ?
3. Define fuel cell. Give the construction and working of KOH fuel cell.
4. Differentiate between low temperature carbonization and high temperature carbonization.
5. Discusss the correction for accurate results of gross calorific value.
6. Explain the characteristics of good fuel.
7. Define fuel and give importance of fuel.
8. Give the classification of fuel.
9. Define calorific value. Explain higher and lower calorific value. Give units.
10. Give the construction and working of fuel cell PAFC/PCMFC

11. Write notes on :
    (i) Bomb calorimeter
    (ii) Boy's calorimeter
    (iii) Calorific value
    (iv) Characteristic of good fuel
    (v) Importance of fuel
    (vi) Fuel cell
    (vii) Advantages and limitations, applications of fuel cell.
    (viii) Gross calorific value and net calorific value

University Questions

1. Draw a neat sketch of Boy's calorimeter and explain Its principle, construction and working.

2. Describe Boy's calorimeter for the determination of calorific value of a gaseous fuel.

3. Describe the determination of calorific value of fuel by Bomb's calorimeter with neat labelled diagram.

4. The following data was obtained in a Boy's calorimeter experiment.
    (i) Volume of gas used = 0.1 m^3 at S.T.P.
    (ii) Weight of water heated = 24 kg
    (iii) Temperature of inlet water = 22 °C
    (iv) Weight of steam condensed = 0.024 kg.
    Calculate the higher and lower (Gross and net) value per m^3 at S.T.P. Take the heat liberated in condensing water vapour and cooling and condensate as 580 kcal / kg.

5. A solid fuel in Bomb Calorimeter give the following data at calorific value determination.
    (i) Weight of coal sample = 1.5 g
    (ii) Weight of water taken = 7009,
    (iii) Water equivalent of bomb and calorimeter = 1300 g
    (iv) Rise in temperature = 3.15 °C
    (v) Coolign correction = 0.05 °C
    (vi) Correction due to acid = 50 Cal
    (vii) Fuse wire correction = 10 Cal
    Calculate hgher and lower (Gross and net) calorific value of fuel containing 5% hydrogen (Take latent heat of steam 587 Kcal / kg).

6. Write short notes on :
   (a) Compare and contrast liquid fuels over gaseous fuels.
   (b) Characteristics of good fuel.
   (c) Advantages of gasous fuels over solid fuels.

Unit 5

Corrosion and its Prevention

- Introduction to Corrosion
- Classification of Corrosion
- Dry Corrosion, other gas Corrosion
- Liquid metal Corrosion
- Wet Corrosion - definition and examples.
- Hydrogen evolution and oxygen absorption mechanism.
- Factors affecting rate of Corrosion
- Testing and measurement of Corrosion by
  - Wet loss method
  - Electrical resistance measurement method
- Prevention of Corrosion
  - Proper design and material selection
  - Metal coatings
    - Hot dipping - Tinning and galvanizing
    - Metal cladding
    - Electro-plating
    - Metallic Spraying
- Exercise

5.1 Introduction to Corrosion

Naturally almost all elements occur in their combined state such as oxides, sulphates, nitrates, sulphides etc. This combined form of the metals is called as ore. In order to obtain the pure metals. It is one needed to carry out many chemical/physical processes and that science is called as metallurgy. Thermodynamically, one can say that, the compounds of metal are more stable (hence less energetic) as compared to the pure metals. In other words if a pure metal is obtained after metallurgy, then slowly if will get converted to its combined form (or compound) naturally. This gives rise to corrosion.

Corrosion (Definition)

The unintentional and undesired destruction of metals by chemical or electrochemical reactions starting at the surface is called as its corrosion.

The products that are formed are oxides (most common), sulphates, nitrates, sulphides etc. are called as corrosion products.

It can be seen from the figure that, there is lowering of Gibb's free energy during corrosion, hence it is a **spontaneous process** (ΔG is negative). There are many applications where metals are used either in pure forms or as alloys that will undergo corrosion spontaneously leading to its destruction. This costs billions of dollars worldwide in replacement, maintenance and repair of machine parts. It should be noted that formation of oxides is most common during corrosion. The oxides are formed by oxidation, hence corrosion is also called as slow combustion.

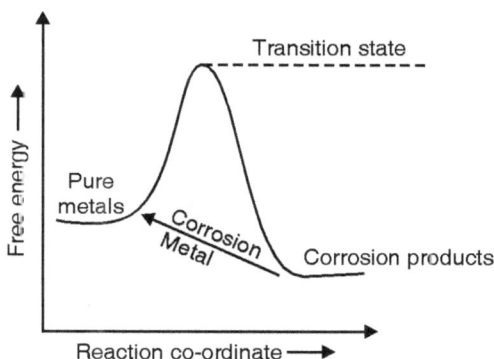

Fig. 5.1 : **Free energy change during corrosion**

5.2 Classification of Corrosion

The corrosion of metals is a result of chemical reaction between metal surface and the environment. Depending on types of attack on metal, corrosion is classified as

(A) Direct chemical corrosion or Dry corrosion or Atmospheric corrosion : The corrosion caused by chemical reaction of gases such as oxygen, halogens, hydrogen, nitrogen and sulphur dioxide with metal or alloy surface is called as dry corrosion.

(B) Electrochemical or Wet corrosion : Corrosion phenomena are electrochemical in nature and involve the presence of an electrolyte in contact with metal. Electrolyte is an aqueous solution of salt, acid or alkali. This type of corrosion of metals occurring as a result of electrochemical reaction between metal surface and electrolyte is called as wet corrosion.

But there is no sharp dividing line between these two general types of attack on metals.

5.2.1 Dry Corrosion or Direct Chemical Corrosion or Atmospheric Corrosion :

The extent of corrosion due to attack of atmospheric gases depends on the chemical affinity between gas and metal as well as on the ability of metal to form a protective film.

(1) Corrosion Due to Oxygen or Oxidative Corrosion :

Surfaces of many metals oxidise very rapidly when they are exposed to air.

$$2\,M + O_2 \longrightarrow 2\,MO$$

Formation of oxide film and their growth is a stepwise process. At the initial stage, oxygen gas is adsorbed on the metal surface. Van der Waal's forces are responsible for this adsorption. Oxidation by gaseous oxygen is an electrochemical process. It is not simply combination of metal with oxygen. After adsorption, oxygen molecules dissociate into atoms or ions. These oxygen ions combine with metal by electron transfer or electron sharing between oxygen and metal atoms. The mechanism of oxidative corrosion is diffusion.

$$M \rightarrow M^{n+} + ne^- \text{ (oxidation)}$$

$$O_2 + ne^- \rightarrow 2O^{n-} \text{ (reduction)}$$

i.e $$M^{n+} + 2O^{n-} \rightarrow MO_2$$

where, n is an oxidation state of metal and it can be +1, +2, +3 ......

This type of adsorption is called chemisorption, it continues till unimolecular oxide layer covers the metal surface.

Mechanism

Corrosion of a metal starts at its surface and a film of corrosion product is formed. This process can be explained as :

(i) Adsorption : When clean and uncorroded surface of a metal is exposed to oxygen, instantaneously it gets adsorbed on the surface. Initially, there is not a chemical bond between the metal surface and oxygen but they are held together by secondary forces of attraction such as weak van der waal's forces.

(ii) Chemisorption : After adsorption, actual process of corrosion starts. Oxygen is an electronegative element and metals are electropositive in nature. So slowly electrons from metal get transferred to oxygen. Hence, finally there is a chemical bond formation between the atom and oxygen. Since this process is also taking place at the surface of metal, it is called as chemisorption.

(iii) Film formation : When chemisorption completes, a strongly adhering film of metal oxide is present at the surface of metal and it is said that the metal surface is corroded. Fig. 5.2 depicts all these three steps in dry corrosion.

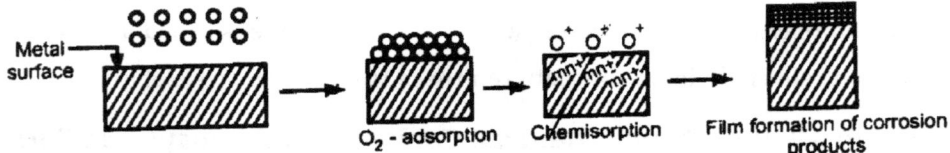

Fig. 5.2 : Mechanism of dry corrosion due to oxygen

The metal will undergo further (complete) corrosion or not, depends on the nature of film formed. Most commonly following types of films are formed.

(1) Stable oxide film. (2) Unstable film.
(3) Porous oxide film. (4) Volatile oxide film.

(1) Stable oxide film : This film is made up of fine particles of oxide and has a compact packing. Such type of film is tightly adhered to the metal surface. It is observed that the volume of metal oxide film formed is greater than that of metal surface. Hence such type of film protects the metal from further corrosion and the film acts as a protective layer for further corrosion.

For example, oxide films on Al, Sn, Cr, Cu etc.

(2) Unstable oxide film : Generally, *such* types of films are observed on the nobel metal surfaces. In these cases, the oxidation reaction is reversible i.e. as soon as oxide of the metal is formed, the reversible reaction i.e. conversion of oxide into metal and oxygen takes place spontaneously i.e.

$$M + O_2 \underset{\text{Reverse corrosion}}{\overset{\text{Corrosion}}{\rightleftharpoons}} MO_2$$

It can be seen that although the corrosion of the metals takes place, they do not get affected.

For example, Al, Ag, Pt etc.

(3) Porous oxide film : Generally, this type of film is observed on the alkali and alkaline earth metals. Some of the transition group elements such as iron also show this type of film. The film formed are porous, so that oxygen from air can diffuse the film and again comes in contact with the fresh metal surface and this leads to chemisorption. This process continues till the metal gets corroded completely. It is observed that for such films, the volume of film is less than that of metal surface. For example. Na, K, Li, Ca, Fe etc.

(4) Volatile oxide film : In this type of film, as soon as the oxide layer is formed on the metal surface, it evaporates. So after some time of corrosion, the oxide layer disappears completely and the new metal surface is exposed to oxygen and further corrosion takes place i.e. if such oxide layer forming metal is placed in the atmosphere, after some time the metal completely disappears. For example, molybdenum.

Pilling-Bed worth Ratio

Protective value or protectivity of films can be decided from Pilling-Bed worth ratio.

$$\text{Pilling-Bed worth ratio} = \frac{\text{Volume of oxide formed}}{\text{Volume of equivalent amount of metal consumed to form oxide}}$$

If P. B. ratio > 1, coating will be non-porous and protective, e.g. Cr, Ni, W, Al, etc.

If P. B. ratio < 1, coating will be porous and non-protective, e.g. Alkali and alkaline earth metals.

Metals on prolonged heating at higher temperature form thick oxide layers called 'scales. They may or may not protect metal from further corrosion.

2. Corrosion Due to Other Gases

Gases like carbon dioxide, sulphur dioxide, nitrogen oxide, chlorine, fluorine under dry conditions corrode metals. The degree of corrosion due to other gases depends upon chemical affinity of metal and above gases, as well as on the protective nature of the films formed on the surface of metal. In case of silver, due to action of chlorine, silver chloride film is formed. It protects the metal from further corrosion.

But chlorine when attacks tin, stannic chloride being volatile, easily escapes as soon as it is formed leaving metal for further exposure. Thus, more and more metal gets corroded due to chlorine attack.

$$2Ag + Cl_2 \rightarrow 2AgCl$$

$$Sn + 2Cl_2 \rightarrow SnCl_4$$

In an industrial atmosphere, all types of contaminants of sulphur in the form of sulphur dioxide and hydrogen sulphide are corrosive. In petroleum industry, hydrogen sulphide at high temperature corrodes steel.

$$H_2S + Fe \rightarrow \underset{\text{Scale}}{FeS} + H_2$$

The burning of fossil fuels generate large amount of sulphur dioxide. Primary cause of atmospheric corrosion is the dry deposition of sulphur dioxide on metallic surface.

$$S + O_2 \rightarrow SO_2$$

$$SO_2 + H_2O \rightarrow \underset{\text{(Sulfurous acid)}}{H_2SO_3}$$

$$SO_2 + H_2O + \frac{1}{2}O_2 \rightarrow H_2SO_4$$

In presence of oxygen and moisture, sulphur dioxide is oxidised to sulphuric and sulphurous acid, which are highly corrosive to metallic equipments. Oxides of nitrogen emitted in combustion process cause atmospheric corrosion.

The basic reaction is,

$$N_2 + O_2 \xrightarrow{1210 \text{ to } 1700\,°C} \underset{\text{Nitric oxide}}{2NO}$$

$$2NO + O_2 \xrightarrow{1100\,°C} \underset{\text{Nitrogen dioxide}}{2NO_2}$$

They react with ozone from atmosphere.

$$NO_2 + O_3 \rightarrow NO_3 + O_2$$

$$NO_2 + NO_3 \rightarrow N_2O_5$$

$$N_2O_5 + H_2O \rightarrow 2HNO_3$$

3. Corrosion Due to Hydrogen

Attack of hydrogen on metals is of two types. This is also studied under wet corrosion as hydrogen damage.

(a) Hydrogen embrittlernent : Action of hydrogen on metals at low temperature is called hydrogen embrittlernent. Under specific environment, as a result of chemical or electrochemical action of metal surface, atomic hydrogen is formed. For example, aqueous solution of hydrogen sulphide reacts with iron surface and evolves atomic hydrogen. This atomic hydrogen diffuses into a metal and collects in voids. There it combines to form molecular hydrogen.

$$Fe + H_2S \rightarrow FeS + 2H$$

Atomic or Nascent hydrogen

$$2H \rightarrow H_2$$

If this process continues, large amount of molecular hydrogen gets accumulated in voids. Some amount tries to escape over the surface which causes blistering in metal and fissure formation. Penetration of hydrogen into metal decreases ductility and tensile strength in metals which is called hydrogen embrittlement.

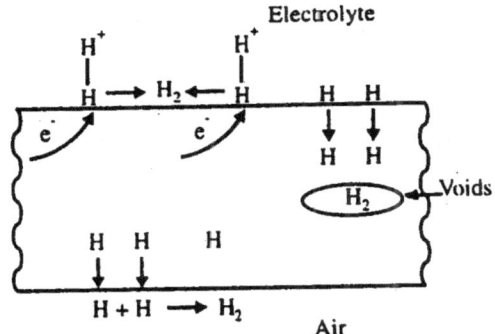

Fig. 5.3 : Hydrogen blistering

(b) Hydrogen attack at higher temperature : At higher temperature, molecular hydrogen dissociates into atomic hydrogen.

$$H_2 \xrightarrow[\text{dissociation}]{\text{thermal}} 2H$$

Atomic hydrogen

At high temperature, atomic hydrogen is chemically very active. It combines with carbon, sulphur, oxygen or nitrogen which are present in metals to small extent.

$$\underset{\text{From steel}}{C} + \underset{\text{Atomic hydrogen}}{4H} \rightarrow \underset{\text{Methane gas}}{CH_4}$$

At high temperature, atomic hydrogen reacts with carbon from steel and forms high pressure methane which causes intergranular cracking, fissuring and blistering. This reduces strength of steel, i.e. the atomic hydrogen eats away C, S. N etc. from around the area where it gets.

4. Corrosion Due to Liquid Metals

Corrosion of metals or alloys by liquid metal is very important along with the corrosion due to gases and electrolytes. In specific examples such as liquid metal fast breeder nuclear reactors. In these types of reactors, liquid metals such as sodium is used as coolant. With passage of time liquid metal in contact with other metals / alloys, attracts the meal and sometimes may lead to their complete destruction.

The corrosion rate of a metal depends on the dissolution rate of a metal in liquid metal. The dissolution rate may lead to simple solution type attack to that of inter granular corrosion. Sometimes a metal may get completely dissolved or one of the metal in the alloy may get dissolved. In both the cases, the destruction of metal takes place.

The factors that may affect the dissolution rate or liquid metal corrosion are,

1. Formation of inter metallic compounds on the surface
2. Presence of impurities in the metal alters the dissolution rate.
3. Temperature gradient.
4. Multimetallic systems can cause the mass transfer from solid to liquid metal.

There are many types of attack of liquid metal on solid metal

1. **Simple solution :** In this type of corrosion, the dissolution of solid metal takes place in liquid metal. i.e. the solid metal acts as solute and liquid metal acts as solvent.

2. **Alloying between liquid metal and solid metal :** Because of high temperature and metal-metal solution formation, the alloy formation takes place. Because of this the physical properties of liquid and solid metal get altered.

3. **Inter granular penetration :** The solid metal becomes mechanically weak because of inter granular penetration.

4. **Impurity reactions :** If impurities are present either in the solid or liquid metal in contact, the side reactions at high temperature may change the chemical nature of metals which is not desirable.

5.2.2 Wet or Electrochemical or Immersion Corrosion

Electrochemical corrosion can be defined as the corrosion caused by exposure of a metal or two dissimilar metals to be in electrical contact, to an electrolytic solution (acid, base or salt). Formation of an electrochemical or galvanic cell governs electrochemical corrosion. Electrochemical cell is set up due to difference in electrode potential between two separate areas out of which one is anodic and other one cathodic.

Anodic area dissolves, corrodes or oxidizes leading to formation of metallic ions or cations and electrons are set free by the reaction,

$$M \longrightarrow M^{n+} + ne^- \qquad \text{...Oxidation}$$

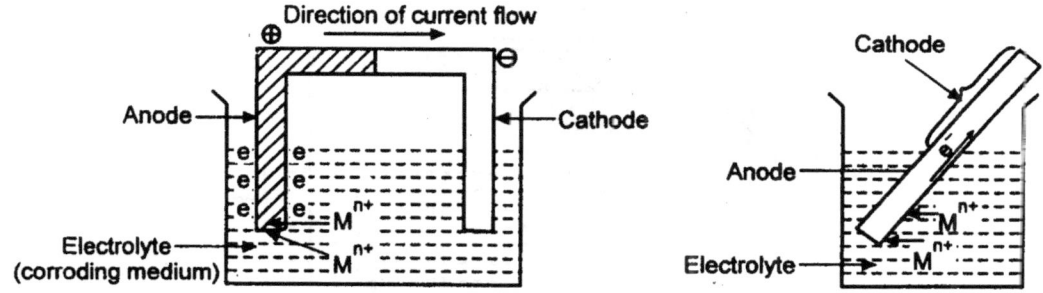

Fig. 5.4 : Electrochemical corrosion

At cathodic area, on the other hand, reduction reaction takes place to discharge anions (e.g. O^{2-}, OH^- etc.) depending upon the nature of conducting or corroding medium (electrolyte).

$$2ne^- + n\,H_2O + \frac{n}{2}\,O_2 \rightarrow 2n\,OH^- \qquad \text{...Reduction}$$

The rate of electrochemical corrosion in general depends upon

1. Solubility of corrosion product
2. Location of corrosion product

Solubility of corrosion product : Corrosion products (metal oxides) are formed by cations generated at anodic area and anions are generated at cathodic area. This process takes place due to diffusion of ions through wet medium. If the corrosion, product is soluble in the corroding medium, rate of corrosion at anode is comparatively faster.

(i) Either in the vicinity of anode or cathode, the corrosion product forms a protective barrier either around anode or cathode and thus corrosion rate is affected substantially.

(ii) In between anode and cathode or away from either of them, corrosion rate is not much affected.

Further, electrochemical corrosion is also influenced by following two factors namely, polarisation of electrodes and hydrogen over voltage.

Galvamic Corrosion or Electrochemical Corrosion

It is wet corrosion. When two dissimilar metals are in electrical contact with each other and are exposed to an electrolyte, a potential difference is created between two dissimilar metals. This potential difference produces electron flow between them. The less noble metal will dissolve and act as anode while more noble metal will act as the cathode. This type of corrosion of metal is called as galvanic corrosion.

In Fig. 5.5, zinc and copper plates arc in electrical contact with each other immersed into a solution of an electrolyte. As zinc has more negative potential than copper, it acts as anode while copper acts as cathode.

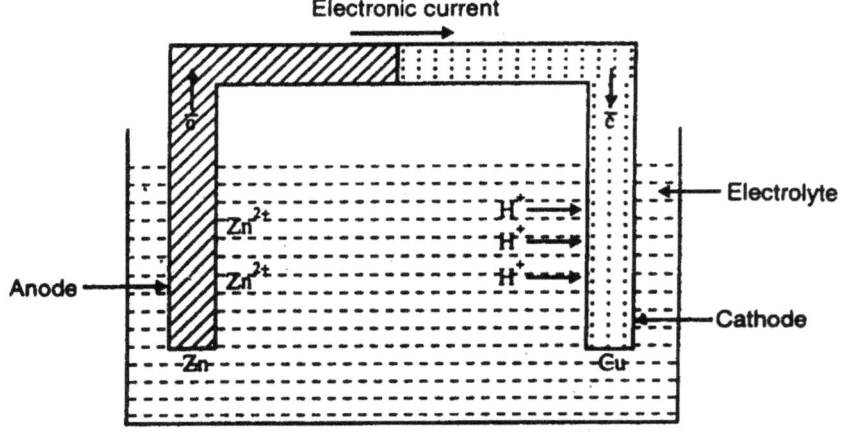

Fig. 5.5 : Galvanic corrosion

The reaction at the anode will be,

$$Zn \rightarrow Zn^{2+} + 2e^-$$

The electric current flows from anode to cathode through metal and corrosion current flows from anode to cathode with dissolution of anode metal. While cathodic reaction is accompanied by evolution of hydrogen or absorption of oxygen in acidic or alkaline medium.

In the galvanic corrosion, cathodic metal is always protected from the corrosion attack. The extent of corrosion depends on corrosive environment as well as the difference in the electrode potential of two contacting metals i.e. their position in the galvanic series. Further apart the metals from each other, more is the intensity of corrosion. Galvanic corrosion depends upon relative areas of anode and cathode. e.g.

(1) Steel screws corrode in contact with brass in marine environment.

(2) Steel pipes corrode preferentially connected to copper plumbing.

Mechanism of Wet Corrosion :

Wet corrosion of metal occurs by electrochemical mechanism. It is associated with flow of electric current between anodic and cathodic areas. At anode, metal dissolves forming corresponding positive ions and electrons.

$$M \rightarrow M^{n+} + ne^-$$

While depending upon the nature of the corrosive environment, cathodic reactions will be of two types :

(1) Hydrogen evolution mechanism   (2) Oxygen absorption mechanism

(1) Hydrogen evolution mechanism : Hydrogen evolution type of corrosion of metals occurs when metals are exposed to acidic environment. It is nothing but displacement of hydrogen ions from the solution by metal ions which can be written as

$$M \rightleftharpoons M^{2+} + 2e^- \qquad \text{at anode}$$

Acid $\rightleftharpoons$ H$^+$

$2H^+ + 2e^- \rightleftharpoons 4H_2$ at cathode

The cathodic reaction consists of evolution of hydrogen gas.

All metals above hydrogen in the electrochemical series will dissolve in acid solution with the evolution of hydrogen gas.

Consider iron plate in acidic solution (See Fig. 5.6). Certain part of metal becomes anodic while certain part becomes cathodic (small area). From iron (anode), electrons flow through a metal to the small cathodic area. Iron will pass into the solution in the form of Fe^{2+} and Fe^{3+}. Hydrogen ions from acid are getting reduced at cathode, they accept electrons from cathode and evolution of hydrogen gas takes place at cathode. In this type of corrosion, cathodes are small points while anodes are of large area.

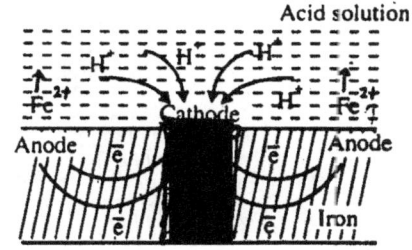

Fig. 5.6 : Mechanism of corrosion - hydrogen evolution

$$Fe \rightarrow Fe^{2+} + 2e^-$$
$$2H^+ + 2e^- \rightarrow H_2$$

This type of corrosion occurs when industrial waste of acidic nature or small copper scrap is stored in steel tank. Copper scrap or industrial waste becomes cathodic while steel becomes anodic and in presence of acid electrolyte, a galvanic cell is formed. Steel corrodes by passing iron ions in solution as above.

In galvanic corrosion i.e. when two dissimilar metals are in electrical contact with each other and are exposed to acidic environment, cathodic reaction will be hydrogen evolution process. In this case, corrosion is more of a uniform type.

(2) Oxygen absorption mechanism : Rusting of iron in water containing dissolved oxygen occurs by oxygen absorption mechanism. At anodic area, iron will dissolve by oxidation.

$$Fe \rightleftharpoons Fe^{2+} + 2e^-$$

The electrons will flow to cathodic area through iron and will be accepted by oxygen.

$$2e^- + H_2O + \frac{1}{2}O_2 \rightleftharpoons 2OH^-$$
$$Fe^{2+} + 2OH^- \rightarrow Fe(OH)_2 \downarrow$$
$$2Fe(OH)_2 + \frac{1}{2}O_2 + H_2O \rightarrow 2Fe(OH)_3 \downarrow$$
$$\text{rust}$$

In this case, anodic areas on the surface of iron are due to presence of cracks in the oxide coating of the metal. The cathodic areas will be the surface of coated metal i.e. cathode will be large while anode will be small area. This results in localised corrosion attack on the exposed iron surface.

If environment is neutral aqueous solution of an electrolyte (NaCl) containing dissolved oxygen.

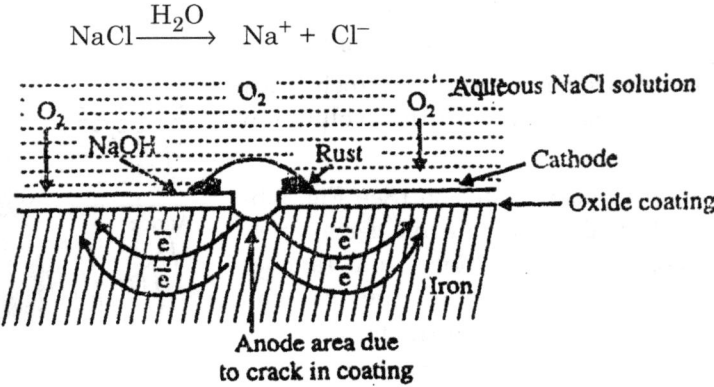

$$NaCl \xrightarrow{H_2O} Na^+ + Cl^-$$

Fig. 5.7 : Mechanism of corrosion - oxygen absorption

At cathode... $Na^+ + OH^- \rightarrow NaOH$, sodium hydroxide is formed.

At anode ... $Fe^{2+} + 2\,Cl^- \rightarrow FeCl_2$, ferrous chloride is formed.

As cathodic product NaOH and anodic product $FeCl_2$ are soluble in water, when they meet, ferrous hydroxide precipitates and in enough oxygen it oxidises to ferric hydroxide.

$$Na^+ + OH^- + Fe^{2+} + Cl^- \rightarrow Fe(OH)_2$$

$$2\,Fe(OH)_2 + \frac{1}{2} O_2 + H_2O \rightarrow Fe(OH)_3 \downarrow$$
$$\text{Ferric hydroxide}$$

Thus, ferrous iron formed is removed as precipitate of ferric hydroxide, the corrosion proceeds till fresh oxygen is available. Oxygen absorption type corrosion is more in strongly aerated solutions. Here corrosion product is formed in the vicinity of cathode although corrosion takes place at anode.

Passivity or Passivation

It is defined as a phenomenon in which metal or alloy exhibits outstanding higher corrosion resistance than its position in the electrochemical or galvanic series. Passivity is the result of formation of highly protective but very thin invisible film on the surface of metal or an alloy, which makes the metal more noble. Metals become passive because of this unimolecular adsorbed film of oxide which is self repairing on the metal surface.

Titanium, aluminium, chromium and stainless-steel alloys containing chromium are passive in oxidising environment. But they become chemically active in reducing environment.

Austenitic stainless steel has corrosion resistance in aerated, dilute sulphuric acid but gets corroded in air free acid. The protective oxide film gets repaired in presence of oxygen, while in absence of oxygen the passive metal becomes chemically active and corrodes. This shows 'passivation' applies only to certain environmental conditions which can maintain the protective oxide film on the metallic surface. Thus, passivation is not a static state but dynamic one which keeps on changing with nature of environment.

By physical isolation of the metal from the corroding environment, pseudo passivity can be achieved which is useful in reducing corrosion. This is due to the deposition of thick protective reaction product films on metal, e.g. Film of lead sulphate on lead in sulphuric acid. Use of inhibitors, anodic polarisation, etc. are different ways of achieving pseudopassivity in metals.

Active metals like Al, Fe when treated with concentrated nitric acid produce protective oxide film. This reduces anodic corrosion making metal passive. But in dilute nitric acid rapid corrosion of metal (i.e. iron) occurs without evolution of hydrogen, as dilute nitric acid stimulates cathodic reaction.

5.3 Factors Influencing Corrosion

Corrosion is destruction of metal through electrochemical action with its environment. So it depends on nature of metal as well as nature of environment.

(A) Nature of Metal :

(a) Position of Metal in Galvanic Series : According to Nernst, all metals have a tendency to pass into the solution in the form of ions. But all metals will not corrode at same rate under similar conditions of environment, corrosion of metals depend upon its position in the electrochemical series and galvanic series. More the negative value of the standard electrode potential, more the metal corrodes, e.g. If zinc, sodium and copper electrodes are dipped in the solution of electrolyte, having same concentration, for some period, it is found sodium corrodes more, than zinc corrodes, copper is noble compared to them as former figures higher in position in galvanic series (having more negative potential) than latter.

(b) Hydrogen Over voltage or Over potential : Over potential of hydrogen plays very important role in corrosion process. Overpotential of hydrogen makes the metal more noble or cathodic with respect to hydrogen evolution than they really are. If overpotential of hydrogen is high, rate of corrosion will be less.

e.g Pure zinc, though it has high negative value will not liberate hydrogen gas in acid solution in the beginning because of hydrogen overvoltage. If drop of copper sulphate is added to acidic solution, hydrogen overvoltage is lowered, evolution of hydrogen gas *is* accelerated. This results increase in corrosion. Hydrogen overvoltage varies from metal to metal.

(c) Relative areas of cathode and anode : The important factor in galvanic corrosion is the area effect, ratio of cathodic to anodic areas. When cathode and anode areas are equal, cathodic and anodic current densities are equal. Corrosion phenomenon will not get accelerated. If cathode area is much larger than anode area, anodic current density will be greater, as a result corrosion of anode metal will be more.

In more easier way we can say that if the areas of cathode and anode are different, the intensity of corrosion of anode is directly proportional to the area of cathode. Thus, the corrosion is more if the area of cathode is larger than the area of anode. This is because if cathode area is larger than anode, the demand of electrons is more for reduction reaction to take place and thus more dissolution of metal at anode takes place.

e.g. Steel rivets in copper plate get completely corroded in corrosive environment because of unfavourable area ratio. (Copper is noble which acts as a cathode).

(d) Nature of protective films : Many metals are susceptible to oxidation when exposed to air and they get covered with oxide films. Depending upon protective nature of film, corrosion continues or stops. If films are porous, metal or oxygen will diffuse and corrosion continues. If films are non-porous, they protect metal from further attack.

Lead forms lead sulphate surface coatings with strong sulphuric acid which protects lead for long time in sulphuric acid environment. Titanium is reactive metal but is resistant to corrosion in many environments because of stability of the TiO_2 film formed.

(e) Purity of metals : The corrosion resistance of pure metal is usually better than that of one containing small amounts of impurities. Presence of impurities accumulated on certain areas of metal are the sources of the potential difference on the metal. In corrosive environment, minute galvanic cell will form and anodic metal will corrode.

e.g. Pure aluminium (99.5 % plus) has good corrosion resistance. But minute amount of impurities even 0.02 % iron and 0.05 % nickel present in aluminium will decrease its corrosion resistance.

But pure metals are expensive (except aluminium), soft and weak, so they have less structural applications.

(B) Nature of Environment :

(a) Temperature : As rates of all chemical reactions increase with temperature, corrosion increases with temperature. Increase in temperature increases ionisation and mobility of all reacting ions and molecules, it also increases diffusion rate. e.g. Intergranular corrosion like caustic embrittlement takes place at high temperature in high pressure boilers. Rate of corrosion of copper and nobel metal is less in boiling sulphuric acid while steel corrodes more in boiling sulphuric acid. Dissolved oxygen is absent in boiling sulphuric acid. For corrosion of copper, oxygen is necessary. In absence of oxygen, corrosion of copper is less. But in case of steel, *oxygen* is necessary to keep steel in passive condition, steel corrodes in absence of oxygen.

(b) Presence of moisture : Atmospheric corrosion of few metals is slow in dry air but it increases rapidly in the presence of moisture. Moisture provides solvent for oxygen or other gases and furnishes electrolyte for setting corrosion cell. In some cases, moisture reacts with metal and oxides.

Corrosion of iron is more in moisture than that in presence of dry air. In moisture primary product of rusting is ferrous hydroxide which oxidises to ferric hydroxide. If moisture contains enough oxygen, ferric hydroxide will oxidise to ferric oxide. If supply of oxygen is limited, corrosion product is magnetite (Fe_3O_4). Rain provides moisture for electrochemical attack. If corrosion products are adherent, they form film. If they are not adherent, rain washes them away exposing new more surface for corrosion attack.

$$Fe^{2+} + 2\,OH^- \rightarrow Fe(OH)_2 \qquad \text{Ferrous hydroxide}$$

$$Fe(OH)_2 \rightarrow Fe(OH)_3 \qquad \text{Ferric hydroxide}$$

$$Fe(OH)_2 \xrightarrow[O_2]{\text{enough}} Fe_2O_3 \cdot 2\,H_2O \qquad \text{Ferric oxide}$$

$$Fe(OH)_2 \xrightarrow[O_2]{\text{limited}} Fe_3O_4 \qquad \text{Magnetite}$$

e.g. Fe_2O_3 is not adherent to iron surface, so corrosion of iron is more in rain. Metals like chromium, stainless steel, aluminium and nickel show good resistance to atmosphere as well as rain.

(c) Effect of pH : Acidic environment is more corrosive than alkaline or neutral environments. Zinc rapidly corrodes in weakly acidic solution but suffers less corrosion in solution having pH 10 to 11. Many metals are readily attacked by acid but are resistance to alkali. By altering the chemical character of corroding medium i.e. pH, corrosion rate of a given metal can be controlled.

(d) Conductance of medium : Stray current is that direct current which has leaked from an electric power circuit and flows through metallic structures in earth. The points at which stray current leaves the metallic structure, become anode where metal dissolves.

In stray current corrosion, cathodes and anodes are remote from each other. If soil contents moisture and soluble salts, it will increase conductivity of soil. Increase in conductivity will increase stray current corrosion. Moisture present in soil also increases conductance of medium, which increases underground soil corrosion of metals.

(e) Nature of electrolyte : The electrolyte itself is a source of potential difference. The solution potential of metal depends on type of ions and their concentration in the solution. So change in concentration of an electrolyte will change electrode potential and in turn will affect corrosion of metal. The corrosion is intense in medium containing chloride ions. Stray current corrosion is more in soil containing soluble salts.

Pourbaix diagram : Redox potentials are useful in predicting corrosion behaviour of metals. Corrosion will not occur till spontaneous direction of the reaction indicates metal oxidation. The applications of thermodynamics or more specifically, half cell potential to corrosion phenomena can be understood by means of potential-pH plots. These plots are known as Pourbaix diagrams, after scientist Pourbaix. He first suggested the use of above plots. The diagram for iron is given in Fig. 5.8.

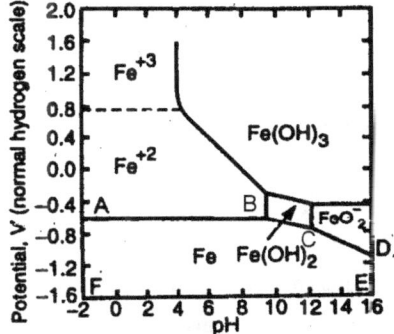

Fig. 5.8 : Potential-pH diagram for Fe-H_2O system given by M. Pourbaix

The electrode potential of a system in which the reactants are not at unit activity can be calculated using Nernst equation,

$$E = E° + 2.303 \frac{RT}{nF} \log \frac{[\text{Oxidised species}]}{[\text{Reduced species}]}$$

where
- E - half cell potential of an electrode
- E° - the standard half cell potential of an electrode
- F - Faraday's constant
- n - number of electrons transferred.

Pourbaix diagrams can be constructed using above calculations. In the above diagram, iron, iron hydroxide, ferrous ions etc. are thermodynamically stable in particular areas. They are in their states of lowest free energies.

Uses of these diagrams are :
1. We can predict spontaneous direction of a reaction.
2. Composition of corrosion product can be estimated.
3. The environmental changes which will prevent or reduce corrosion attack also can be predicted.

In the above diagram, the area ABCDEF, indicates that iron is inert under these conditions of potential and pH.

5.4 Testing and Measurement of Corrosion

Testing and Measurement of Corrosion is important because one can

1. Monitor the corrosion taking place in the industrial plant.

2. To evaluate the quality of specific material so that it can be decided that the material may or may not be used under the given environmental conditions.

3. To study the mechanism of corrosion.

4. To study the effect of environment on corrosion rate.

The corrosion tests that can be used to achieve above objectives can be divided into three categories.

(a) Service tests in natural environmental (on-site tests).

(b) Simulated service tests : In these type of tests, the actual environmental conditions are simulated in the laboratory and corrosion tests are carried out.

(c) Accelerated Tests : These are of theoretical use such as to predict the corrosion mechanism. The corrosion of a metal is done under sever conditions (fast corrosion) and the test is carried out.

The most important methods to measure corrosion rate are :
(a) Weight loss method.
(b) Measurement of electrical resistance.

(a) Weight loss method :

- This method is most commonly employed to measure the corrosion rate. However, this method gives only approximate value of corrosion rate under given conditions.
- In this method, a clean metal piece (or metal coupon) is taken and its dimensions (length and breadth) are measured. Then it is weighed accurately and exposed to corroding medium for specific time. (pre-determined time)
- During this period, the corrosion of metal takes place and after this specific time, the metal is removed from the medium.
- The corrosion products are removed and the metal is reweighed and loss in weight is calculated.
- The corrosion rate, R is calculated using following formula.

$$R = \frac{kW}{ATD}$$

where k = Corrosion constant,   W = Weight loss,

A = Area of corroded part of metal,   T = Exposure time

and   D = Density of metal.

(b) Electrical resistance method:

This method is based on the fact that, if corrosion products are formed and deposited on the surface of a test metal which is in the form of a strip or wire, then the cross-sectional area for conducting metal decreases and hence electrical resistance increases. The rise in the electrical resistance can be monitored continuously and the observed value of electrical resistance between two ends of the specimen can be used to determine the corrosion rate. It should be noted that the rise in the electrical resistance has nothing to do with the electro-chemistry and redox reactions taking place during corrosion. The electrical resistance (or conductance) is only the bulk property of metal under test.

5.5 Prevention of Corrosion

After learning about the ill effects of dry, electrochemical and atmospheric corrosion, it is appropriate to study corrosion prevention and corrosion control. As you have already learned that corrosion, its extent and rate depends upon :

- Nature of metal,
- Nature of environment and
- Design of the specimen under study.

It is practically impossible to avoid corrosion entirely but it can be controlled by

- Retarding either the anodic or cathodic reactions known as cathodic and anodic protection.

- Conditioning of metal which is done by either coating of metal or by alloy formation.
- Conditioning of corrosive environment which mainly includes removal of oxygen from the electrolyte, modification in pH, use of inhibitors, modification in temperature which is more relevant for wet corrosion.
- Application of various types of organic coatings which include use of paints, polymer films.

It is of prime importance that periodic inspection of metallic machines and structures is done and reports be documented as; the optimum design for corrosion resistance will often vary with the material used. In a repair application, there is usually less opportunity for redesign, and the principal decision factors will be centered on delivery time and ease of fabrication in the field. It is also advisable to estimate the remaining life of the equipment so that the repair is not over-designed in terms of the corrosion allowance. Inspection normally refers to the evaluation of the quality of some characteristic in relation to a standard or a specification. As products and their manufacturing processes have grown complex and divided among many departments, the job of inspection has also become complex and distributed.

'Prevention is better than cure' it is best to prevent corrosion rather than controlling the rate of corrosion. Given below are some methods of corrosion prevention.

Prevention of bimetallic corrosion :
- By isolating the metals electrically using insulators.
- By isolating the metals from the environment using a coating.
- By choosing metals that are close together in the table or coating one of them to achieve this.

5.5.1 Methods of Controlling Corrosion

(A) Proper Selection and Design of Material:

The selection of the proper metal or alloy for a particular corrosive environment and sound engineering design are the best means of controlling and preventing corrosion.

The criterias in the design selection are :

1. Noble metals should be used in surgical instruments, ornaments as they are most immune to corrosion.
2. The use of two dissimilar metal contacts should be avoided.
3. If two dissimilar metals have to be used, they should be as close as possible in the galvanic series.
4. Weld rather than rivet tanks and other containers.
5. The anodic metal should have as large area as possible while cathodic material should have much smaller area (nuts, bolts..... etc.).

6. An insulating material should be applied to prevent access of an electrolyte to the junction, but it should not be porous, as porous materials absorb and hold liquids.

7. Avoid electrical contact between two dissimilar metals to prevent galvanic corrosion.

8. Design tanks and other containers such that it provides for easy draining and easy cleaning.

9. Sharp corners and recesses should be avoided because they favour accumulation of solids.

10. During designing, presence of crevices between adjacent parts of structure should be avoided.

11. The corrosion resistance of pure metal is usually better than that of one containing small amounts of other elements. So pure metals should be used. But pure metals are expensive and are soft and weak, so can be used in few cases. Exception is aluminium metal, it is not expensive and can be used in fairly pure state, 99.5 % plus purity.

(B) Cathodic and Anodic Protection Methods :

Cathodic Protection : The science of cathodic protection was born in 1824, when Sir Humphry Davy made a presentation to the Royal Society of London about the rapid decay of the copper sheeting on ships of war, and Davy succeeded in protecting copper against corrosion from sea water by the use of iron anodes. From that beginning, cathodic protection has grown to have many uses in marine and underground structures, water storage tanks, gas pipelines, oil platform supports, and many other facilities exposed to a corrosive environment. Recently, it is proving to be an effective method for protecting reinforcing steel from chloride-induced corrosion.

Principle

Cathodic protection has become a widely used method for controlling the corrosion deterioration of metallic structures in contact with most forms of electrolytically conducting environments, i.e. environments containing enough ions to conduct electricity such as soils, sea water and basically all natural waters. Cathodic protection basically reduces the corrosion rate of a metallic structure by reducing its corrosion potential, bringing the metal closer to an immune state. From a thermodynamics point of view, the application of a CP current basically reduces the corrosion rate of a metallic structure by reducing its corrosion potential towards its immune state as shown here for iron and steel or for aluminium and its alloys.

Another and popular method of cathodic protection is Sacrificial Anode method. In ships, materials of different electrochemical potentials - the steel of the hull and the bronze of the propellers - coexist. Once bathed in the sea water and electrically connected by the internal structures, phenomena of corrosion induced by galvanic coupling appear. These phenomena create currents in the water around the ship and induce, in the conducting sea water; a static electric field called "Underwater Electric Potential Field (UEP)" and a static magnetic field associated called "Corrosion Related by Magnetic Field (CRM)", harmful to the electromagnetic silencing of the ship. In order to protect the hull and the other sensitive anodic parts of the ship against corrosion.

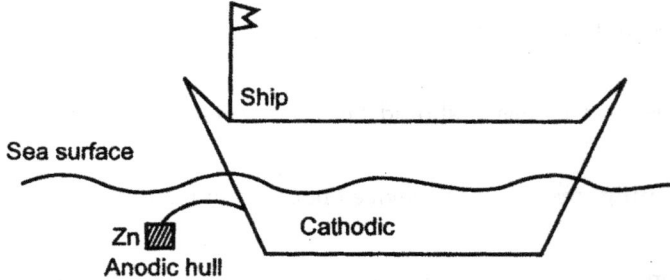

Fig. 5.9 : Sacrificial anode-cathodic protection

(a) **Method of Cathodic Protection** : Cathodic protection is a method of preventing metal corrosion in an electrolyte solution by supplying external current. The metal to be protected is made cathode. It can be explained by considering the corrosion of metal M in acid environment. Electrochemical reactions occurring are dissolution of metal and the evolution of hydrogen gas. Cathodic protection is achieved by supplying electrons to the metal structure to be protected. Addition of electrons to metal structure will suppress metal dissolution and increase the rate of hydrogen evolution.

$$M \rightarrow M^{n+} + ne^-$$
$$2H^+ + 2e^- \rightarrow H_2 \uparrow$$

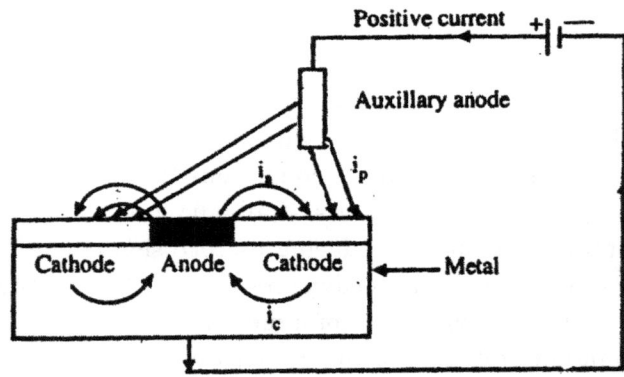

Fig. 5.10 : Cathodic protection

Suppose a piece of corroding metal is to be protected cathodically by an applied current from an auxiliary anode. The battery shown in the circuit produces protective current. The negative end of the battery is connected to the metal to be protected while positive end is connected to auxiliary anode i.e. anode placed in corrosive environment. Current from the anode passes to the protected metal through an electrolyte making it cathodic. From the anodic area on the metal surface, local corrosion current flows to cathode.

To prevent corrosion of metal, an impressed current is applied from auxiliary anode to nullify the corrosion current. This stops corrosion of metal by making it cathodic.

Cathodic protection is the most effective method of corrosion control, in fact prevention of corrosion.

There are two ways to protect a structure cathodically : (1) By an external power supply and (2) By appropriate galvanic coupling.

(1) Cathodic protection by external power supply (Cathodic protection by impressed current) :

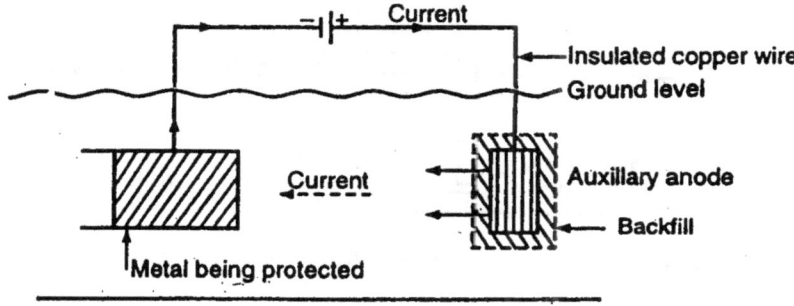

Fig. 5.11 : Impressed current protection of underground tank

Underground metallic structure can be protected by this method. Here external dc power supply is connected to underground metallic tank or pipe line to be protected. Negative terminal of the current source is connected to the tank and positive end to an inert anode like graphite, immersed in corroding medium. Anode is surrounded by backfill consisting of gypsum or bentonite to improve contact between anode and surrounding soil. Current from the anode passes to metallic structure through an electrolyte and corrosion of cathode is suppressed. This cathodic protection by impressed current is economical where electric power supply is cheap.

(2) Cathodic protection by galvanic coupling : In this method, the structure to be protected is connected by wire to metal which has more negative potential i.e. anodic with respect to metal to be protected. The anodic metal gets corroded while cathodic metal is protected.

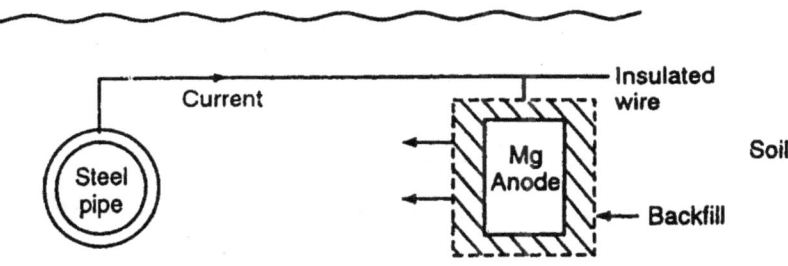

Fig. 5.12 : Cathodic protection by galvanic coupling

Magnesium is anodic with respect to steel and corrodes preferentially when galvanically coupled with steel. The anode in this case is called sacrificial anode, since it is consumed during protection of steel structure. Cathodic protection using sacrificial anodes can be used to protect buried pipelines as shown in Fig. 5.13. Anode selection for cathodic protection is based on engineering and economic considerations. Among several sacrificial anodes (steels, graphite, silicon, iron, magnesium), magnesium is widely used.

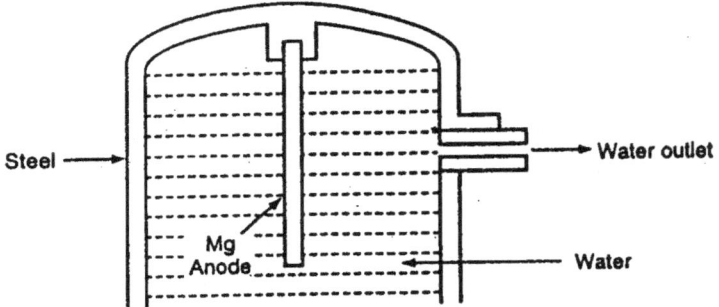

Fig. 5.13 : Cathodic protection of domestic hot water tank using sacrificial anode

(b) Anodic protection : Anodic protection is based on the formation of a protective film on metals by externally applied anodic currents, i.e. by passivating the metal. Actually the application of anodic current to a structure increases dissolution rate of metal. This type of behaviour occurs except for metals exhibiting active-passive transitions. Anodic protection can be applied for metals like nickel, chromium, titanium and their alloys as they exhibit active - passive transitions. If carefully controlled anodic currents are applied to above metals, they are passivated and the rate of metal dissolution is decreased.

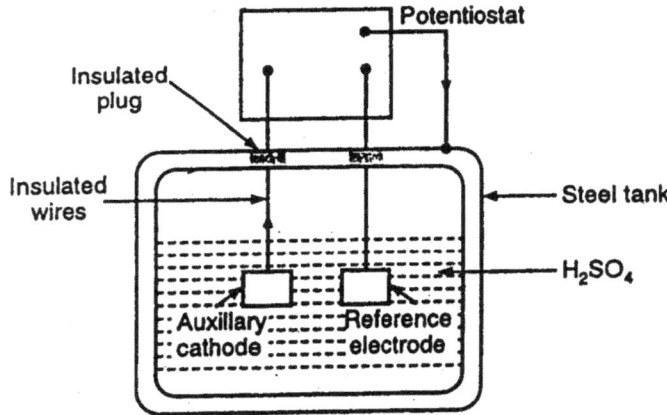

Fig. 5.14 : Anodic protection of steel storage tank

To protect structure anodically, an electronic device potentiostat is used. Potentiostat maintains a metal at constant potential with respect to reference electrode. Out of three terminals of potentiostat, one is connected to the metal i.e. tank to be protected, another to an auxiliary cathode (platinum) and third to reference electrode. (Calomel electrode). Potentiostat maintains a constant potential between tank and reference electrode.

Anodic protection is limited to passive metals and alloys, it requires low current and is applicable in extremely corrosive environment. Cathodic protection is applicable in moderately corrosive conditions and current requirement for this is high. Installation cost for cathodic protection is less while for that of anodic protection is high.

(C) Protective Coatings Methods:

The surface of engineering material can be protected from corrosion by covering it with metallic, inorganic or organic materials.

Properties of good protective coatings :

- They provide satisfactory barrier between metal and its environment.
- These coatings impart mechanical properties, thermal insulating properties, electrical properties and oxidation resistance to the protected surface. Coatings are used for decoration also.
- The effectiveness of these coatings depend on their thickness, type of environment and required degree of protection.

Surface Preparation or Surface Treatment Methods :

To obtain excellent surface adhesion and service behaviour, surface treatment is a must.

For application of any type of coating, the surface to be coated must be free from dirt and other corrosion products and it must be properly prepared. Cleaning and preparation of metal surface for coating is done in steps.

(a) Removal of greases and other impurities : Oils, greases and fatty substances present on metal surface are removed by using organic solvents like naphtha, xylene, toluene, acetone, etc. Then surface is cleaned with steam and hot water containing wetting agents like alkalies. After alkali cleaning, the surface is washed with water followed by water containing 1 % chromic acid to remove last traces of alkali.

(b) Removal of oxides, scales and corrosion product : Mechanical cleaning is done by bristle brush and detergent, knife scrapers, grinder and cutters followed by hot water. This removes dirt and scales. Loose scale is removed by flame heating and mechanical brushing while oxide scale is removed by sand blasting. Sand blasting consists of introducing sand into an air stream under pressure. The blast impacts on the surface to be cleaned and removes scales present on the surface.

For complete removal of scales, metals are immersed in various pickling solutions. Acid pickling is more convenient method of scale removal than mechanical cleaning and sand blasting. Temperature of bath, time of immersion and composition of pickling solution depend on type of scale to be removed.

Plane carbon steels are pickled in dilute warm sulphuric acid, then cold hydrochloric acid with inhibitor and finally with alkaline solution of soda ash or lime.

Metallic Coatings

Metal coatings are applied by electrodeposition, flame spraying, cladding, hot dipping or vapour deposition. Spraying is followed by baking or firing at elevated temperature. The complete barrier must be provided. Porosity or defect in coating results in accelerated localized attack on metal. Metal to be protected is called base metal while the metal used for protection is called coating metal.

Methods of Applying Metallic Coatings on Base Metal:

(1) Hot dipping : Hot dip coatings are applied on base metal by immersing them in molten metal bath covered by molten flux layer of $ZnCl_2 \cdot 3\,NH_4Cl$. This method is useful for producing coatings of metals having low melting points, on the metals having high melting points. Zinc, tin and lead are used to coat steel, iron and copper. Hot dipping coatings are of two layers, first layer is alloying layer adhering directly to metal while second layer is of pure coating metal. For proper adhesion, base metal surface must be cleaned properly.

For coating lead on iron, first iron is coated with thin coating of tin by immersion method and then by hot dipping lead is applied on it to form second layer.

Galvanized steel is a popular example of steel sheets having thin coat of zinc. Zinc prevents steel from corrosion due to atmosphere. But galvanized iron has poor acid resistance. Galvanized wares cannot be used for preserving food-stuffs as zinc will form toxic compounds with food preservatives.

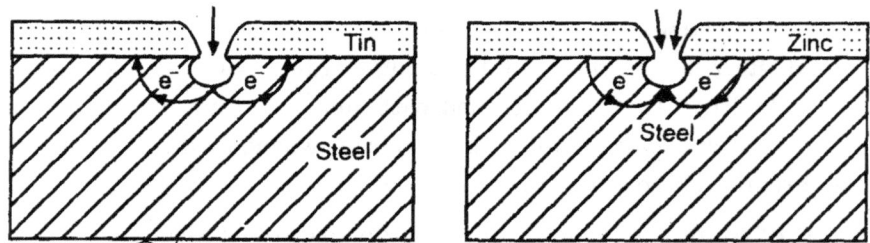

Fig. 5.18 : Galvanic corrosion in tin and
zinc coated steel Arrows indicated corrosive attack

Tin is applied on iron in a similar way as zinc is applied on iron. But tin cannot protect iron like galvanized iron, as tin coating cannot cover the iron surface completely. When coated surface is exposed to air, iron being anodic to tin, rapid corrosion of iron takes place (See Fig. 5.18). Tin can be used for coating over mild steel. Tin-coated containers can be used for storing and preserving food-stuffs because tin has corrosion resistance to dilute acids and water and it is non-toxic.

By hot dipping method, thickness of the coating produced on base metal is more. Afterwards, the coated part is heat treated to form an alloy bond between coating and base metal.

(2) Metal cladding : It is the process by which dense homogeneous layer of metal is bonded firmly and permanently to the base metal on one side or both sides. The protecting layer of the covering metal is called the cladding metal. Thin sheets of base metal and coating metal are passed through roller under pressure and high temperature. The two metals form a composite material. The choice of cladding metal depends upon environment in which it is to be used. Mild steel clad by stainless steels, nickel, nickel alloys, copper, copper alloys, platinum is used in many environments. Sandwich rolling, hot pressing, fusion welding are the different ways of metal cladding.

(3) Electroplating : It is one of the most important methods for the application of metallic coatings on the metals. In this method, coating metal is deposited on the base metal by immersing base metal in a solution of coating metal and passing direct current between base metal and another electrode.

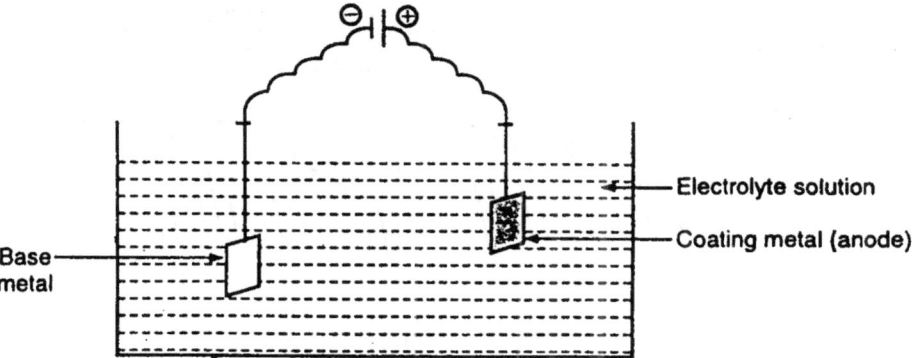

Fig. 5.15 : Electroplating bath

Electroplating consists of immersing a part to be coated in a solution of salt of coating metal and passing a direct current between the part and another electrode. The base metal is made cathode of an electrolytic cell and anode is of coating metal. The metal to be plated electrolytically is cleaned and surface is made proper. Then it is made cathode of an electrolytic cell. The electrolytic solution is of soluble salt of metal to be coated. Direct current is passed after immersing cathode and anode in electroplating tank. Metal at anode dissolves and ions migrate to cathode and get deposited on base metal. Thus, a thin coating layer is formed on base metal. Properties of coating depend on the concentration of plating solution, agitation, temperature of solution and its pH.

Electroplating is one of the most important methods for commercial production of metallic coatings. Zinc, lead, nickel, iron, tin, chromium and copper are frequently used for metallic coating. Precious metals like gold, silver, platinum are used for plating to smaller extent. Recently certain alloys like lead - tin, tin - copper, tin - zinc are used in electroplating.

Types of Metallic coating :

Depending upon position of coating metal in the electrochemical series with respect to base metal, the coatings are called cathodic coatings or anodic coatings.

Anodic coating : In anodic coating, coatings are produced from metals which are anodic to base metal. Aluminium, zinc, cadmium have their solution potentials greater than that of steel. So they are used to coat steel anodically. If any scratch is developed on zinc coated steel, a galvanic cell is formed between zinc and exposed iron. Zinc being anodic to steel, it will dissolve protecting steel or iron. Thus, iron is protected cathodically by sacrificial zinc. No attack on iron or steel occurs till all zinc gets corroded almost practically.

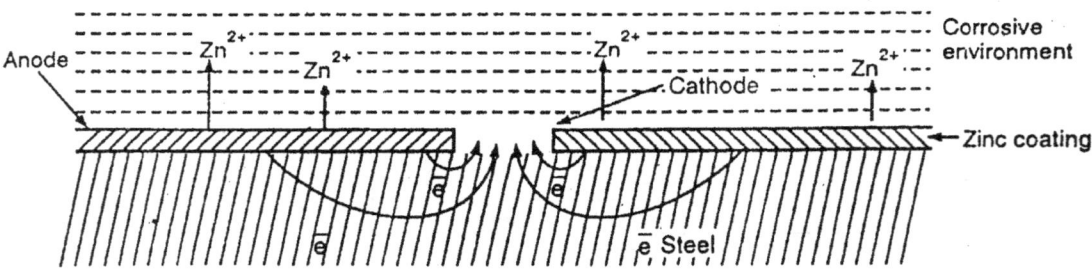

Fig. 5.16 : Anodic coating

Cathodic coating : Cathodic coatings can be obtained by application of more noble metal than base metal, for coating of base metal. They protect base metal because they have more corrosion resistance than base metal. Gold, copper, platinum, nickel, silver and chromium are the metals which can be used for cathodic coatings. Only continuous and pore-free coating gives protection to the base metal. If pores are present on the cathodically coated iron, iron being anodic to coating, intensive localized attack at the pores will take place. This will result severe pitting.

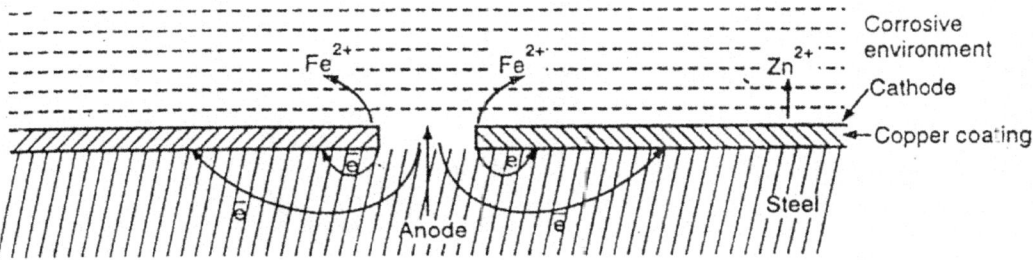

Fig. 5.17 : Cathodic coating

(4) Metal spraying or flame spraying : Metallized coatings are obtained by spraying heated metal particles on the roughened surface of base metal. This can be achieved by using spraying guns or by powder method. When the molten metal particles strike the metal surface, they flatten and fill up the surface irregularities. Finely divided molten metal particles are obtained by feeding metal wire through a melting flame. Oxyacetylene flame is commonly used for melting the metal. The atomized metal is then blown out into a fine spray with the help of compressed air. Thus, the sprayed metal adheres to the surface of base metal. This method is limited to low melting metals like zinc, lead, tin as coating metals. Coatings produced by spraying are uniform but porous, so they are less protective under severe corrosion attack. Sprayed metal provides a good base for paint.

Exercise

Long Answer Questions

1. What is wet corrosion. Discuss the mechanism of wet corrosion.
2. Discuss different factors affecting corrosion rate.
3. Define corrosion. Discuss different types of corrosion.
4. Explain two different methods of testing and measurement of corrosion.
5. Discuss different methods of controlling corrosion.
6. Discuss anodic and cathodic protection methods of corrosion.
7. Give the properties of good protective coating. Give surface treatement methods.
8. Discuss different methods of applying metal coating on base metal.

Short Answer Questions

1. Define corrosion. Explain different factor affecting corrosion.
2. Explain hydrogen evolution and oxygen adsorption mechanism of electrochemical corrosion.
3. Differentiate between anodic coating and cathodic coating.
4. Explain non-metallic coating.
5. What is dry corrosion? Explain its mechanism.
6. Discuss corrosion due to CO_2, SO_2, NO_2, Cl_2 and F_2.
7. Explain corrosion due to hydrogn.
8. Discuss corrosion from liquid methods.
9. How is the Pourbaix diagram used to understand corrosion behaviour of metals.
10. Write a note on passivity.
11. Discuss weight loss method to measure corrosion.
12. Explain resistance method to measure corrosion.
13. Discuss how nature of metal is responsible for corrosion.
14. How is nature of environment responsible for corrosion ?
15. Discuss use of inhibitor in controlling corrosion.
16. Explain the principle fo cathodic protection. How is corrosion prevented ?
17. Discuss the principle of aniodic protection. How is corrosion prevented ?
18. Discuss electroplating method.
19. Explain anodic and cathodic coating of metal.
20. What is electroless plating ? Give it's applications.
21. Write short not on : (i) Inorganic barriers ; (ii) Organic barriers.

University Questions

1. Define corrosion. Explain the mechanism of hydrogen evolution in electrochemical corrosion.
2. Discuss factors affecting the rate of corrosion.
3. Explain the importance of design and material selection in controlling corrosion of metallic material.
4. Explain electroplating process in corrosion prevention.
5. Define corrosion. Explain oxygen absorption mechanism of electrochemical corrosion.

6. Explain the process of galvinising in corrosion prevention.
7. Give two methods of cathodic protection.
8. What is corrosion? Explain mechanism of oxidation corrosion.
9. What is hot dipping ? Explain process of galvinizing with schematic diagram
10. **Write short notes on :**
    (a) Cathodic protection (b) Atmosphereic corrosion.
    (c) Electroplating   (d) Factors influencing corrosion.

Unit 6

Metallic Materials and Green Chemistry

- Metallic Materials
  - Introduction
- Alloys
  - Definition of Alloy
  - Purposes of Making Alloys
  - Classification of Alloys
  - Ferrous alloys : plain carbonsteel (mild, medium and high), Stainless steel
  - Non Ferrous alloys :
  - Cu alloys
  - Aluminium alloy (Duralumin, Alnico),
  - Nicked alloy (Nichrome)
  - Tin alloy (solder)
- Green Chemistry
  - Definition
  - Significance
  - Industrial applications
  - Goal of green checmistry
  - Basic components of green chemistry research.
- Excercise

6.1 Metallic Materials :

6.1.1 Introduction :

The term material indicates the matter present in universe. There are different types of engineering material present in universe from which useful things can be prepared. Engineering materials include metallic, ceramics composite, electronic and chemical materials. The metallic material is discussed in this chapter.

Metallic Materials :

The word metallic material includes pure metals, alloys of metals and metal ores. Man was familiar with metals and their alloys since ancient times. In modern erra of science and technology metallic materials have tremendous importance. The metals and non metal have demand as engineering material for the manufacture of machines, vehicles, aeroplanes, spare parts, railways, instruments etc. without which the life is impossible. Among the metallic material, iron and their alloys are most important and widely used because of its wide occurrence, useful and simple properties and cheap as compared to other metals. The Classification of metallic material is as follows :

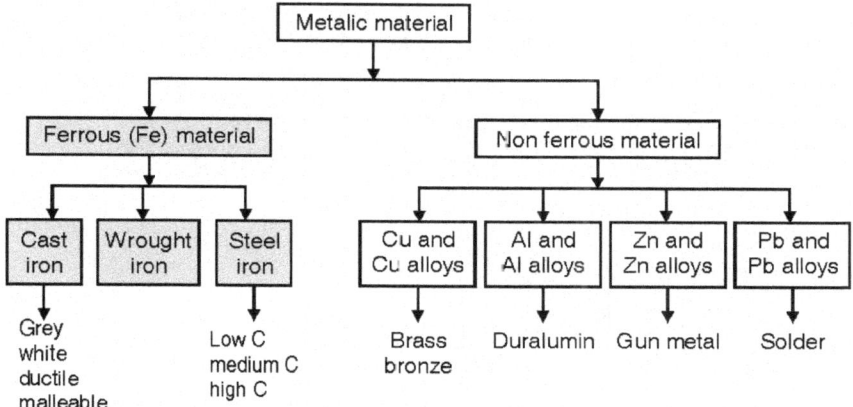

The metallic material should be properly selected depending on engineering purpose for which the material is used. It depends on the structure and properties of materials, temperature etc. Engineer must be familiar with the detail knowledge of metallic material.

Occurrence of Metallic Materials :

Elemental form :

The metals generally do not occure in nature in elemental form. There are few exceptions like gold and silver which occur in uncombined form. Metals occur in nature in combined form as chemical compounds and using the chemical reactions, compounds are transformed to metal.

Minerals :

The metals occur in different forms in nature called as minerals. They are oxides, sulphides, carbonates silicates, halides and sulphates. They may be present in combined form. e.g. $CaCO_3$ (calcite), SiO_2 (Quartz), CaF_2 (Fluorspar) ZnS (Spalerite), (FeO, Cr_2O_3) (chromite) etc. The minerals are associated with other material like Clay and sand.

Ores :

If the process of extraction of metal from the mineral is economical then mineral is called as ore. The ores are used to extract metals using different industrial extracting processes.

Metallurgy :

Metallurgy is the process of extracting metals from their ores and refining them to pure metallic state. Metallurgy also includes the preparing of alloys of different metals. Metallurgy includes wet and dry processes.

6.2 Alloys :

Pure metals are not useful for the manufacture engineering material like machines, vehicles, bridges, airoplanes, railways, etc. Among the metals very few have useful properties.

Properties of metal can be changed and improved by mixing the metal with some other metals or nonmetals. We can prepare the mixture of metal and other element having desired properties called alloys. Alloys can be defined in different ways.

Metal present in higher proportion in an alloy is called principal or base metal while other element is called alloying element.

6.2.1 Definition of Alloy :

- Alloy is defined as the homogenous mixture of two or more elements at least one of which must be a metal.
- Alloy is a solid solution of metal and other elements in which solvent is element present in higher proportion and solute is the other alloying elements of lower proportion.

6.2.2 Purposes of Making Alloys :

1. Alloying to change abundance : Alloying increases the abundance of metals. The metals have different abundance. Some metals like Fe, Cu are abandent and some metals are rare. The abundance of rare metals can be increased by alloying rare elements like Au, Pt etc.

2. Alloying to change the economy of material making : Some elements are very costly e.g. gold, silver, platinum etc. and use of these elements in pure form in material making is very costly and uneconomical. The cost of material can be lowered by alloying such metals with other metal of lower cost.

3. Alloying to make the substance of desired properties : The properties of the metals which are not useful for definite purpose can be modified to useful by alloying the metal with some other metal or metals or nonmetal.

4. Alloying to modify colour : Colour is the characteristic property of the metal e.g. Cu-Red, Ag-White, Au-Yellow, Zn-Silvery white, Sn-Silvery white etc.

The colour of the metal can be modified to different desired colour shade by alloying the metal with other suitable metal. e.g.

- Copper is red, zinc and tin are white but its alloy brass is yellow but when 10% Al is added to Cu, colour changes from red to golden.
- Both silver and tin are white but the alloy of two is pink.
- Gold is yellow and silver is white but its alloy is purple.

5. Alloying to reduce melting point : The characteristic property of metals is their melting point which is generally very high. The casting generally require the metals of low melting point. The melting point is lowered by adding other metal as impurity in a base metal. The lowering in melting point is proportioned to the amount of % of added metal. e.g. solder alloy.

Melting point of Sn is 232 °C and that of Pb is 327 °C.

The alloy of 67 % Sn and 33 % Pb has melting 183 °C.

6. Alloying to change the chemical character : The reactivity of metals can be lowered or increased by alloying the metal with other metal. e.g. Na and K are highly reactive with water. The reactivity with H_2O is lowered by amalguming Na and K with mercury metal. Reactivity of Al metal is increased alloying with mercury metal.

7. Alloying to increase hardness of metal : The pure metals are generally soft in nature e.g. gold, silver, copper etc. are soft metals.

Hardness of these metal increases when alloy is formed with other metal. When small amount of Cu is added to Au, hardness increases and resists wear and tear of gold ornaments. The Fe becomes hard on addition of very small amount of carbon to iron.

8. Alloying to increase tensile strength of metal : The tensile strength of metal can be increased by addition of other metal.

Addition of metals like Cr, V, Ni etc. increase the tensile strength of metal by alloying.

- When 1% Ni is added to mild steel, increases the tensile strength many fold.
- Tensile strength of iron metal is increased ten time by addition of 1% C to it.

9. Alloying to decrease ductility and malleability of metal : Ductility and malleability can be controlled by alloying the metal. e.g. ductility and malleability of gold is reduced by addition small amount of Cu to it.

10. Alloying to increase corrosion resistance of metal : The resistance of metal can be increased by alloying. e.g. brass and bronze (alloys of copper) are more corrosion resistant than pure Cu metal.

11. Alloying to obtain good casting : For casting, the melting point should be low and it should expand on solidification. Alloying fuses the metal at lower temperature and expand on solidification e.g. Gun metal which is an alloy of Cu, Sn and Zn has very good casting properties.

6.2.3 Classification of Alloys :

The alloys can be Classified in four different ways.

1. This is main Classification based on wheather iron is present in alloy or not as base metal.

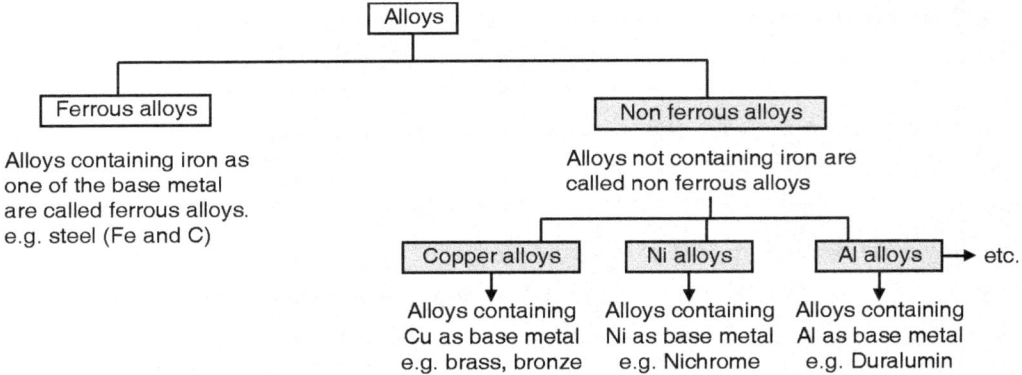

2. This Classification of alloys is based on metallurgical structure whether alloys have single phase or two or more phases.

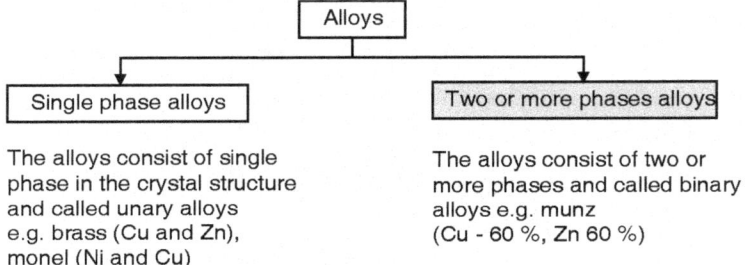

3. This Classification is based on the method of fabrication of alloys. Alloys are fabricated by different processes.

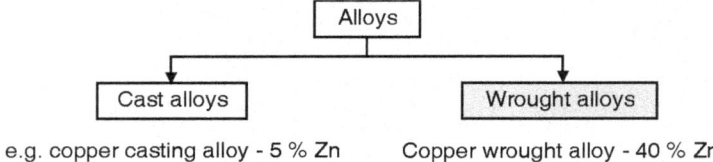

4. This Classification is based on the purpose or application of the particular alloy.

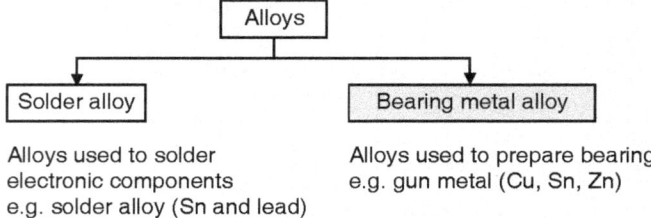

6.2.4 Ferrous Alloys (Steel) :

Steel is the alloy of iron and carbon. The properties of steel when depends on the % of carbon content in it is called straight or plain carbon steel. There are mainly three types of plain steel. (A) low carbon content steel (B) medium carbon content steel (C) high carbon content steel and (D) stainless steel

[A] Low carbon steel :

This type of steel is also called as mild steel. It contains very small amount of carbon.

Composition :

Fe – 99.95 to 99.7%, C – 0.05 to 0.3%

Properties :

- It has low hardness. Brinell hardness number varies from 110 to 400.
- It has low tensile strength.
- It is non brittle.
- It can be cast.
- It is ductile and malleable.
- It has moderate corrosion resistance property.

Mild steel can be subdivided into two categories depending on carbon %.

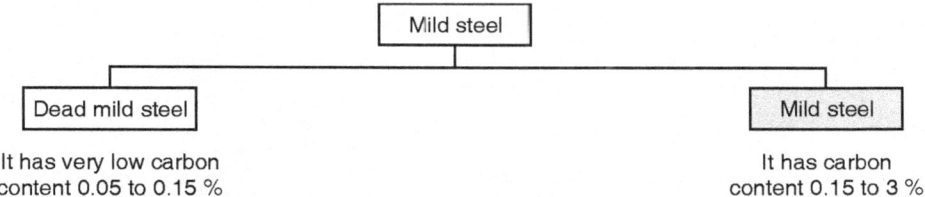

Dead mild steel — It has very low carbon content 0.05 to 0.15 %

Mild steel — It has carbon content 0.15 to 3 %

Dead Mild steel	Mild steel
Properties :	**Properties :**
1. Tensile strength is ~ 40 Kg mm^{-2}.	1. It can be hardened.
2. Good malleable property.	2. It can be easily welded by gas or electric welding.
3. Incapable of hardening.	3. It is tough and brittle.
Uses :	**Uses :**
1. It is used to prepare wires automobile body sheets which can be pressed.	1. It is used to prepare wheels, axles, rods, shafts, barrel, ropes, spokes, Clutch plates and springs for heavy machines.
2. It is used to prepare chains, nails and pipes.	

[B] Medium carbon steel :

This type of steel contains carbon from 0.3 to 0.6%.

Properties :

- It is hard and Brinell hardness number range from 150 to 400.
- It has high tensile strength. It varies from 700 to 1200 Kg mm^{-2} which depends on carbon content in steel.
- It has medium hardness.
- It has high tensile strength which varies from 42 to 55 Kg mm^{-2}.
- It is shock resistance.
- It cannot be easily welded.
- It is tough and non brittle.
- It has good heat response.

Uses :

- It is used for railway engineering to manufacture axles, shafts, wheels, fish plates etc.
- It is used to prepare barrels, agriculture equipments, heavy machines, armatures etc.

[C] High carbon steel :

It has high % of carbon. It is tool steel.

Composition :

Fe – 99 to 98.5% , C – 0.6 to 1.5 %

Properties :

- It is extremely hard and tough.
- It is brittle.
- It can produce cutting edge.
- The tensile strength is high.
- It has excellent wear resistance.

Uses :

- It is used to prepare chisel, files, hammer, punches, blades, drills springs, wood cutting tools and high speed cutting tools.
- It is used to produce high tensile wires and wires for musical instruments.

[D] Stainless steel :

Stainless steel is also called as corrosion resistance steel. It is an alloy of steel and chromium along with other metals like nickel, molybdenum. The alloying metals are highly corrosion resistant, chemical resistant and atmospheric corrosion resistant. The presence of chromium in the stainless steel form dense and tough film of chromium oxide at the metal surface which protect it from corrosion.

Composition of stainless steel :

Mild steel - 74%, Chromium - 18%, Nickel - 8%. The stainless steel containing Cr - 18% and Ni - 8% is commonly known as 18/8 stainless steel.

Properties :

(i) It does not tarnish due to its great strength and roughness.

(ii) It is non magnetic.

(iii) It has heat resistance and corrosion resistance properties.

Uses :

(i) It is used to manufacture of household utensils.

(ii) It is used in food industry to prepare and store food.

(iii) It used in diary to carry and store milk and milk products.

(iv) It is also used in chemical industry to manufacture different chemical and pharmaceutical products.

Different Types of Stainless Steel :

(I) Austenitic Stainless Steel :

Composition :

Chromium - 15 to 20%, Nickel - 7 to 20%, Carbon - 0.15% and remaining mild steel 70-78%

Small quantity molybdinium and very little quantity of titanium or niobium or both are added to increase corrosion resistance and stabilization properties.

Properties :

(i) It cannot be hardened by heat treatment

(ii) It is nonmagnetic and stable at all service temperatures.

Uses :

(i) It is used to prepare household utensils, sink etc.

(ii) It is used to prepare dental and surgical instruments.

(II) Martensitic Stainless Steel :

Composition :

Chromium - 10 to 14% and mild steel 86 to 90%

It can be hardened by heat treatment

Properties :

(i) It is tough, wether resistant and water resistant.

(ii) It can be worked easily upto 800°C and even in cold state.

Uses :

(i) It is used to make blades, scissors, cutters and surgical instruments.

(III) Perritic Stainless Steel :

Composition :

Cromium - 14 to 18%, Mild steel 82 to 86% or cromium 23 to 30%, mild steel 70 to 77%

Properties :

(i) It is better corrosion resistant.

(ii) It cannot be hardened by heat treatment.

(iii) It can be easily forged, machined and machines.

Uses :

(i) It is used to make chemical equipments and automobile parts.

6.2.5 Non-ferrous Alloys :

(A) Cu alloys : Metallic copper has low strength and toughness, high malleability, ductability and electrical conductivity. These properties are not suitable to use copper for technological purposes in industries. These drawbacks of copper metal can be overcome by alloying it with other suitable metals. The most important alloys of copper are brass and bronze which are used since ancient times. We will study here brass alloy of copper.

(I) Brass : The principal alloying constituents of brass alloy are copper (Cu) and zinc (Zn) metals. The metals like tin(Sn) and lead (Pb) in small proportion are also present in some brass alloys along with copper and zinc. The zinc is mainly added to copper to improve its properties to make suitable for technological application.

(i) Zinc increases the strength and ductability of Cu.

(ii) Zinc reduces the thermal and electrical conductivity of copper.

(iii) Zinc import excellent corrosion resistance to alloy.

Composition : The ordinary brass has useful composition as, Copper (Cu) : 60 to 80%, Zinc (Zn) : 20 to 40%

In some brass alloys other metals are present along with Cu and Zn in small proportion are,

Tin (Sn) : 1%

Lead (Pb) : 3.5%

General Properties :

(i) Melting point of brass varies from 800 - 1000°C.

(ii) It has typical yellow brass colour.

(iii) Brass can be forged in hot or cold condition.

(iv) Brass is salt and ductile.

(v) Brass has high tensile strength. It increases with increase of % of Zn in alloy.

(vi) Brass is non magnetic.

(vii) Brass can be rolled into sheets and drawn into wires.

(viii) Brass can be extrued into bars and can be casted.

(ix) Brass are corrosion resistance.

General Uses :

(i) Brasses are used to prepare household utensils

(ii) Brasses are used to manufacture,

(a) Hydranlic fittings.

(b) Pump linings

(c) Bearings and

(d) Bushes.

(iii) Brasses are used to prepare joints required in marine fittings

(iv) Brasses are used to caste valves.

(v) Brasses are used to prepare parts of locks, valves, gears, pipe urinary, electrical components.

Types of Brass :

There are three types of brass

(I) Brass : Copper (Cu) - Zinc (Zn) alloys.

(II) Tin brass : Copper - tin - Zinc alloy

(III) Lead brass : Copper - lead - Zinc alloy

Commercial types of brass :

(I) Brasses are available wih commercial names

(a) Dutch metal (Low brass) :

Composition : Cu - 80%, Zn - 20%

Properties :

(i) It has golden colour.

(ii) It has high malleability and ductility

Uses :

(i) It is used in preparation of cheap jewellery.

(ii) It is used in drawing and forging operations.

(b) Spinning brass (Cartridge brass) :

Composition : Cu - 70%, Zn - 30%

Properties :

(i) It is good corrosion resistance.

(ii) It has high stiffness.

Uses :

(i) It is used to prepare household utensils.

(ii) It is used to prepare condenser tubes.

(iii) It is used to prepare cartridge cases.

(c) High brass :

Composition : Cu - 66%, Zn - 34%

Properties :

(i) It has high tensil strength.

Uses :

(i) It is used to prepare articles using drawing and stamping operatioins.

(d) Muntz brass :

Composition : Cu - 60% Cu, Zn - 40%

Properties :

(i) It can be rolled.

(ii) It can be casted.

(iii) It is suitable for hot working.

Uses :

(i) It is used to prepare marine fittings.

(ii) It is used to prepare casting valves.

(II) Tin brass

(a) Admiralty brass :

Composition : Cu - 70%, Zn - 29%, Sn - 1%

Properties :

(i) It is corrosion resistance particularly to saline water.

Uses :

(i) It is used to manufacture marine fittings.

(b) Naval brass :

Composition : Cu - 60%, Zn - 39%, Sn - 1%

Properties :

(i) It can be rolled and casted.

(ii) It can be not worked.

(iii) It is saline water resistant.

Uses :

(i) It is used to manufacture

(a) nuts

(b) bolts

(c) joints.

required in marine fittings.

(III) Lead brass

(a) Leaded brass :

Composition : Cu - 60%, Zn - 36.5%, Pb - 3.5%

Properties :

(i) It has high strength.

(ii) It has high corrosion resistance.

(iii) It has machinability.

Uses :

(i) It is used to prepare electrical components.

(ii) It is used to prepare parts of locks and Clocks.

(iii) It is used to prepare microgears and valves.

(iv) It is used to prepare pipe unions.

(B) Aluminium Alloys :

(a) Duralumin : It is interesting and important alloy of nonferrous aluminium alloy.

Composition :

Al – 93 to 95%,   Cu – 3.5 to 4.5%,   Si – 0.3 to 1%,

Mg – 0.4 to 1%,   Mn – 0.3 to 1%.

Properties :

- Duralumin is light alloy and somewhat brittle.
- Duralumin is ductile and machinable.

- Duralumin can be harden by precipitation.
- The tensile strength of duralumin alter from 180 Nmm^{-2} to 400 Nmm^{-2}.
- The shear strength of duralumin alters from 125 Nmm^2 to 260 Nmm^2.
- The brinell number of duralumin changes from 45 to 1.5.
- When duralumin is heated to higher temperature and cooled, it becomes hard at a temperature little above the room temperature. This property exhibited by duralumin is called age hardening.

Uses :

- Duralumin is useful to manufacture sheets, bars, tubes and bars.
- The windows and partition frames can be prepared from duralumin.
- Duralumin is used in structural work particularly of air-craft.
- Duralumin may be useful in ship and vehicle building.

(b) Alnico : The principal alloying constituents of Alnico are

(i) Aluminium (Al) (ii) Nickel (Ni) (iii) Cobalt (Co)

(iv) Copper (Cu) and (v) Iron (Fe).

There are different compositions of above metals in Alnico alloys as given below. These composition are commercially important magnetic materials.

(a) Alnico - I :

Composition : Al - 12%, Ni - 20%, Co - 6%, Fe - 62%

(b) Alnico - II :

Composition : Al - 10%, Ni - 18%, Co - 12%, Cu - 6%, Fe - 54%

(c) Alnico - III :

Composition : Al - 12%, Ni - 25%, Fe - 63%

(d) Alnico - IV :

Composition : Al - 12%, Ni - 28%, Co - 5%, Fe - 55%

(e) Alnico - V :

Composition : Al - 8%, Ni - 14%, Co - 24%, Cu - 3%, Fe - 51%

Preparation of Alnico :

Alnico alloy is made by precipitating very small particles of magnetic material i.e. iron rich phase into a non magnetic matrix of aluminium. The non magnetic matix consists of Al - Ni - Co compositions. The alloy is directionally solidified and subsequently given heat treatment in a magnetic field.

Properties :

(i) Alnico possesses high magnetic stability.

(ii) Alnico alloys are machinable or non machinable.

(iii) Alnico alloys possess resistance to action of external magnetic field.

(iv) Magnetic properties are stable with temperature, time and shock.

(v) Alnico can be shaped easily by casting and grinding process.

Uses :

(i) Alnico are commercially important magnetic material.

(ii) Alnico are used to make permanent magnets.

(iii) Alnico are used to manufacture powerful permanent magnets by casting technique.

(iv) Alnico are used to manufactured small magnets by powder metallurgy.

(C) Nickel Alloys :

Nichrome :

Major constituents of nichrome is nickel. It is also called as chromel. There are two types depending on composition of alloy.

(a) Chromel A – Composition : Ni – 80%, Cr – 20% and

(b) Chromel C – Composition : Ni – 60%, Fe – 26%, Cr – 12% and Mn – 2%

Properties :

- Nichrome has high electrical resistance. This property depends on composition.
- Nichrome has high thermal stability. This property depends on composition.
- Nichrome is resistant to chemicals.
- Nichrome is resistant to heat.

Uses :

- Nichrome is mainly used to prepare heating elements which work at a temperature > 850°C in electrical appliances like iron, toaster, coffee pot, heaters.
- Nichrome is used to make heating coil in furnaces.

(D) Solder Alloys :

The constituents of solder alloy is tin and lead having melting point much lower then the melting points of tin (232°C) and lead (327 °C). The soft solder has different compositions of tin and lead metals.

Composition :

(i) Sn – 50%, Pb – 50%

(ii) Sn – 40%, Pb – 60%

(iii) Sn – 67%, Pb – 33%

Properties :
- Solder has low melting point.

Uses :
- Used extensively in electronic industries for soldering electronic components.

6.3 Green Chemistry :

(i) The develpoments in all fields of science and technology in last 50 years is tremendous. Chemists, physicists, biologists, engineers all have played a role in these developments. All these efforts are for improving the human life.

(ii) Chemistry has played a very important and significant role in all developments of modern civilization. In the field of agriculture, manufacturing of pesticides, fertilizers on large scale increased the production of food grains, sugar cane, cotton, vegetables and fruits. In the field of engineering, chemistry palyed important role in the production of cements, polymers, composites, metallic materials, dyes, paints, rubber, electronic products, ceramics, alloys etc. In medical science manufacture of synthetic drugs and other instruments required for surgery has improved life of people in the world with the help of chemistry. Chemistry has also played a role in the other fields like environment monitoring, preservation of food, atomic energy production and even the latest nano technology.

(iii) The manufacture of chemicals and production of different by products on very large scale resulted into production of hazardus chemical waste. Along with this environmental pollution, polluted drinking water, unsafe and toxic atmosphere resulted. The annual chemical waste production is more than 50 million tons and millions of dollars requires for their disposal and treatments.

(iv) Above results lead to think scientists for designing the chemical processes in different ways without dangerous by products. This emerged a new branch of chemistry in recent years called Green Chemistry.

(v) The American scientists Paul T. Anastas in 1994 proposed the concepts of Green Chemistry. The Green Chemistry is also called as Clean chemistry, Benign Chemistry and Chemistry with good atom economy.

6.3.1 Definition of Green Chemistry :

The term Green Chemistry can be defined in different words.

(i) Green chemistry is defiened as the proper use of chemistry for environmental pollution prevention by proper designing chemical processes and chemical products that eliminate or reduce the use and generation of toxic as well as hazardous substances.

(ii) Green chemistry is defined as the designing chemical products and processes to decrease or eliminate the use and generation of hazardous chemicals.

6.3.2 Goal of Green Chemistry :

(i) The green chemistry can be used to avoid organic solvents and use ecofriendly solvents for the chemical processes.

(ii) The green chemistry can be used for making chemical products that protects the environment and health.

(iii) The green chemistry can be used to develop reactions that use non toxic reactants.

(iv) The green chemistry can be used to develop the processes that take place at low temperature and pressure and improves energy efficiency.

(v) The green chemistry can be used to produce biodegradable products and by products.

(vi) The green chemistry can prevent the pollution during the design stage of chemical production rather than preventing after its production.

(viii) The green chemistry can be used for developing catalyst resposible for the synthesis of organic compounds in greener way.

6.3.3 Significance of Green Chemistry :

The chemical waste produced by chemical industries exceeds fifty million tons and millions of dollars require for their treatment and disposal. This chemical waste pollute our environment to a great extent. Therefore it becomes necessary for chemists, chemical engineers and researchers to think of improved reaction path ways and chemical technology to produce harmless products and nontoxic by products. The green chemistry has served the purpose.

Green chemistry is finding new reaction paths and technologies to save our environment. Use of green chemistry reduces the waste and reduce the efforts to handal the waste and its disposal.

6.3.4 Basic Components of Green Chemistry (Principles of Green Chemistry) :

There are twelve principles of green chemistry as follows :

1. Prevention of Waste : The most important principle of green chemistry is to prevent the production of hazardous material rather than destroying it afterwards. Green chemistry gives better path ways than traditional. Disposal of waste increases the cost of material.

In the manufacture of polycarbonates by traditional method, phosgene and solvents are used. Phosgene and solvents produce environmental problem. The green chemistry gave new process using suitable catalyst which enables high yield and high product of polycarbonates without the use of hazardous phosgene.

2. Atom Economy : Barry Trost introduced the term atom economy. The term atom economy is introduced to understand 'green-ness' of a chemical reaction without the need of experimental results. It represents the extent of starting material incorporated in the final product. If the number of atoms present in starting material are incorporated in the final product is high, the atom economy is high and pathway is better.

The percentage atom ecomy (PAE) is calculated using the following formula.

$$\% \text{ Atom econopmoy} = \frac{\text{Molecular weight of desired product}}{\text{Sum of molecular weight of all reactant}} \times 100$$

For the reaction P + Q ⟶ R

$$\text{PAC} = \frac{\text{Molecular weight of R}}{\text{Molecular weight of P + Molecular weight of R}} \times 100$$

The PAC of rearrangement reactopms amd additional reactions is 100%. PAC of substitution reactions is < 100%.

3. Use of safer solvent and auxilliers : The traditional chemical route requries large amount of solvents and seperating agents. These substances are used once only and evaporated to atmosphere producing harmful effects to environment and human health. The green chemistry suggests chemical routes that do not require solvents or multimple use of solvents and seperating agents. In green chemistry solvent water is used. The solvents like benzene, chloroform, carbontetrachloride which are highly inflammable and carcinogenic should not be used in the synthesis. The ionic solvent (, BF_4^-, $FeCl_4^-$ etc.) can be used.

4. Synthesis with less hazardous material without using organic solvents : Green chemistry try to investigate path ways that uses and produces less hazardous and toxic substances. These pathways are safe and do not damage the environment and human health.

5. Designing safter chemical products : The chemical process should be designed to prepare product having maximum expected functions and minimum toxicity. The insecticide like DDT is highly dangerous to human health should be replaced by safe biological or natural pesticides. The antibiotics with side effects should be replaced by different antibiotics with same function prepared by safter pathway.

6. Energy efficient design : The traditional simple reactions use the high energy in the form of heat and electricity. The green chemistry considers in getting the desired product by consuming minimum energy and considers economic and environemental effects.

Designing of energy efficient process, the systhesis should use low pressure and temperature and catalyst. The starting material should be renewable.

7. Renewable feed stock : The green chemistry demands the use of renewable raw material or feed stock as the starting material. e.g. D-glucose can be used for the synthesis of adipic acid instead of health hazardous benzene which can not be reused.

8. Reduce derivatization : The chemical synthesis shoud have minimum number of steps to get final product. This reduces derivatization. Derivatization requires use of blocking groups, protection and deprotection of groups, temporary modification. Derivatization should be avoided because it consumes more time, requires more reagent, produces waste and increases the cost of product.

9. Use of Catalyst : Green chemistry suggests the use of catalyst for synthesis. Catalysis accelerate the reaction rate, decrease the energy requirement and if selective can produce single required product. It generates minimum waste. The catalyst can be reused and saves the reaction cost.

The green route of synthesis of adipic acid using glucose platinum is used as catalyst. In this systhesis the by products are formed and number of steps are reduced.

10. Use of safer chemicals and conditions : In green chemistry the reagents and conditions of synthesis should be risk free. There should not be occurance of accident such as fire, explosion, release of poisonous gases or gases which cause irritation of skin and eyes.

11. Analytical methods : Green chemistry suggests for the investigation of new analytical methods to allow real time, in process monitoring and control to the formation of dangerous chemicals.

The release of poisonous substances can be prevented by perfectly monitoring the reaction controls in the synthesis of ethylene glycol.

12. Degradation : The substances like plastic, some polymers are not biodegradable. They have very long life. They pollute our environment. In green chemistry chemical products are designed in such way that products undergo degradation and produce less harmful product after their use. The green chemistry tries to produce biodegradable end products.

Industrial Applications :

(1) The most important applications of green chemistry is in chemical industry for the synthesis of desire product utilising renewable and cheaper material eliminating hazardous by product. The catalysts are preferred and organic solvents eliminated.

For example : Synthesis of adipic acid.

(a) Traditional Synthesis : Adipic acid is prepared from benzene. In the first stage hydrogenation of benzene at high pressured to cyclohexane and then oxidation of cyclohexane to cycloheanol and cycloheanone. In second stage, oxidation of cyclohexnol by HNO_3 gives adipic acid.

Step 1 :

Benzene + 3 H$_2$ $\xrightarrow[\text{Ni} - \text{Al}_2\text{O}_3]{\text{High pressure}}$ Cyclohexane + $\xrightarrow[\text{CO} \cdot \text{O}_3]{\text{Low pressure}}$

Cyclohexnone + Cyclohexanol

Step 2 :

Cyclohexnone + Cyclohexanol + $\xrightarrow[\text{HNO}_3]{\text{Cu, NH}_4\text{VO}_3}$ HOOC―(CH$_2$)$_4$―COOH + N$_2$O

Adipic acid

The starting material benzene and by product N$_2$O are both hazardous substances. Benzene is non renowable starting material. The synthesis requires costly high pressure equipments.

(ii) Green Synthesis of adipic acid : The starting material is glucose. It is converted to muconic acid by using bacteria and then easily reduced to final product.

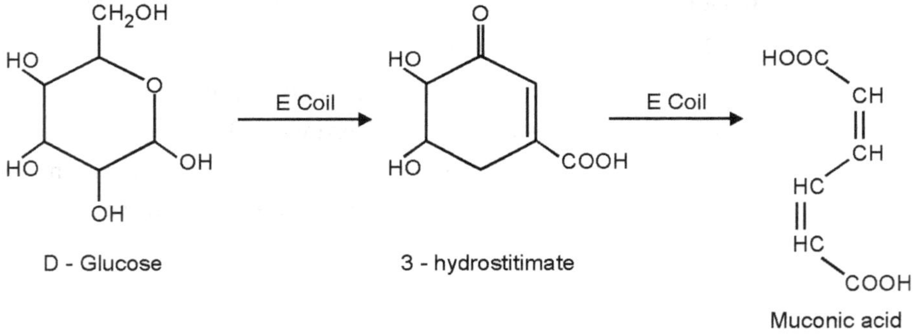

D - Glucose $\xrightarrow{\text{E Coil}}$ 3 - hydrostitimate $\xrightarrow{\text{E Coil}}$ Muconic acid

$\xrightarrow{\text{Pt / H}_2}$ HOOC―(CH$_2$)$_4$―COOH
Adipic acid

In this synthesis D-glucose is used as starting material which is cheap, nontoxic, renewable feed stock and uses water as solvent. The method gives desired product with the formation of non-toxic by products.

(2) The green chemistry is applied for the production of green fuel, green propellants for rockets etc.

(3) Microwave induced Green synthesis : The use of microwaves has led to the substantial savings in time for many synthesis in industry. Microwave induced reactions can be carried out in water or organic solvents. The organic solvent if used are required in very small quantities. These reactions can be carried out in solid state without the use of solvents.

For example : Saponification of esters.

$$R-C(=O)OR^* \xrightarrow[\text{(i) KOH (ii) HCl}]{\text{Microwave 4 to 10 min}} R-C(=O)OH + R^*OH$$

This reaction takes place in very short time (10 minutes) using microwave irradiation. In routine process reaction requires about six hours for comletion. This process is also energy efficient.

(4) The polymers are most important material required for the manufacture of plastics, yarn, resins, paints, many articles in different industries. There are many green methods developed for the manufacture of polymers.

For example : Synthesis of polycarbonate.

Polycarbonate is thermoplastic polymer.

It has special properties. It can be easily worked, moulded and thermoformed. It has optical clarity and resistance to heat. It is used to prepared windows, platic parts of household appliances, automobile parts spectacles etc.

(a) Traditional Synthesis : It is prepared by the polycondensation reaction between bisphenol A and phosgne. The reaction requiers solvent methylene chloride and water. Teritary anime or quaternary ammonium salt is used as catalysis for the process.

$$n\,O=C(Cl)(Cl) + n\,HO-\langle\text{Ar}\rangle-C(CH_3)_2-\langle\text{Ar}\rangle-OH \rightarrow (-\langle\text{Ar}\rangle-C(CH_3)_2-\langle\text{Ar}\rangle-O-C(=O)-O-)_n$$

Phosgene   bisphenol A

Fig. Polycarbonate

In this reaction very toxic gas phosgene as well as low boiling corcinogenic solvent methylene chloride are used. Both these chemicals are dangerous and spoil the environment. Also large quantity of water is required for salt removal.

(b) Green Synthesis : In green synthesis, polycarbonate is prepared from ethylene oxide, carbondixide and bisphenol A in solid state without the use of solvent. First bicarbonate is formed which reacts with Bisphenol A to form polycarbonate.

Polycarbonate

The end product is in crystalline form and of high quality. The process does not use harmful chemicals and is ecofriendly.

Exercises

Long Answer Questions

1. Define and Classify the alloys. What are the purposes of making alloys ?
2. Discuss different types of steel.
3. Define Green Chemistry, Discuss goals of Green Chemistry.
4. Explain four basic components of green chemistry.

Short Answer Questions

1. Applications of Green Chemistry.
2. Give the significance of Green Chemistry.
3. Write Notes on : (i) Stainless Steel (ii) Brass alloy (iii) Brass
4. Give purposes of making alloys.
5. Define alloy. Give the Classification of alloy.
6. Give the composition and properties of low C steel / medium C steel / high C steel/ Stainless Steel.
7. Give the composition and properties of alloys, Brass / Duralumin / Nichrome / Solder alloy/ Alnico.

University Questions

1. What are alloys ? Describe various purposes of alloying.
2. Describe the properties and uses of mild steel and high carbon steel.
3. Explain setting and hardening of portland cement.
4. What is brass ? State composition and uses of different varieties of brass.
5. What is plain carbon steel ? Explain w.r.t. composition, properties and uses.
6. Give composition, properties and uses of medium carbon steel.
7. Explain composition, properties and applications of different varieties of steel.

❑❑❑

www.ingramcontent.com/pod-product-compliance
Lightning Source LLC
Chambersburg PA
CBHW081919170426
43200CB00014B/2769